Masks of Tradition

MASKS *of* TRADITION

*Women and the Politics of Writing
in Twentieth-Century France*

Martha Noel Evans

Cornell University Press
Ithaca and London

Cornell University Press gratefully acknowledges a grant from the Andrew W. Mellon Foundation that aided in bringing this book to publication.

First published 1987 by Cornell University Press.

Excerpts from *The Lesbian Body*, by Monique Wittig, translated by David Le Vay, are reproduced by permission of the publisher, Peter Owen, London.

Excerpts from *The Vagabond*, by Colette, copyright © 1955 by Farrar, Straus and Young, are reprinted by permission of Farrar, Straus and Giroux, Inc., and Martin Secker & Warburg, Ltd.

Chapter 2 is a slightly revised version of Martha Noel Evans, "Murdering *L'Invitée*: Gender and Fictional Narrative," *Yale French Studies* 72 (1987). Chapter 3 is a slightly revised version of Martha Noel Evans, "Writing as Difference in Violette Leduc's Autobiography, *La Bâtarde*," in *The (M)other Tongue: Essays in Feminist Psychoanalytic Interpretation*, edited by Shirley Nelson Garner, Claire Kahane, and Madelon Sprengnether, pp. 306–17. Copyright © 1985 by Cornell University. Used by permission of the publisher, Cornell University Press. Chapter 5 is a substantial revision of Martha Noel Evans, "*Portrait of Dora*: Freud's Case History as Reviewed by Hélène Cixous," *SubStance* 11, no. 3 (1982), 64–71.

International Standard Book Number 0-8014-2028-8
Library of Congress Catalog Card Number 87-6685
Printed in the United States of America
*Librarians: Library of Congress cataloging information
appears on the last page of the book.*

*The paper in this book is acid-free and meets the guidelines for
permanence and durability of the Committee on Production Guidelines
for Book Longevity of the Council on Library Resources.*

*To Germaine Brée
and Amelia Kerrigan*

Contents

Preface

In 1979, when I attended a summer seminar sponsored by the National Endowment for the Humanities and directed by Germaine Brée at the University of Wisconsin, it did not occur to me that a book might result from my experiences there. The seminar, "The Problematics of 'l'Écriture Féminine' from Colette to Hélène Cixous," was the first one devoted specifically to women's issues that the NEH had ever supported. All the participants were women and all were committed feminists, each in her own way. As Brée had obtained special permission to admit an extra participant beyond the usual dozen, we joked about being a coven and went about our work with a zeal and a sense of mission that indeed did not belie that appellation.

It was an awakening and agonizing summer for most of the participants in the seminar as we struggled to recognize, interpret, and explain literary texts—and sometimes ourselves—in a way we never had done before. What we were trying to get at had not been talked about much in the United States at that time and so lacked a language, a logical matrix, a context in which it could make sense. We floundered a good deal and often went in circles as we attempted to get at this thing that the French called *l'écriture féminine* and that had something to do with the special and specific ways in which women put themselves into writing.

It was, in a sense, the very frustration and incompleteness of that summer's work that impelled me to turn aside from psychoanalysis and nineteenth-century literature, which had been my special interests up to that time, in order to try to find some answers to the questions that had both plagued and

Preface

eluded me and my colleagues. This book is the record of my effort to arrive at understanding.

In the years since the seminar, many people have preceded me in this effort, and without them I would not have been able to complete my own work. But, as much as has been said about the recent writing of French women, who have exercised an important influence in England and the United States, no one has yet, I believe, attempted to bring them together in a single, coherent study. *Masks of Tradition* will contribute, I hope, to the enterprise of understanding the ways in which women may approach, enter, and thus transform not just literature but all institutions that we have, up until recent years, played small roles in defining.

In addition to the two women to whom this book is dedicated, I thank the members of the NEH seminar, especially Suzanne Relyea and Hélène Wenzel, who over the years have generously shared their own work and ideas with me and supported me with their friendship.

In the early stages of writing, Carolyn Hildebrandt read, criticized, challenged, and offered encouragement. I welcome this opportunity to express my gratitude to her.

My thanks go also to the Mednick Memorial Foundation and to Mary Baldwin College for helping to defray the expenses of research and typing.

Bernhard Kendler of Cornell University Press has been unfailingly helpful, patient, and fair in his role as editor.

My mother, my children, and my husband—Josephine Noel and Rachel, Justin, and John Evans—all loved and endured throughout the work on this book, and to them, especially to John, I am deeply thankful. I hope it will all have seemed worthwhile.

M. N. E.

Lexington, Virginia

Introduction

Of course a woman will mark her work with her femaleness, because she's a woman and because when one writes, one writes with one's entire being.

—Simone de Beauvoir

When a white, middle-class woman in a Western industrialized country sits down to write with the hope of having what she writes published and then appreciated by the people in her society who are in the habit of reading, her intention puts her at the intersection of a complex set of intangible forces. She may experience some of these forces as outside pressures coming from material necessities, literary ideals, or expectations of people around her. Others she may consider as originating inside her: some urge to create, a desire to be recognized, a need to tell a story. But whether she experiences these forces as coming from outside her or not, they are all finally internalized and go to make up what we might label her "desire to write." Whether or not she is consciously aware of all the components of this complex network of energies, they will nevertheless be present in what she writes—in the story she imagines, the characters she invents.

The hypothesis posited by this book is that the particular component "woman" in this network of forces will play a capital role in the shaping of the desire to write and therefore in the fictions created by that desire. It will play a capital role not only because in our society the desires of women have been shaped differently from those of men, but also because,

3

with respect to writing, women's desires have been assigned a place different from men's. Although the outward appearances may be the same, although, that is, a woman may write, publish, be reviewed, and become famous like her male colleagues, both the content and the context of these events will be different for her precisely because she is a woman.

To sum up, as a result of the differential roles assigned to men and women in our society, as a result, specifically, of the preeminent place assigned to men in written language and literature, women writers face a special set of circumstances and problems with respect to their writing. As the imaginative projection of their place in the world and the focus of their desire to write, literary works by women thus bear the imprint of these circumstances and problems as well as their reactions to them. It is this imprint—the reflection or trace of what one might call the politics of gender and literary tradition—that I propose to explore in this book through readings of six twentieth-century literary works by French women.

The Politics of Selection

For reasons that I examine later, French authors have recently played an important role in the shaping of both literary and theoretical discourse in this country. This literary continental drift has left in its wake a large body of scholarship. French feminist writers, in particular, have stirred Americans to consider the larger issues involved in women's writing; to ask, for instance, whether there is indeed such a thing as "women's writing" at all. In turn, many American critics have focused their attention on French writers, bringing to bear the fruits of a richly evolved discipline that barely exists in France: feminist academic literary criticism.

Masks of Tradition is a product of those exchanges. In it I attempt to approach recent French women writers with a critical technique that has been shaped both by continental theoretical writing and by American feminist academic criticism. This cultural confrontation and mix will generate new in-

4

sights, I hope, about the specific literary works studied, as well as about the more general issue of women's writing.

Brought together for the first time, the authors studied here have in common their nationality, their gender, and a historical moment. Beyond those considerations, my selection was to a large extent dictated by personal preference and by the very politics of literary tradition I wish to examine. Colette, Simone de Beauvoir, Marguerite Duras, and, to a lesser extent, Violette Leduc are already established in the hierarchy of writers as among the most significant French women authors of this century. My choice of Hélène Cixous and Monique Wittig as representatives of a younger generation was influenced by another kind of literary politics: they are probably the most widely known of the younger French writers in American academic and literary circles.

Because my aim was not only to identify and analyze the strategies women use to negotiate the tangle of contradictory pressures facing them as writers but also to see whether there were common patterns among them, I chose to study one text each by the selected authors: *The Vagabond* (1911) by Colette, *She Came to Stay* (1943) by Beauvoir, *La Bâtarde* (1964) by Leduc, *The Ravishing of Lol V. Stein* (1964) by Duras, *Portrait of Dora* (1976) by Cixous, and *The Lesbian Body* (1973) by Wittig. Among these texts are a play, an autobiographical work, and four novels.

The books were selected for their virtues as exempla of the various ways women have gone about making a place for themselves in writing. They thus tend to share at least one characteristic: each represented a milestone in the publishing career of its author. As a first book or a turning point, each text presents in a particularly intense and concentrated form the fundamental questions and conflicts confronting each author as she encountered the full force of her vocation as a writer.

It has not been my aim to develop a historical perspective on these texts, although such a perspective would be a possible and eventually necessary extension of my approach. While contextual issues have in some respects been taken into account, each text is considered as a moment, a moment of significant encounter between a woman and (her) writing.

Gender and Art

What this book assumes—that being a woman plays an inevitable, important, and specific role in the creation of art—has been and still is often put into question. For literally thousands of years, the role of what we now call gender was held to be basically irrelevant in art. Art is universal, this belief says; art tells us about general human experiences and has nothing to do with the gender of either the person who creates it or the person who perceives it. This belief is so ancient, so well established, that it is no wonder it still prevails not only among critics but among artists as well, many of them women.[1]

The observation that the claim of the universality or neutrality of art has been demonstrably and consistently accompanied by the near exclusion of women from its production and dissemination might well lead us to conclude, however, that there is some flaw, some fallacy in the system. The tendentious current of this inconsistency between theory and practice is obvious. Leaving aside the issue of bias for the moment, though, let us look at what is more important, even crucial, to the argument of this book: the actual merit of the claim of neutrality in art, particularly in literature.

The question at stake here involves no less than the immensely complicated network of relationships, including those of cause and effect, linking the self, gender, social structures, and language. These relationships have held center stage in a number of disciplines for many years. The literature on the subject is so vast that a full account of it here would be impossible. I will attempt, rather, to outline the premises of

1. Gail Godwin, review of *The Norton Anthology of Literature by Women*, *New York Times Book Review*, April 28, 1985, pp. 13–14; Elaine Showalter, "Women Who Write Are Women," *New York Times Book Review*, December 16, 1984, pp. 1, 31–33.

6

my own writing, "premises" being used in the double sense of presuppositions and the place I inhabit as a critic.

Language, Sex, and the Self

The division of physical and emotional labor according to sex appears to be a universal phenomenon. Although the attributes and activities assigned to each sex vary widely from society to society and may thus said to be culture-bound, in virtually every society that we know about, past or present, all individuals have been assigned to one or the other of the sexes and have been treated in a differential and specific way according to sex from the first moments of life.2 Biological sex and its culturally constructed meaning, gender, thus form a universal binary system for the marking of the place of individuals in social organization. From the moment of birth when someone says, "It's a girl" or "It's a boy," a set of mutually exclusive alternatives shapes each individual's behavior; neutrality, in all senses of the word, is impossible.

Furthermore, because the given of biological sex is only one element in this process of social marking, the development of a psychological or social gender identity is not automatically continuous with anatomy. Indeed, far from being a given, psychological gender identity is presented to the child as a *goal* to be achieved. The development of this identity is therefore the result of a complicated and, in a sense, laborious process influenced by the ongoing sets of signals people receive from their bodies as well as from the surrounding environment. Although this gender identity continues to modulate throughout life and although it may, in rare cases, be in contrast with biological sex, apparently the core—which might be expressed by the simple sentence "I am a female" or "I am a male"—is

2. For one of the earliest descriptions of systems of gender markings, see Margaret Mead, *Sex and Temperament in Three Primitive Societies* (New York: Morrow, 1935).

set quite early, probably between the ages of eighteen months and three years.[3]

As we have just observed—"It's a girl," "I am a female"—language plays a central role in the defining and teaching of gender distinctions. It is not accidental, it seems, that psychological gender identity and language are acquired simultaneously. As we grow up and learn to speak, part of that process includes learning the place assigned to us in language, and one of the main positioners in language, along with age, family membership, and social class, is gender. Our taking a position in society, our self-definition, begins with the use of gender-coded personal pronouns and names. The use of the word "subject" to denote both the psychological self and the enunciator of a sentence suggests this relationship between psychological and grammatical identity.

Gender, language, and social structure are thus all mutually implicated as instrumentalities in what may at first appear to be a highly personal process of self-definition. Furthermore, none of the elements in this process is separable from the other either theoretically or practically. The marking and expression of gender difference in the individual reflect the marking and expression of gender difference in language and in society and vice versa.

On the other hand, while they all structurally imply one another, self, gender, language, and social organization are not reducible to one another either. Although, for instance, language may be necessary in the definition of identity, the self is not reducible to language. Nor does saying that language reproduces the discontinuous and alternative structures of gender mean that language is reducible to that principle of difference, any more than asserting the structuring of gender by political organization means that it is the same as that organization. What we are dealing with, rather, is a matrix of mutu-

3. John Money and A. A. Eberhardt, *Man and Woman, Boy and Girl* (Baltimore: Johns Hopkins University Press, 1972); Robert J. Stoller, *Sex and Gender*, vol. 1 (New York: Science House, 1968); vol. 2 (London: Hogarth, 1975).

ally defining relationships, at once real and symbolic, in which each element simultaneously participates in and represents the others, without, however, merging with them.

If gender is, as we have seen, a profound and integral part of personality, an essential component of the process of positioning we call the self, then it follows that gender is necessarily a part of all subjectivity, of all self-expression. To emphasize the gender-bound nature of self-expression is not to claim it as the sole determinant of subjectivity, but rather to insist that it be considered as an essential and legitimate object of study for anyone who interprets the production of human meaning.

To reject the relevance of this consideration in the study of literature is to repeat the very process by which women were excluded from it in the first place. The theoretical denial of the particularity of women as subjects in language is the correlate of the practical denial of women as agents, that is, as the origins of meaningful action. We have already noted the relationship between the claim of neutrality in literature and the exclusion of women from its practice. Another pertinent example of the linking of the erasure of women as agents in political and linguistic practice is seen in the exclusion of women, until recently, from the status of legal adult, including the right to make contracts and to vote, and their treatment in language as objects and/or projections of male fantasies.[4]

The symbolic nature of language makes it function as the symbol of the symbolic relationships we have just noted among the self, gender, and social organization. This representational function of language puts it at the center of the claims

4. See Sally McConnell-Ginet et al., eds., *Women and Language in Literature and Society* (New York: Praeger, 1980). A particular illustration of the nullifying of women in language has been presented by two French anthropologists who demonstrate that the language used by ethnologists to describe women is the same as that used for inanimate objects: Claire Michard-Marchal and Claudine Ribery, "Enonciation et effet idéologique: Les Objets de discours 'femmes' et 'hommes' en ethnologie," in *L'Arraisonnement des femmes,* ed. Nicole-Claude Mathieu (Paris: Editions de l'Ecole des Hautes Etudes, 1985).

of women to be recognized as authentic subjects. Women's authority to speak and to write, to be heard and to be read as the origins of meaning, logically underlies and is fundamental to all the other demands they may make to achieve status as agents in the *polis*. Until a woman can become the subject of her own sentences, specifically as a woman and not as an instance of a universalized mankind, she will continue to be a reflection of the males who have been given the responsibility to stand in for her; in her own right (write), she will be seen as a babbler and a scribbler, at best frivolous, at worst a silent hole in discourse.

Feminist literary critics, myself included, have thus insisted on the fundamental role played by language in the expression and enforcement of the power structures of society, including the hierarchical marking of gender. The analysis of language use, particularly in literature, opens the possibilities of understanding the hidden traces of those markings as well as the breaches and slippages between symbolic systems that make change possible. Our practice as literary critics implies, then, a political enterprise whose very goal is the rejection of our own neutrality.

Who's a Woman?

If we accept the premise that consideration of gender, for instance the gender of authors, is legitimate in literary criticism, and if we go on to state our aims as the study of the writing of women, an apparently absurd but nevertheless vital question presents itself: Whom are we going to consider as women? Writers with the proper body parts? Writers who sign themselves as women whether they are biological women or not? Writers who, although they sign themselves as men, nevertheless write in what we might call a woman's mode? Launched by Hélène Cixous's famous footnote in "The Laugh of the Medusa," in which she names Jean Genet as one of the three writers of the twentieth century who have "inscribed

10

femininity," vigorous debates over this issue in feminist literary criticism continue into the present.[5]

Although the strands of sex, identity, and language seem to tangle into a knot here, the very fact that one can pose such questions reveals the point at which gender and language both overlap and separate. Gender is simultaneously a fact of language and a fiction in it. What is at stake in this study, therefore, is not matters of individual psychology but patterns of discourse. The most relevant criterion for our purposes in deciding who is a woman ends up being, paradoxically, biological. Only people identified as biological females at birth are in a position to feel the entire weight, the entire force—to use the word we started out with—of that gender in the meaning system constructed around the difference of the sexes. If what interests us, then, is the interplay of social gender ideals and self-definition, people who are biologically female are in a unique and privileged position to experience the force of the female gender as it is impressed upon them and expressed by them in language.

The Hierarchies of Gender and Language

As one of the main repositories of the history of meaning in Western culture and also as the fundamental practice of the creation of symbolic relationships, the significant if not key role of literature in expressing and transforming women's place in language should now be apparent. But as we set out to read the inscriptions of women in literature, we must recall once more that this key to symbolic systems is itself embedded in a history of symbolic relationships reflecting the very values it both shapes and represents. Written language in gen-

5. Hélène Cixous, "The Laugh of the Medusa," in *New French Feminisms,* ed. Elaine Marks and Isabelle de Courtivron (Amherst: University of Massachusetts Press, 1980), pp. 248–49. See also Peggy Kamuf, "Replacing Feminist Criticism," and Nancy K. Miller, "The Text's Heroine: A Feminist Critic and Her Fictions," presented as a dialogue in *Diacritics* 12 (Summer 1982), 42–53.

eral and literature in particular are part of a system of binary marking differentiating them from spoken language. Following the principles we have just outlined, this binary marking of written and spoken language symbolically reflects the marking of sexual difference. The same divisions and hierarchical arrangements apply to them both, placing written language above speech and making it, therefore, the domain of men.[6]

This tradition of reserving written language for men means that writing, in and of itself, represents a forbidden activity for women. The marks women make on the paper as they write seem the very trace of a transgression. In *The Madwoman in the Attic*, Sandra Gilbert and Susan Gubar demonstrate this point brilliantly. Revising Harold Bloom's concept of the anxiety of influence and applying it to the particular situation of women, they conclude that the anxiety experienced by women writers of the nineteenth century was a specific response not so much to their predecessors, as was the case for men, as to their art itself. The women authors Gilbert and Gubar write about felt so menaced when they crossed over the forbidden boundary into male territory that the images of themselves they projected into their writing took the grotesque shapes of monsters and madwomen.[7] When they wrote in the only language available to them—that is, the written language reserved for men—they were forced to distort themselves, to twist themselves out of shape. Inherent in women's experience of writing, then, one finds not only the terrors or the lure

6. For three very different readings of the hierarchical valuation of writing and speech, see Erich Auerbach, *Mimesis: The Representation of Reality in Western Literature*, trans. W. R. Trask (Princeton: Princeton University Press, 1953); Jacques Derrida, *Grammatology*, trans. Gayatri Chakravorty Spivak (Baltimore: Johns Hopkins University Press, 1976); and Sandra Gilbert and Susan Gubar, "Sexual Linguistics: Gender, Language, Sexuality," *New Literary History* 16 (Spring 1985), 515–43.

7. Sandra Gilbert and Susan Gubar, *The Madwoman in the Attic: The Woman Writer and the Nineteenth-Century Literary Imagination* (New Haven: Yale University Press, 1979); also Harold Bloom, *The Anxiety of Influence: A Theory of Poetry* (New York: Oxford University Press, 1973).

of transgression but also the anguish or the ecstasy of mutilation.

Crucial as it may be, however, the anxiety of writing may not be the fundamental problem facing women writers with respect to literary tradition. For within literature, there is another hierarchical, binary marking that differentiates the "higher" forms of literary practice from its "lower" forms. And here we discover, not unexpectedly, that literary conventions controlling genre correspond to social structures governing gender, the higher forms of literature, such as tragedy and epic poetry, being reserved for men, while the lower forms, such as the novel, are made available to women.[8] Women have not actually been excluded, then, from the house of literature, but they have been welcomed in a particularly demeaning way—through the back door, the service entrance.

The Problems of Negative Inclusion

The exclusion of women from the practice of literature operates not directly, then, but in the impure, convoluted form of *negative inclusion.* As a result, the woman writer must come to terms with herself in relation to literary tradition not as an absence—which might in fact bestow on her a certain freedom of self-definition—but rather as a trivialized and distorted presence.[9] This situation snarls her in a seemingly inextrica-

8. The filtering out of women from places of recognized importance in the institution of literature continues today, despite the great increase in the numbers of women who are publishing books. Germaine Brée has documented the discriminatory process of selection by gender in anthologies in *Women Writers in France: Variations on a Theme* (New Brunswick, N.J.: Rutgers University Press, 1973), pp. 73–75. The same patterns of heirarchization and exclusion are found in other arts as well: in the eighteenth and nineteenth centuries in France, for instance, there was a sharp increase in the number of recognized women painters, but only in genre and portrait painting, the "heroic" category of history painting being reserved for men.

9. Some recent theorists, including Jacques Lacan, postulate women as the absence, the unknowable Other that allows male discourse to function: see Lacan, *Encore* (Paris: Seuil, 1975), pp. 13–15, 68–71. This interpretation of the exclusion of women from discourse stops short of a full analysis of the

ble tangle of double binds that turn her writing into a snare of self-contradiction and self-betrayal. The very term "woman writer" is a kind of mongrel construction, recalling the endless sniggering that greets women when they want to be taken seriously—remember, for instance, Johnson's bipedal dog.[10]

Beyond the label "woman writer," marking her off as special, she encounters other, even more negative stereotypes representing her as a whore or as an unnatural women who has failed to fill her proper sexual role as wife, or who has substituted writing for her "normal" biological function, having children.[11] These caricatures of the woman writer, related to a similarly reductive classification of women in the *polis*, suggest that women have access to only one kind of meaning: all female desire and activity, including writing, are read in terms of women's sexual nature and its extension in reproduction. Women's writing is thus emptied of its content and reduced to a gesture, itself reductively interpreted as being only sexual in intent.

An extension of this monothematic, not to say monotonous, view of the woman writer is the perhaps even more common image of her as a frivolous scribbler. If, in the present hier-

---

situation, even in its own terms. Women are silenced, but only relatively; they return, and continue to return, to speak as a *symptom*. Women's function as a symptom in male organization explains why women have not been silenced totally, but are allowed to murmur on the margins, allowed to speak and write specifically as the manifestation of someone else's malady. The function of women as symptom in discourse will be taken up later in the introduction.

10. James Boswell, *The Life of Samuel Johnson*, ed. Arnold Glover, 3 vols. (London: J. M. Dent, 1925), 1:307: "Next day, Sunday, July 31, I told him I had been that morning at a meeting of the people called Quakers, where I had heard a woman preach. Johnson. 'Sir, a woman's preaching is like a dog's walking on his hind legs. It is not done well; but you are surprised to find it done at all.'"

11. See Mary Jacobus, ed., *Women Writing and Writing about Women* (New York: Barnes & Noble, 1979), *passim*. Margaret Lawrence (*The School of Femininity* [New York: Stokes, 1936]) states, on the one hand, that "writing [by women] is always tinged with harlotry" (p. 6) and, on the other, that "it has been seen in the lives of historic women writers that all of them were damaged biologically in some form" (p. 340).

14

archy of sexual differentiation, a woman can have no meaning
other than her biological existence, anything she may attempt
in any other sphere will, by definition, be trivial. Since she has
no cultural meaning, nothing she may say or do can possibly
have any interest.[12]

In order to assert their authority to write, their claim to be
taken seriously, women writers must somehow extricate
themselves from this sticky web of belittlement glued to the
act of writing. Furthermore, the very language, indeed the only
respected literary language, they have to rebut these debased
and debasing images is itself the principal instrument used to
construct and transmit those images. Women writers find
themselves, therefore, in the precarious, emotionally damag-
ing, and logically impossible position of having to find a way
of expressing themselves by means of the very instrument that
codifies their oppression.

Language Tradition in France

The role language plays in the inscription of women in cultural meaning also makes it the locus of possible shifts or
changes in that mode of meaning. It is in this respect that the
example of French writers becomes particularly relevant, for
their cultural inheritance includes a valorization of language
that at once differentiates it from that of other Western na-
tions and makes it their epitome. In other words, the inten-
sification by the French of the generalized practices and values
we have just explored makes explicit in their language tradition what is concealed elsewhere.

At once a product and an expression of a highly centralized
and authoritarian political organization, the French language
was institutionalized during the seventeenth century as an

12. In an excellent study done in France, Verena Aebischer shows that no
matter how much or how little women talk and no matter what they say,
they are perceived as "babblers" (*Les Femmes et le langage* [Paris: Presses
Universitaires de France, 1985]).

essential element of France's cultural superiority. The French Academy, founded in 1635, began the codification of rules enforcing the values considered to be inherent qualities of the French mind: clarity, exactness, the complete correspondence of language and thought. Correctness of spoken and written language according to the rules established by the elite Academy were viewed as bestowing worth both on the nation and on the individual.[13]

Language was conceived, then, in a context of stated national and personal ideals. When language use conformed to those ideals, it was considered to be worthy, "pure"; when it was deviant, it was labeled non-French.

The closure and rigidity of this aristocratic notion of language have resulted in an elegant but relatively impoverished fund of words and grammatical invention in French. Specifically, the paucity of vocabulary—relative to English, for instance—results in and reinforces a highly abstract mode of expression. Modern literary French is the product of this long process of strenuous sifting which has resulted in a kind of official written language barricaded off from its own vernacular.

The French authors we are going to read are all legatees of a cultural estate in which words and who uses them are questions of paramount importance. Since the bestowing of personal worth through language is highlighted in their national tradition, it is no accident, I think, that from the beginning of the recent feminist movement, the French were the first to insist on the importance of writing as a central political issue in women's lives.[14] But while they may have made such a

13. Alain Fantapie, "Le Français miroir des Français," *Le Vif: L'Express,* March 28, 1986, pp. 62–74.

14. The call for an *écriture féminine,* a women's writing that would inscribe the female denied in male discourse, was made compellingly in France by Hélène Cixous in "The Laugh of the Medusa" and with Cathrine Clément in *La Jeune née* (Paris: Union Générale d'Editions, 1975); also Annie Leclerc, *Parole de femme* (Paris: Grasset, 1974), and Hélène Cixous, Madeleine Gagnon, and Annie Leclerc, eds., *La Venue à l'écriture* (Paris: Union Générale d'Editions, 1977).

16

claim because of the special role of language in their own country, their assertions are applicable in a general way. Because the French national inheritance makes explicit the hidden agenda in other, apparently more democratic traditions, such as that of the United States, the impasses confronting women who seek authority in French are symptomatic of the problems women meet in other language traditions.

These impasses are the result of a series of logical moves explicitly stated by the French but characteristic to the value system underlying all proprietary models of language use. First, correct use of language, especially written language, is seen as conferring value on the writer both as an individual and as a member of the national cultural community. Second, sexual difference, absorbed into a hierarchical system of political organization, is defined in essentialist, oppositional terms. Third, correct written language is characterized by features associated with maleness, that is, clarity, exact expression, and a high level of abstraction, while "impure" or trivial language is associated with the vernacular, domestic, practical spheres assigned, by definition, to women. Like the strategy of negative inclusion, this logic subtending traditional ideals puts women in the cruel situation of having to sacrifice either their gender, their status as agents in language, or their links to the community. In other words, it is a logical impossibility to be a woman, an origin of meaning, and a member of the cultural community all at the same time.

Women as the Leak in Language

The obstacles specific to women in language practice are still highly visible in current French psychoanalytic and literary theory. The authoritarian, male-centered values underlying a theory of language as rich and overtly radical as Jacques Lacan's, for instance, have been addressed by feminist critics.[15] Even the aspect of Lacan's thought which involves a

15. Jane Gallop, *The Daughter's Seduction: Feminism and Psychoanalysis* (Ithaca: Cornell University Press, 1982); Luce Irigaray, "La Misère de la psychanalyse," in *Parler n'est jamais neutre* (Paris: Minuit, 1985), pp. 253–79.

postmodernist revision of French language ideals—his notion of the self—ends up being assimilated by Lacan himself into previous mythologies of gender that reify the difference between the sexes and exclude females, as females, from language.

Developed from Freud's first conceptualization of psychical structure, Lacan's theory represents the self as a radically divided, decentered agency. It is impossible, in this view, for *anyone* to achieve full self-definition, as there will always be an Other part of one's being split off, not speaking, but *spoken by* the language of the unconscious. Here the role of language as a mediator of social and psychic structures tips over into another, more tyrannical version of language as an uncontrollable, foreign presence within the psyche. As Alice Jardine has pointed out, the splitting and passivizing of the self characteristic of current psychoanalytic theory problematizes the identity and gender of the speaking subject "beyond recognition."[16]

This problematizing of the speaking subject has produced two results that highlight the traditional underpinnings of current theory and are relevant to our study. The first result, characteristically pushed to its theoretical extreme by the French, is that it has cut off debate about gender in language as an irrelevant distinction, the self already being so pulverized that questions of gender no longer apply. A return, from the far side, to the assertion of neutrality—now called "indeterminacy"—of the speaking subject has thus been effected.

The second result, apparently contradictory to the first but nevertheless a consequence of it, is the reification of the split self precisely according to old definitions of gender, the unsayability of the subject being treated as specifically *feminine*. Women are made to symbolize the limits of discourse. More specifically, women's pleasure is theorized as the great un-

16. Alice Jardine, "Gynesis," *Diacritics* 12 (Summer 1982), 57 (her book by the same title was published by Cornell University Press, 1985). My discussion of current theory in France owes a great deal to Jardine's excellent presentation.

18

sayable, the great unknowable, even by women themselves—a particular result of their anatomical differences from men[17]—and is maintained as unsayable in English by the retention of the French word *jouissance* by American critics. This ultimate ecstasy, the essence of women, represents what the French call *un point de fuite,* the place where the system leaks out of itself into chaos.

The association of women with the dark, the unsayable, the mysterious, the chaotic, is as old as history and has the effect of justifying once again the presumed essential antinomy of women and language.[18] While these theories assert the preeminince of language as the organizer of human meaning, women are again disqualified from participating in the creation of meaning because they are defined precisely as its horizon—the hole, the leak, the point of nonfunctioning that, paradoxically, founds the system.

Attempting to Write as a Negative Presence

The contradictions and impasses that characterize women's position in language become immediately apparent as we turn to the present series of books by twentieth-century French women writers. In fact, the central narrative strand in each of these texts tells precisely the story of each writer's attempts to negotiate the shallows she has been stranded in by literary tradition.

Her initial position is already fraught with dilemmas, since she must start by using the language bequeathed to her by a tradition that transports with it, as we have seen, debased, distorted, caricatural images of women. She is alienated not

17. Lacan, *Encore,* pp. 68–69; Eugénie Lemoine-Luccioni, *Le Rêve du cosmonaute* (Paris: Seuil, 1980); and Michèle Montrelay, *L'Ombre et le nom* (Paris: Minuit, 1977).

18. See Simone de Beauvoir, *The Second Sex,* trans. H. M. Parshley (New York: Knopf, 1953), pp. 192–94, 256–60. For a review of the position of women in psychoanalysis as nothingness or chaos, see Juliet Mitchell, *Women: The Longest Revolution* (New York: Pantheon, 1984), pp. 305–6.

only *from* her own language but *in* it as well. To speak is to speak ill of herself.

The degree to which these authors have internalized the traditional negative images of the woman writer can be measured by the self-loathing they express as they set out to write. The narrator of Colette's *Vagabond* characterizes herself in contradictory but equally negative versions of the writer: the bluestocking and the whore; Beauvoir represents her female world as a realm of dank, dangerous vegetation, and eventually equates her writing with a crime; Leduc calls herself a "slug"; the transgression of writing drives both Duras and her main character to the edge of madness; Cixous identifies with an adolescent hysteric; and Wittig feels so fragmented by the language she must use that she slashes all first-person pronouns in two. The ultimate vision of herself as a woman in male literary tradition takes the form of someone who smiles graciously while her insides are torn out.

Wittig's trope of disembowelment literalizes the horror these writers feel upon realizing that the ugly, debasing images of women are parts of themselves. Because the distorted reflections of women in male tradition are not just outside them, but inside as well, these writers cannot simply ignore them or put them aside. Their attempts to establish a positive place for themselves as writers inevitably involve, then, not only a struggle with exterior forces of domination but an inner conflict as well. That conflict is particularly agonizing in that it pits a part of themselves that is loathsome but acceptable to the community against a part of themselves in which they take pride but which, ironically, leaves them isolated and alone.

The mutually canceling elements of this conflict structure the writer's erotic project of connection and communication as the contradiction of her individual pride. Wedged between pride and isolation on the one hand and shame and community on the other, Beauvoir symbolically kills off the unruly, independent part of herself in order to remain linked to traditional ideals. The other writers negotiate this cruel dilemma

20

in ways we will investigate later, but loneliness, or at least some form of solitude, figures inevitably in each resolution.

Autonomy and Connectedness

The efforts these writers make to redefine themselves in relation to male literary tradition and to break the spell of the grosteque images that that tradition has graven in them represent, finally, two versions of the same enterprise. While the paths they follow and the solutions they arrive at are very different, they tend nevertheless to adopt a common mode of action in their attempts to rescue themselves from the past. The mode of action they employ has something to do, I conclude, with the conditions of their gender, since it is quite different from the male patterns described by Harold Bloom in *The Anxiety of Influence* and by Renato Poggioli in *The Theory of the Avant-Garde*.[19] The observation of a general gender difference in the negotiation of literary conflict or antagonism confirms the conclusions of other critics and suggests a transference of patterns of social conduct into literary behavior.[20]

As Bloom and Poggioli describe them, male patterns of literary identity are dominated by notions of separateness and the writer's need to establish his autonomy over and against the writers who preceded him. The male need to assert independence by undoing the past means that rivalry will be the main mode of relationship in literary tradition. Models of antagonism figure prominently in critical discourse, and military metaphors are often chosen to characterize the confrontations between authors. Bloom describes the field of literary influence as if it were a battlefield where writer-warriors go into combat "even to the death" (p. 5). While this macho version of how literary influence works may be exaggerated, it has the

19. Bloom, *Anxiety of Influence*; Renato Poggioli, *The Theory of the Avant-Garde*, trans. G. Fitgerald (Cambridge: Harvard University Press, 1968).
20. Elizabeth Abel, "(E)Merging Identities: The Dynamics of Female Friendship in Contemporary Fiction by Women," *Signs* 6, no. 3 (1981), 433–34.

virtue of bringing to the surface and highlighting the territorial paradigms of exclusionary power implicit in male fantasies of writing.

The twentieth-century French women writers we are going to study are equally concerned with personal autonomy and are equally ready, in my judgment, to act aggressively with respect to male predecessors. But the modes of struggle are different and proceed from other models of engagement. First, in all of these texts, personal autonomy is envisioned as embedded in, rather than separate from, a network of relationships, and the definition of self as over and against the other is regarded as a defeat (Colette) or a crime (Beauvoir). Even Wittig, who explicitly declares her intention of cutting off contact with male tradition, constantly refers to that tradition in *The Lesbian Body*, if only to modify it.

The female model of self-definition does not involve fighting toe to toe or slaying the other and leaving him to rot, but rather a process of mutual transformation made possible precisely by the special configuration of women's relationship to language. Because their self-consciousness has been both shaped and fragmented by their negative inclusion in cultural tradition, these writers never think of themselves as intact beings separable from their representations in language. Language is not a mask they can shed to reveal the true, authentic self underneath. Or rather, language *is* a mask, but of a special kind because it adheres to the face like makeup. The comparison, made explicitly by Colette and Leduc, between language and makeup demonstrates how a specifically female everyday experience may shape perceptions in widely different areas of life to reveal a common link among them. In this case, women's experience of needing to beautify (hide) themselves translates simultaneously their sense of unworthiness and the special porosity, the indistinction and merging, that characterizes their relationship to language. Writing, like makeup, melts into them until face and mask are one.

While the melting of self and language may inspire fears of invasion (Beauvoir), temptations to subservience (Colette), or the anxiety of formlessness (Duras), it also provides a remarkable possibility of change, for if one element of the interlocking system changes, the other must too. The model of change developed by these authors involves, then, a notion of themselves and writing as two mutually defining beings in an interdependent, binary system. If language is inside them, they are also inside language.

Transforming Tradition

The transformation of women's place in male tradition is not achieved, as we have seen, through rivalry, or even by subversion, since both these models suppose the existence of two separate and self-defining entities. Change is achieved, rather, by a process the writers describe variously in terms of metamorphosis (Colette, Wittig), exchange (Duras, Leduc), and eating (Wittig). The stories of their subjection to male tradition get turned inside out and become the narration of their subjection in another sense, that is, their coming to the place of the subject. In *The Vagabond,* the letters of Renée's lover became part of her own narration; Duras's male narrator is transformed into a character in the story of his female main character; and Freud is transmuted from master into an instance of Dora's hysteria.

Along with these twists of inside and outside in narration, the projections of the writer in her own story also shift. Character and context change although, strangely, the words remain the same. When the author redefines herself positively, though she uses the old negative words featured in male tradition, the shock waves of the change shudder down the signifying chain, setting off a whole series of transformations. As a writer, Duras assumes, for instance, the role of whore, but a new kind of whore who plies her trade not for money, not even quite for pleasure, but with a mixture of determination and indifference that revises the whole economy of exchange. Cixous takes on the role of hysteric only to discover in that disease a whole new world of possibility. Each of these writers in her own way thus assumes the mask of the past but/and shapes it into new possibilities of meaning.

The Metamorphosis of Metaphor

Transformations in plot and attitude take place finally as a shift in language, and are made possible by the shiftiness of language itself. Tradition—what is handed over from generation to generation—is transfigured by metaphor, a carrying across of another kind. Apparently trapped in writing as its silence, these writers use the opening in language which they themselves represent as its hole, its horizon, to transport metaphor itself to another level of meaning.

When they assume the labels of the past and turn them into a new reality, they are changing not only their own status but the status of the word as well: they have literalized a metaphor. By taking language at its word, as a reality and not a fiction, they turn metaphor inside out; it becomes a symbol of itself, a teller of its own tale. No longer a mediating function between two distinct entities but the place where they implode on each other and mutually modulate, metaphor becomes the figure of its own possibilities of transfiguration.

This process of metamorphosis, of carrying forms across, words across, is a fearsome one. For, as we saw, the thing to be transmuted or transformed is not separable from the movement, the energy of change. There is no dialectic here, no cause and effect, no orderly progression, but rather an anarchic shifting of everything at once in which the writers themselves participate. What they experience as a free fall between two forms sweeps them into a rift between being and language, self and words. For Beauvoir's Françoise, this rift is her own voracious desire for power; for Leduc, it is being unmasked by another's word: for Duras's Lol V. Stein, it is a ravishment into madness; for Wittig's narrator, it is the panic of feeling herself literally going to pieces.

In this moment of catastrophe when form flows away, when words fail, language is also swept into lawlessness. Set adrift

24

from its old moorings, it becomes a free floater. No longer the warship of the ruling class, but an old whore of a boat consorting with anyone, language opens and becomes not a trap but a gift.

The realization that language belongs to no one but is free for the taking constitutes a capital moment of discovery in many of these books. In *The Vagabond*, it comes to Renée in a garden in southern France; to Leduc, in a twirling dance by the Seine: to Dora, in a dream. Since they realize at last that they are not stealing anything from anyone, are not transgressing any rules, guilt and self-loathing flow away. Helping themselves to what has been theirs from the beginning, they and their words are liberated in the same jubilant gesture. All the rules, all the fear, everything else has been a joke: the women in Wittig's *Lesbian Body* laugh until they cry.

From History to Myth

The rift in language itself turns inside out and emerges not as a gap but as full of meaning; it becomes the symbol of an experience of radical change that marks, in a way, the beginning of these stories. Words have not really failed, they just come later.

Because these writers have been separated from their own words for so long, the tardiness of language is particularly vivid for them. They have, in a sense, a whole lifetime to make up, and many of them make voyages into the past to recoup, to recuperate what had been left unsaid. Lol V. Stein's pilgrimage to the casino, Renée's trip to southern France, Leduc's autobiography, Dora's analysis, Wittig's descent to the underworld, all are attempts to vivify the numb spots of preempted experience, to encounter and live their past, really, for the first time. The texts we read are the products of the writers' efforts to put their stories into their own words. Their quest for the past is thus an enterprise that is at once formal and erotic: it is the embodiment of a desire to gather fragments together, to connect what had been separated, to unify self and story.

The attempt to recover a chronology inevitably leads these writers in the direction of a beginning, an origin. As they reconnect to the past, they also link up with their desire for it. The historical process of reconstructing a narrative thus coincides with an effort to locate and understand the energies of transformation they themselves have awakened. History and myth merge at a point of common origin: the story of their story's beginnings.

The telling of stories has always been, in a way, the telling of the first story, the story of our being here, and it is just so for these twentieth-century French authors. Many of them imagine encounters with parental figures as a way of understanding themselves and their desire for an origin. Renée's return to her homeland, at once mythic and real, and her rediscovery of herself as her parents' child endow her with what she lacked before: an empowering inheritance, a tradition that puts her at the center of its desire. Leduc's re-creation of her grandmother and Wittig's evocation of Sappho represent similar reconnection—in these cases, to a specifically maternal past—which is symbolically life-giving.

As these authors reposition themselves with respect to the tradition of male written language, they generate, then, another past, this one explicitly female and anterior to the male tradition, which in retrospect appears to be a deviation, a perversion. They thus extricate themselves from the patriarchal line of inheritance in which they must, by virtue of their gender, constitute a hiatus, in favor of a woman-centered history that makes them the recognized child of their parents' desire. The discovery of themselves as a link in an erotic history, as a child of desire rather than its debris, has the effect of a symbolic birth, an awakening, a liberation into life.

The Myth of Maternity

The mothers whom these writers evoke are not, for the most part, other writers. The absence of a reference to a female literary past is not surprising: the felt absence of female predecessors is precisely the problem. Nor is it surprising that they bypass Judeo-Christian tradition in their search for a mythic grounding, since the patriarchal character of that tradition, its emphasis, especially for women, on self-effacement and self-sacrifice, make it a sterile source for stories of female creativity, entitlement, and authority. They awaken, rather, the ancient goddesses of the pagan past—Demeter, Diana, Athena, Aphrodite—as images of empowerment. Wittig's Sappho, the last in the line, constitutes a significant development in the reconstruction of a female mythological tradition, itself a new beginning, since she represents the place where a goddess figure and the writer coincide.

While the experience of rebirth is a central, perhaps the essential, moment in these narratives, it constitutes neither the culmination of the story nor the final mythic model of the writer. All of the narratives proceed past epiphany to the difficult and troubled juncture where the moment of revelation tumbles back into time. I have already pointed out the difficulties women writers may have in integrating their stories into communally recognized patterns of meaning. What is important to notice here is that their moving beyond birth as the founding of desire takes place not only on the level of story but on the level of writing as well. The discovery of a new filiation, the rebirth of a female line, dazzling as it may be, does not end up as the constitutive paradigm of literary creation. In other words, these writers do not identify (with) the mother as the origin of language, or if they do, it is with a motherhood so reinterpreted and reconceived that it no longer resembles our current notions of that role. Beauvoir and Leduc both confront the old maternal models in their books, and in each case the encounter is a disaster.

The mother—or rather the Mother—as she is mythologized in our culture, in psychoanalysis for instance, is an all-powerful figure. But for those who have been mothers in reality or who can assume motherhood as an actual possibility, the enormous power imputed to the maternal figure is triply flawed. First, it conceals the self-sacrifice required of actual

27

mothers. Second, it doesn't match the lived experience of women giving birth to and caring for children. Third, it implies the child as a helpless object who may be needed or loved but never desired in the full erotic sense of the word; the child cannot be, therefore, part of an exchange. In other words, the myth of the powerful mother originates with someone else, not the woman herself, and, in contradiction with first appearances, ends up alienating her from internal sources of empowerment.[21]

In the traditional maternal paradigm of creation, the child-text is seen as an inert, passive product. The power of the mother-writer is, therefore, power-over, and reproduction (of children, of texts), in a reversal of the apparent process, is not a paradigm of other kinds of production but rather a reflection of them. The stifling, suffocating effects of this power model of creation and of the aggression, not to say violence, it entails is vividly played out in Beauvoir's *She Came to Stay*.

Coming Together

The act of writing is represented in these texts not as a reproduction of the self according to the traditional paradigm of production but rather as an intersubjective process, an exchange of and in desire, explored symbolically through a variety of relationships between adults. Reinterpreted in the context of newly imagined erotic ties that do not include the eventual domination or possession of one of the partners, the relationship of the writer to her writing suggests the coming together of two mutually desiring and defining subjects.

While the possibilities and dynamics of intersubjectivity are tested through human relationships in these stories, the role

21. In *Of Women Born* (New York: Norton, 1976), Adrienne Rich presents a compelling account of the contrast between the myth of motherhood and the way it is experienced by women. See also Susan Rubin Suleiman, "Writing and Motherhood," in *The (M)other Tongue* (Ithaca: Cornell University Press, 1985), pp. 352–77, for an excellent treatment of motherhood and its troubled relationship to writing.

of lover is ultimately played by writing. This metaphoric substitution, made explicitly by Colette, for one, puts language in the place of a desiring subject needing and moving toward the writer, just as she needs and moves toward it. No more Pygmalions and mastery; no conquests or abandonment of an elusive muse. An opening (Cixous), a dance (Leduc), a dream of whoring (Duras), a fearsome confrontation with freedom (Beauvoir)—the endless metamorphic potentials of this relationship are made explicit by Wittig.

The model of the mutual cofounding of the self and writing as desiring subjects generates two significant corollaries. First, the self is de-reified without being constituted as radically decentered or alienated. Second, sexual difference is transcended as the model of difference per se and thus as the paradigm of desire.

While self-identification or self-coincidence as a female subject in language is the founding moment of discourse in these texts, self-presence is neither the essence nor the goal of the narrative. To envision the female self as an entity to be attained and preserved would be to return it finally to the status of object or Other as projected in traditional male discourse.[22] But while the self is not a fullness here, neither is it fractured, for the second represents, essentially, a disappointed version of the first.

Earlier I discussed the function of women in male discourse as the location of the leak or hole that founds desire in that system. While Duras appears to come close to that kind of configuration in her presentation of Lol V. Stein as a kind of absence, Lol's blankness is finally revealed as the result of her removal from male discourse, and is the reverse side of a persistent and insistent female desire. All of the writers represented here similarly describe experiences of longing, frag-

---

22. Cixous, presents a version of this essentialist view of women's writing in "Laugh of the Medusa." Such a view has been widespread, even dominant, in France. The very fact that Cixous's fictional presentation does not correspond to her theoretical position is a strong argument for the interpretation I am proposing here.

mentation, and lack, but those experiences do not constitute for any of them the nature of (their) desire any more than self-presence does.

The female self is founded by and in these texts precisely in the mode of language and therefore resembles something one might call a symbol. Some core identity, some "I" is implied, but as a changeable presence always in relation to an equally shifting system of meaning outside it. The self is thus always in situation, always embedded in a network of implied significance that I have here called "tradition." The female self is a paradoxical construct, therefore, including a self-coincidence that is constantly shifting and within which difference is inscribed. To state the case more radically and also more precisely, the female self is the symbol of difference itself.

Looking in the Mirror

We may begin an exploration of the meaning and ramifications of this formula by a test case, that is, an example that puts stress on the system: the inscription of the female body in language. Women's bodies have, throughout Western history, played the role of the instantiation of matter, of the biological—a role reinforced, as we have seen, by women's maternal function: *mater = materia*.[23] Ignoring the cultural process by which women's bodies have arrived at this status, men continue to regard them as the point at which the human rejoins the animal or the objectal. Matter without consciousness, women's bodies may represent the forces of nature, but never to themselves, since they are, by definition, nature itself. Thus even women's pleasure, their *jouissance,* is deemed unsayable.

The only relation of women's bodies to themselves adumbrated in this system suggests a shimmer of self-consciousness, but a consciousness so absorbed in itself that its solipsistic reflection is plunged once more back into the abyss of matter. Women were first defined as bodies, and then allot-

23. Beauvoir, *Second Sex*, pp. 144–51.

ted consciousness and desire only as a function of the body's reflection of itself. Confined in this narcissism, closed out of a symbolic system of exchange except as its money, women's bodies became either scraps, refuse, or a kind of solipsistic ecstasy.[24] In this traditional view, women's writing is assimilated to a reflection of this self-reflection.

In these circumstances, it doesn't seem accidental that our first text, *The Vagabond*, opens with a woman looking into her mirror. In the course of the novel, however, this narcissistic gesture of the main character becomes a self-reflection of another kind. The image Renée sees in her mirror speaks to her, and as she progresses in her self-discovery, the voice in the mirror becomes her own. At the end of the book, the mirror is no longer a locus of anxious self-reference but a surface on which Renée writes messages for others.

Leduc's preoccupation with her body as refuse in need of concealment and/or embellishment reveals, through a negative example, the flaws in the mirror of narcissism. Leduc tries to become the perfect object but cannot, and, as a result of her failure, achieves the glorious transmutation of her body into words.

The place where culture could not penetrate, the very locus of resistance to language, the female body becomes in these texts the origin of a meaning. As the authors restate and reinstate their bodies, the materiality of both the self and writing is rescued from separation. Neither the absence of meaning nor the place where it explodes into ecstasy, the female body is revealed, rather, as gesture. In addition, concurrently with the body's recovery of expressivity, written language reincorporates the gestural quality of speech. The reinscription of the female body and spoken words as at once origins of writing and symbols of it takes its most explicit form in Wittig's *Lesbian Body*.

24. For a psychoanalytic version of the narcissistic nature of women, see Béla Grunberger, "Outline for a Study of Narcissism in Female Sexuality," in *Female Sexuality*, ed. Janine Chasseguet-Smirgel (Ann Arbor: University of Michigan Press, 1970), pp. 68–83.

The recovery—in the sense of both a retrieval and a healing—of their bodies as the subject of desire means that neither their bodies nor their words are any longer a disability, an inability to mean. Indeed, it reveals the female illness of narcissism to be itself a reflection—the inverted projection of another self-love. In other words, women have functioned in male discourse as the denial of its own narcissism. By locating an inverted image of their narcissism outside discourse and outside themselves—that is, in women—men have attempted to hide its omnipresence within.

The Self as Difference

The first point about the de-reification of the female self thus leads us to the second point about difference, for narcissism is founded precisely on the denial of difference. In the Western tradition of writing that we are discussing, whatever differs from the white males of the ruling classes is simply ejected from discourse as its impossibility. Any divergences are ruled unsayable and therefore remain unregistered, insignificant in the meaning system of the community. This point has been made many times;[25] what I would like to add here is precisely what the present texts by twentieth-century French women writers have to teach us about the implications of the denial of difference in traditional discourse.

In their fictional works, the authors begin, as we have seen, with what tradition has bequeathed to them, that is, a language organized around a specifically male experience that represents itself nevertheless as universal. They approach language, then, as its outside. When these women come to language as the subjects of their own consciousness, they enter it, then, precisely as the consciousness of (its) difference. In the terms of male discourse itself, women enter language as its

25. For recent formulations, see Luce Irigaray, *Speculum of the Other Woman*, trans. Gillian C. Gill (Ithaca: Cornell University Press, 1985), and, by the same author, *This Sex Which Is Not One*, trans. Catherine Porter and Carolyn Burke (Ithaca: Cornell University Press, 1985).

opposite; and once more we find ourselves face to face with the models of rivalry, alterity, and antagonism we met in Bloom and Poggioli.

But the liberation into language of the denied female self reveals the traditional opposition between male and female to be a lure, a symptom, a defense that serves to protect male narcissism against a difference even more threatening: a protean, desiring diversity *already within*. The mutually exclusive marking of male and female as "opposite" sexes cannot properly serve as a metaphor for all difference, then, since it turns out to be its denial. As the symptom that at once hides and expresses the real principle of difference within language, women do not in fact enter writing as its opposite, but rather rejoin themselves where, in a sense, they always were.

The expression of a principle of difference which founds the relation of the subject to herself and to language but which is not based on the dichotomies of sex or dialectic can be found most vividly in the homosexual models presented by Leduc and Wittig. The lesbian lovers in their books constitute a kind of minimal pair, that is, a pair where difference is reduced to its smallest degree and where, therefore, it is most perceptible. The model of difference emerging from the similar is apparent also in other texts, such as *She Came to Stay* and *The Ravishment of Lol V. Stein,* in which women struggle to define themselves in relation to other women.

Women and Writing

We find in these books a model of difference which is, in a sense, an incarnation of its own function, a symbol of itself. The female self as difference includes difference within it. It cannot coincide with itself, but marks, rather, *a border*—and I use the term both in the context of sewing and in the context of national divisions—a place of distinctness where exchange and elaboration can occur.[26] Since it already includes the het-

26. The concept of the self developed here bears a strong resemblance to

erogeneous within it, as the paradoxical example of homosexuality demonstrates, the border is not a closing but an opening, a place of crossing over, the locus, precisely, of metaphor.

The structures of the female self—difference, desire, and writing—all resemble and imply one another both as movements across and as already including within them that which they are moving toward. One of the astonishing results of the configuration of the female self is that it reveals an unexpected privileged relationship between women and written language, linked to one another by their common function as the loci of difference denied in traditional male discourse. The special relationship of women with writing reverses the traditional association of women with spoken language, and even with preformal speech.[27] Women are not closer to nature than men, closer to the biological through their function as mothers; quite contrary to these ancient and still current caricatures, they actually represent the principle of difference that founds culture's symbolic order.

Casting a look back at the phenomenology of motherhood, we now can see that the revelation of women's symbolic function radically restructures their relation to the biological. When reproduction is seen not as the antinomy of discourse but rather as a process of desire, the mythologized oneness of mother and child yields to other forms. Although the baby is literally a part of the mother during pregnancy, she may very well think of it as different from her, as an other—protégé or parasite; it does not merge with her. Physically, too, the baby is maintained as a separate system within the mother by the placenta, which acts as the border between the two. The organ that both keeps them apart and acts as the locus of all exchange, the placenta becomes a throwaway at birth, the sym-

---

the notion of being as a primordial relationship with otherness, as presented by Martin Heidegger in *Identity and Difference,* trans. Joan Stambaugh (New York: Harper & Row, 1969). His formulation of the relationship among identity, difference, and language is on pp. 37–38.

27. Julia Kristeva, *La Révolution du langage poétique* (Paris: Seuil, 1974).

bolic trace of the marking off of motherhood from collapse into an abyssal Nature.

From a biological as well as a social point of view, women function as the trace of difference, the origin of the symbolic. Being the subject of difference, however, means that women will never simply coincide with themselves, even as women, and that their special relation to the symbolic function of language is itself liable to change. The border between women and writing, mutually defined but embedded in an open network of relationships, may shift. The meanings of the self and of words are perpetually in flux, irresistibly modified by the swell of numberless exchanges. The meeting place of the individual and the community, neither the self nor any word in any language will ever reach final definition.

Living on borders, living as a border, is not easy. With the threat of chaos on one side and fear of going over the edge on the other, one finds a sense of danger everywhere in the books we are going to read. But finally, they tell us, the risk of catastrophe is preferable to paralysis, to silence, to the terrible violence of defending one's frontiers, to the perversion of turning away.

And, in the end, the danger is not so great. As these writers approach the edge of themselves, of language, the threat of the Other melts away, a phantom of fear. What one meets instead is uncannily familiar: something forgotten but already known. The border may be the edge of chaos, but it is also the place where desires meet, where words are exchanged.

As if in reminder of that perception of themselves as a border always being redefined, each of the writers here ends with a new beginning—the threshold of another space to be entered. It is there, in that specifically imagined space, that we as readers can move toward them, each in the difference of our own desire, drawing our borders with them. The present book is the exploration of that other space—at once a coming together and the border marking a new desire.

1

Colette:
The Vagabond

Colette has always resisted classification. Music-hall performer, writer, actress, journalist, wife and mother, cosmetics entrepreneur, *grande dame*, Colette moved from genre to genre, husband to husband, gender to gender, with a gusto and determination that defied definition. She evaded classification as a writer, too, minimizing her own vocation, insisting writing was only one way among others to make a living.[1] Having begun her career under duress—literally a writer in spite of herself—Colette remained determinedly silent in an age filled with authors who theorized about their own work. Even in her letters to other authors, she talked little about her writing, and when she did, her comments were on the most practical level: trouble with editors, lost manuscripts, the tiresome necessity of writing to make a living.[2] Here was a woman who spent almost sixty years of her life writing every day and who insisted she would as soon turn out a carefully made pair of shoes as a well-written page.[3]

If she shunned male patterns of artistic heroism and intel-

---

1. Quoted in Michèle Sarde, *Colette libre et entravée* (Paris: Stock, 1978), p. 463.
2. Colette, *Lettres au petit corsaire* (Paris: Flammarion, 1963) and *Lettres de la vagabonde* (Paris: Flammarion, 1961), *passim.*
3. Sarde, *Colette libre et entravée*, p. 463.

36

lectual pretentiousness, Colette did not fit the stereotype of a woman writer either. She wrote in a persistent and work-manlike way that belied the conventional frivolousness at-tributed to women writers. And although she wrote about traditional female subjects—love, nature, animals—she also wrote about forbidden topics—homosexuals, prostitutes, the backstage world of vaudeville—with a frankness that her au-dience found shocking.

Colette did not fall easily into any established category. The result was that she was, and continues to be, regarded as a kind of anomaly: a great writer, but strangely marginal, outside the mainstream of literary history, influenced by no one and influ-encing no one.[4]

One cannot help feeling some perplexity in the face of this woman who wrote so tenaciously while denying the impor-tance of her writing, who, while publishing prolifically, veiled her vocation in silence. This same puzzling mixture of vigor and elusiveness is prominent in Colette's novel *The Vaga-bond*.[5] Published initially as a serial in *La Vie parisienne* be-tween May 21 and October 1, 1910, *The Vagabond* is the first novel that Colette wrote after her separation from her first husband, Willy, in 1906, and the first one that she signed with her own name, Colette Willy, or more precisely, the name she chose for herself—a combination of her father's surname and her husband's nickname.

Having begun to write in the shadow of a man as her hus-band's ghostwriter, with this novel Colette fashioned for the first time a story that would belong to her, publicly, legally, and emotionally. This first signed novel reflects in a way that perhaps no other of her works does what it meant to Colette to be a writer.

The Vagabond is a first-person narrative. The narrator is

4. Anne Ketchum, *Colette, ou La Naissance du jour* (Paris: Minard, 1968), pp. 49–54.
5. Colette, *The Vagabond*, trans. Enid McLeod (New York: Farrar, Straus & Young, 1955; rpt. Westport, Conn.: Greenwood, 1973). All references are to this edition. Modifications of the translation are indicated by "TM."

Renée Néré, a writer and recent divorcée, who is now making a living as a pantomime artist in music-hall productions. An upper-class admirer of her performance, one Maxime Duffe-rein-Chautel, approaches her and by his gentle persistence eventually succeeds in gaining Renée's trust. She falls in love with him. Although they experience moments of intense erot-icism, they do not become lovers.

A crisis in the relationship occurs when Renée is asked to go on tour with her act. Maxime tries to dissuade her from leav-ing. They reach a compromise: she will go on tour, he will wait for her, and when she returns she will become his mis-tress, perhaps his wife.

While Renée is on tour she and Max exchange many letters, several of which are included in the text. During her absence from Max, however, Renée begins to look at their relationship with more and more distance, confronting some of the prob-lems she was not able to look at in Max's presence. She is troubled by his idle life, his hostility to her work, his wish to possess her.

As she travels from Paris into the spring of southern France, she finds herself awakening in a new and intense way to the world around her. Slowly a decision formulates itself. When she returns to Paris, instead of seeing Max, who has now pro-posed marriage, she will send him a letter breaking off their relationship. She has chosen to be unattached, to be a vaga-bond, in order to possess herself and her own work.

The story line is clear. What is not is the status of the text the author has given us to read. Nowhere in the book does Colette create a fiction to account for or to explain what we are reading. Its informal tone, its close following of events, its reflection on intimate thoughts and feelings, all give it the feel of a journal. Yet there are moments when this impression is directly contradicted. From time to time the narrator explains herself or reviews her past in a way that would be unnecessary or out of place in a *journal intime* (see pp. 30–35). On other occasions she addresses the reader directly. The first time she does so, she speaks to the reader as one familiar with her former novels (Renée Néré is the author of three books), and reassures him that she will not write another novel as bad as her last one (p. 31).

This purposeful blurring of genres—private journal and public text—parallels a blurring of fact and fiction on another level. Colette's appeal to the fictive reader, who, she says, is already familiar with her work, raises the question of the actual reader, who was also—her former husband had seen to that—very familiar with the events of Colette's life. Her divorce and music-hall career had been a public scandal. The many similarities between her own life and the life of Renée Néré cannot have been lost on her contemporaries.

Colette seems to take some pleasure in this blurring of autobiography and fiction. She gives the name Brague to her mime master and partner, whose name in real life was Wague.[6] Colette was more discreet in other areas of her life, however: at the time she wrote the book, she was in love with a woman called Missy and not with a man named Max.

The final bluff that Colette presents to the reader as she situates her text is the narrator's perplexing statement that she has in fact given up writing: "A woman of letters who has turned out badly: that is what I must remain for everyone, I who no longer write, who deny myself the pleasure, the luxury of writing" (p. 14). Writing is a luxury that Renée has abandoned because she now must earn her living. Her present "writing" is therefore a puzzling kind of nonwriting, a writing denied, which records precisely the impossibility of being an author.

These perplexing denials and tantalizing transmutations add up to a text that gives the strange impression of floating in an undefinable zone between personal journal and public writing, between autobiography and fiction, between existence and nonexistence. Both the position of the narrator and our

6. The blending of life and fiction operated in the other direction as well. Several months after the publication of her novel, Colette began to address Wague by his fictional name, and she continued to do so throughout the rest of their lives. See Colette, letter of April 10, 1911, in *Lettres de la vagabonde.*

position as readers are mobile, multiple, confusing. Colette's writing attracts us and simultaneously keeps us at bay. She camouflages herself in order to make us want to see her: it is the writing of a tease, a flirt. These ambiguities of text and reality, author and reader are translated by Colette into a spatial metaphor of movement which she uses like a game of hide-and-seek to conceal herself while waiting to be found. The ultimate issue is one of concealment and revelation.

Associated with the wantonness of showing themselves in public, writing has often been thought immoral for women. From this point of view, it seems particularly significant that the career Colette chooses for her narrator as a substitute for writing is a career as a music-hall dancer, in which she both tantalizes and shocks her audiences by undressing partially on stage (as Colette herself did at this time). Renée's career symbolically lays bare one of the most strictly enforced taboos concerning women's writing: the sanction against the propriety of publication.[7] Emphasizing the scandal of visibility which is fetishized specifically because women are not allowed to speak, Colette represents this defiant exhibition of herself as a kind of self-punishing replacement for language.

While the status of the text is undefined, it furnishes nevertheless a metaphoric space, a stage that Colette, the symbolic shadow of her protagonist, mounts to perform, to show herself—but disguised—in public. Paradoxically, like Renée, the more naked she appears, the more invisible she declares herself to be: "And where others adorn themselves, I disrobe, trained as I have been, first as Taillandy's model and then as a dancer, to avoid the dangers that lie in nudity and to move naked under the light as though it were a complicated drapery" (p. 194). Nakedness is an illusion, a lure. Trained by her former husband, Renée has learned how to be an object and to be in control at the same time. In other words, she has learned how to alienate her mind from her body while she is being

7. See Joan DeJean's article "Lafayette's Ellipsis: The Privileges of Anonymity," *PMLA* (October 1984), 884–902.

40

used/using herself as an exhibition. She has learned how to be seductive.

The anger involved in this fragmentation, this splitting of mind and body for the use of another's desire, the anger involved, then, in seduction becomes explicit as Renée dances one night at a private party. The audience is made up of her former husband's friends. Feeling resentment toward them, she discovers a new way of revenging herself:

> But there is something more worthwhile than humiliating them; I want, for one moment only, to seduce them! It needs only a little more effort: already their heads, under the weight of their jewels and their hair, sway vaguely as they obediently follow my movements. At any moment now the vindictive light in all those eyes will go out, and the charmed creatures will give in and smile at the same time. [P. 48]

As Renée learns how to manipulate her audience, she humiliates them by charming them; she exercises her power by getting them to desire her. Her very artfulness, then, is a measure of her distrust and anger.

This model of the relationship between a female artist and her audience is rooted in the dynamics of the heterosexual seduction that it uses as a metaphor. And those roots are planted in a soil bitter with anger and humiliation. That Colette associates humiliation specifically with being a female who desires men becomes explicit in what she reports about Renée's relationship with her husband and with Max.

Renée's marriage to Adolphe Taillandy, whom she loved deeply, was a disaster. Having chosen her as a mate, Taillandy then betrayed her openly with other women, even going so far as to seek her complicity in his infidelities. Renée naturally felt humiliated by this behavior, wounded by the blatant rejection of one who had claimed to love her, overwhelmed by his arbitrary cruelty.

As a result of this traumatic wounding of her love and pride, Renée distrusts the love of all men and anticipates in their desire her future betrayal and humiliation. That Taillandy's treacherous behavior has shaped Renée's reactions to other men becomes clear in her relationship with Max. Expecting to be betrayed precisely because he desires her, Renée in turn experiences her desire for Max as humiliating. In order to please Max and protect herself at the same time, she anticipates her humiliation by inflicting it on herself. Exaggerating her docility and defusing it with playful irony, she nevertheless associates love between a man and a woman with mastery and submission: "Maxime has remained on the divan and his mute appeal receives the most flattering of responses: my look of a submissive bitch, rather shame-faced, rather cowed, very much petted, and ready to accept the leash, the collar, the place at her master's feet, and everything" (p. 127).

As presented by Colette in *The Vagabond*, heterosexual love is, then, a highly ambivalent affair, a contrast between two contradictory modes of desire—one treacherous, one trusting—in which women, precisely because they are trusting, are bound to be harmed. Being in love with a man not only implicates Renée in a highly complex love/hate relationship—she habitually calls Max her "dear adversary"—it also sets her at war with herself. When she desires a man, she puts herself in danger; the more womanly she becomes, the more she feels undone.

No wonder, then, that Colette describes female erotic pleasure as the opening of a wound: "And once again there is born that exacting pain that spread from my lips, all down my flanks as far as my knees, that swelling as of a wound that wants to open once more and overflow" (p. 126). The analogy that Colette has suggested between love and writing-reading extends to this association of female pleasure with pain. Just as erotic pleasure is felt in terms of wounding, so the "luxury" of writing reminds Renée of an "old scar" (p. 15). The expression of a deep desire and the reminder that harm has been done, female genitals and female writing both share the same story of trust, betrayal, humiliation, and desire renewed. One is the inscription of the other.

In this nontext that we are yet reading, in this ambivalent,

42

seductive writing, Colette writes for her audience the same way she would act toward a man: her readers are at once adversaries and lovers. And just as desire and submission are bound together in her love of men, so she writes and yields her pen in the same gesture of surrender: "It takes up too much time to write. And then, I'm no Balzac . . ." (p. 15, TM). The suspension points, omitted in the English translation, tell a long story. A sigh of resignation, of hopelessness: a lapse into silence. I'm not a great man, I'm not a great writer. I can't measure up, so why should I try? The presence of a powerful male predecessor is felt by Renée to be so overwhelming that it drowns her own desire to write.[8]

Later on, Renée compares her ex-husband with the novelist, characterizing Taillandy as "that Balzacian genius of lying" (p. 26, TM; the English translation omits Balzac's name). Balzac may be a genius, but, it appears now, his special talent, like her husband's, was for prevarication. Writer and husband are both betrayers and masters of humiliation who reduce her, if not to silence, at least to a truncated, alienated version of her own speech and action.

By equating the dynamics of marriage with her situation as a woman writing in a male tradition, Colette sets up an ultimate and essential conflict between female authenticity and male power. In order to be loved, desired, read, and interpreted, she must yield both her pride and her own language. As she carefully prepares her "text" for Max to read, Renée furnishes a model for the kind of filtering and manipulation in which a woman must engage when she writes for a male-dominated audience. Renée censors her speech to avoid shocking Max, persuaded that her natural self would be repellent to him:

8. Here Renée appears as the negative expression of Colette's powers, as the expression of her reticence. Colette was a great admirer of Balzac, but rather than feeling overshadowed by him, she regarded him as an example, even a kind of refuge: "Balzac, my cradle, my forest, my voyage." She writes also of his "warm imperfection," his "robust bad taste," and never describes feeling undone by his genius (quoted in Nicole Houssa, "Balzac and Colette," *Revue d'histoire littéraire de la France*, no. 1 [January–March, 1960], pp. 18–48).

Sometimes it seems to me that it is you who are being deceived here, and that I ought to tell you . . . to tell you what? That I have become an old maid again with no temptations, and that the four walls of my dressing-room at the music-hall are for me a cloister?

No, I shall not tell you that because . . . you are a *man*. . . . I don't know how to talk to you, poor Dufferein-Chautel. I hesitate between my own *personal* language, which is rather brusque, does not always condescend to finish its own sentences, but sets great store on getting its technical terms exact—the language of an ex-blue-stocking—and the slovenly, lively idiom, coarse and picturesque, which one learns in the music-hall. . . . Unable to decide, I choose silence. [Pp. 82–83]

Renée can find only negative terms to describe herself as an independent woman who is absorbed by her career and has a particular care for self-expression: she calls herself an "old maid" and an "ex-blue-stocking." When thus filtered through the sieve of male language and attitude, her devotion to her career and her interest in words can become only negative characteristics.

Besides her tendency to clam up at odd moments, the aspect of her language which she foresees as unacceptable to a male reader is the "slovenly, lively idiom, coarse and picturesque," of the music hall. This language would be unseemly for her to use with her suitor because of the social expectations that women will use more pure, more correct, more polite language than men.[9]

Renée has an idiom of her own that she cannot use with Max precisely because he is a man. This female idiom is eclectic and transgresses the rules governing conventional female language in several ways. It is at once technical and vulgar; it includes the unfinished and the unsayable, not as an expression of confusion but out of respect for the component of silence in language.[10] Because her own female language would

9. See Robin Lakoff, *Language and Woman's Place* (New York: Octagon, 1976).

10. This description of Renée's idiom is, of course, a perfect depiction of

44

make her unacceptable or even repellent to a man, Renée must hide, conceal, censor, and even silence it. The appearance and language she presents to her male lover-reader is, then, a kind of false front, a translated (betrayed) version of herself: a mask.

This denied writing that we are reading, this false document, this seductive text, falls into a perfectly analogical relationship with the makeup that plays so important a role in Renée's life. Her writing and her makeup serve the same purpose of hiding and reshaping a part of her natural being and expressiveness whose direct, naked appearance would drive a male reader-lover away.

Essential to her presentation of herself to a male audience, Renée's makeup is a perpetual worry. She becomes anxious about it even, or perhaps most especially, at the most intimate moments. At one point Max has caught her sleeping and, embarrassed at being seen in so unprotected a state—which Max has indeed found shocking—Renée quickly seeks her makeup: "'I say, do pass me the hand-mirror, there on the little table, and the powder puff: I must look a sight, what with the champagne, the sleeping, and no powder on my nose'" (p. 106).

As she goes riding in the country with Max and a friend, feeling free, exhilarated, she happens to notice Max's wrinkles and compulsively reaches for her mirror to verify her "face" (p. 115). When she once lets down with Max, revealing her panicked fear of abandonment, she immediately pleads:

"Don't look at me, my darling, I'm ugly, my eye-black has got rubbed off and my nose is red. I'm ashamed to have been so foolish." . . . Relying on the dusk to hide my face whose ravages I have hastily restored, I sit on his knee and let him drink from

---

Colette's own writing not only in *The Vagabond* but in her other books as well. Her perfectionism and independence of convention in her writing are accompanied paradoxically and persistently by her assertion that she writes *incorrectly.* She is proud of herself as a writer and at the same time insists (ironically) on deprecating her talents. She wrote, for instance, about her collaboration with Leo Marchand: "My victim learned only one thing from me, but something important: the art of writing badly" (*Lettres de la vagabonde,* p. 292).

my lips the breath that is still uneven from my sobs a moment ago. . . . I leave him, to go encircle my eyes again with the blue outline which makes them velvety and shining. [Pp. 157–59]

Each time her deepest, most spontaneous feelings threaten to emerge in Max's presence, Renée runs for her makeup as if to cover up her nakedness. She associates makeup, then, with control not only of appearances but of her feelings: "Two habits have taught me how to keep back my tears: the habit of concealing my thoughts, and that of darkening my lashes with mascara" (p. 20).

Makeup and its analogical kin, language, constitute a special kind of mask, a peculiarly ambiguous mode of concealment peculiar to women in their status as objects. For although they may hide the face in one sense, makeup and language, as used by women, are not finally separate from the face itself. A foreign substance, makeup nevertheless eventually sinks into the skin and becomes one with the face it was meant to hide. In a continuous process of fading, the mask of makeup is never entirely separable from the reality it is designed to hide. False self and real self blend, become indistinguishable, because, in a sense, the female face is already its own mask.[11]

If the female self, including her language, is a mask, an object constructed to present to a male audience, then the distinction between appearance and reality does not hold for women. There is no authentic self hidden behind the public mask; as Renée anxiously imagines, face and makeup may indeed melt into one runny mess:

Me. As that word came into my head, I involuntarily looked in the mirror. There's no getting away from it, it really is me there behind the mask of purplish rouge, my eyes ringed with a halo of

11. It is worth noting that when Colette began writing articles for the neswpaper *Le Matin*, she did not sign her name but used a mask as a signature (Sarde, *Colette libre et entravée*, p. 300). Colette's commercial venture into her own line of cosmetics later in her life is well known.

46

blue grease-paint beginning to melt. Can the rest of my face be going to melt also? What if nothing were to remain from my reflection but a streak of dyed color stuck to the glass like a long muddy tear? [P. 7]

As a result of the objectification of women by and for men, women lose a sense of themselves. The frontiers between dress and disguise, speech and lie, face and mask become indistinguishable. Identity and travesty blend into each other. She can identify the "me" that is Renée only by exterior verification, by looking in the mirror. When she tries to look more deeply, the "me" dissolves into a question, leaving behind only a congealed residue, the equivalent of a wordless sob.

Just as her makeup melts into Renée's face, so the distinction between fictional character and the person who signed the book breaks down. As we noted earlier, Colette has hopelessly scrambled fiction and autobiography in *The Vagabond*. And that very confusion, anxiety-producing as it may be, serves the author's original seductive strategy of concealment and revelation. If Renée as mask blends into Colette's face, if the narrator's discourse is not distinguishable from the author's, then they become reflexive but unlocatable versions of each other. Blatant self-revelation of the one makes a perfect hiding place for the other.

The author raises the stakes of this game of hide-and-seek by stating explicitly what she is doing. She teases the reader into looking for her by announcing that she has purposely put him off. Analyzing her own writing career, Renée comments on her third and last novel:

As for the third, *The Forest Without Birds*, it fell flat and never picked up again. Yet this one is my favorite, my private "unrecognized masterpiece." It was considered diffuse and muddled, incomprehensible and long. Even now, whenever I open it, I love it and wholeheartedly admire myself in it. Incomprehensible? Perhaps it is for you. But for me its warm obscurity is clear as day: for me a single word is enough to create again the smell and colour of hours I have lived through. It is as sonorous and full of mystery as a shell in which the sea sings, and I would love it less,

I think, if you loved it too. But rest assured, I shall not write another like that. I never could. [P. 28]

In this passage Colette represents the text as the locus of a kind of game between author and reader in which the author's aim is precisely to remain unrecognized by the reader while enjoying meeting and loving herself in her own language. Here the lure of public language becomes specifically a protective measure she uses to construct a private place in the shape of a seashell whose "warm obscurity" would be violated by the presence of anyone else. Two realities, two sets of expectations, confront each other in this text; what is defined as "diffuse and muddled" by the public seems to the author "sonorous and full of mystery." The same language that appears "flat" to the reader is to her evocative, a singing seashell.

Although she provocatively asserts that she would never write another book of that sort, Colette describes two mutually exclusive kinds of reading: one a dangerous, aggressive reading that, by definition, misconstrues her; the second a reading modeled on the author's own reading of herself, evoking rich memories and producing love and acceptance. There is an alternative version, then, of the female genitals/writing as the inscription of a wound, the tracing of a scar. In this other kind of discourse, destined not for a man but for herself, female genitals/writing delineate a rich, resonant space, the source of an intensely intimate, lyrical pleasure. The richness of language here and the joyfulness it expresses are themselves a result of this self-reading. At the same time that she asserts she will never write "like that" again, Colette in fact does so as part of her denial.

While the text of *The Vagabond* can be read as a false writing, a mask, a seductive lure offered to a male audience, it can also be read as a dialogue of the author with herself, a place where she can meet herself and relive the "smell and colour" of past hours. Seen from this point of view, her writing is a kind of reflecting pool, a mirror in which she can observe, admire, and love herself "wholeheartedly." That Colette must create an exteriorized version of herself specifically in order to accept and take pleasure in herself may be less a measure of her narcissism and vanity, as the traditional view of women would have it, than a result of the fragmentation and splitting produced by her ambivalent dialogue with men.

The authentic female subject, the "I" who can write her own language, is indeed a stranger to the "me" presented as a mask to the world. Fragmented and at war with herself precisely because she acts like a woman, Colette reflects and reads herself in her writing in order to learn to recognize her own face and voice. Colette dramatizes this self-reading in *The Vagabond* in a series of encounters between Renée and other versions of her self. Her first meetings with another self occur in a conventional way as she looks in her mirror. But the image Renée sees in her mirror talks to her and gives her advice.[12] Renée calls this reflective-reflexive self her *conseillère* (ill translated in the English version as "mentor"). Colette's use of the word *conseillère* to refer both to the mirror and to the woman she sees reflected there cannot help recalling to the French reader the well-known periphrasis the seventeenth-century *précieuses* created to substitute for the word "mirror": *la conseillère de grâces.* By using this term Colette makes an intertextual reference to a former tradition of female language and culture with which she is establishing a link. The denomination is used ironically here, however, for instead of being graceful, precious in language, the voice in the mirror is a very tough talker. While the *précieuses* sought refuge from male violence and vulgarity in extremes of refinement, for Colette that very refinement has itself become a trap.

This tough-talking *conseillère* tells Renée what she knows and doesn't want to hear. And it tells her in directly quoted speech. The voice of the mirror thus set off in quotation marks achieves a special status in Renée's denied writing. The first

12. In "Colette: The Mirror Image" (*French Forum* 3 [September 1978]) J. H. Stewart comments on the reflective role of Colette's writing and notes particularly "the introverted and reflexive" character of the name Renée Néré, which suggests closure and a turning round on the self (p. 196).

instance of acknowledged, authored female speech, it erupts like a well-defined truth in the ambiguous, elusive wash of Renée's words. The more obfuscated this discourse has become in Renée's language, the more clearly defined and pointed its projected version becomes.

Speaking woman to woman, the mirror voice represents the self-centered language that Renée has forsaken for Max. Reflecting her life and her identity back to her in the form of a question, the mirror emphasizes the relationship of self-sacrifice and silence:

> "Is that you there? All alone, there in that cage where idle, imprisoned hands have scored the white walls with interlaced initials and embellished them with crude, indecent shapes? On those plaster walls reddened nails, like yours, have unconsciously inscribed the appeal of the forsaken. Behind you a feminine hand has carved *Marie*, and the name ends in a passionate mounting flourish like a cry to heaven." [Pp. 5–6]

By imprisoning herself in a "cage" of silence as a mime, Renée has limited her writing to graffiti, the literature of the dispossessed. The mark of her identity, her very name, will become a cry of hopelessness.

The lucid and "dangerous" (p. 6) voice of the mirror is a reflection, but a transformed reflection, of this desperate writing. As it describes the crude dressing room, it transmutes it into an eloquent and passionate appeal. The mirror's speech provides a model of woman's writing that is not a strategy of concealment but rather a mode of revelation and recovery.

While Renée is immobilized emotionally by "thinking too much" (p. 83)—that is, by thinking from others' points of view—the mirror speaks in a full voice not fractured by indecision or even concern for others. It represents to Renée a call to remembrance, to lucidity, drawing her away from her "obsession with . . . *ifs* and *buts* and *howevers*" (p. 130).

The last long speech of the mirror occurs in the middle of the book, just before Renée sets out on her voyage. It is an angry, indignant speech, recalling to Renée the misfortunes of her first love (p. 129). The mirror now becomes a *"conseillère sans pitié,"* a pitiless adviser, who exhorts Renée to be realistic. But strangely, while this obdurate voice urges her not to trap herself in the deceptions of Taillandy's love, it suggests at the same time that that love was necessarily deceiving. The association between Renée's first love and Taillandy begins to unravel in the mirror's speech as the references of the masculine singular pronoun in French become more and more ambiguous:

> " 'You, who have found me once,' he [love] says, 'will lose me forever!' Did you think when you lost him [it] you had reached the limit of your suffering? It is not over yet! In striving to resuscitate what you once were, savor your fall [disgrace]: try to stem, at each feast of your new life, the poison flowing from the first, the only love! . . ." [P. 129, TM]

Religious language and references abound in this speech. The first love is a paradise of trust, giving, and true feeling. The loss of that love is a fall from grace, and all of life is poisoned by the memory of what is lost. As Taillandy becomes overshadowed and finally replaced in this speech by love itself, the suggestion that Taillandy himself was a replacement becomes stronger and stronger. His love was poison to Renée because it was a substitute for the nourishment of a former love. Renée was betrayed by Taillandy not so much because he was an unfaithful backguard but because his love already was, in and of itself, a betrayal.

At the beginning of the book Colette suggests that Renée's distrust of men in erotic relationships was the result of a particular bad experience and was therefore remediable; here she proposes a less contingent explanation. All love of men is essentially tainted, poisonous, because it cannot provide the total trust and acceptance given by the one who first furnished love and nourishment together. The love not only of Taillandy but of all men must by definition be a deception because it can never reproduce the mirroring the mother gave. Mistakenly

51

seeking that kind of nourishment and acceptance from men, Renée has alienated and sacrificed the very wholeness she sought.

While the mirror denounces loss and separation, it also creates in its speech a medium in which those losses, faced and acknowledged, can be recovered. For the mirror symbolically restores in its precise, tough, loving message the lost gift of the mother: self-knowledge.

Just as forgotten knowledge of herself comes to her from the mirror, other lost parts of Renée appear to her in the outside world. The return of these lost selves casts them indeed as ghostly *revenants* whose appearances, or rather apparitions, have an uncanny, intense quality precisely because they represent the familiar as unrecognizable. These phantoms are not figments of the author's imagination but fragments of her lost self returning to her in the mirror of her writing. Their return, like that of the specters they recall, must always by definition be unexpected. However fleeting these encounters with lost selves may be, they possess a vividness and intensity that come from the full presence they create:

> I look at my hand hanging down as though it did not belong to me. I don't recognize the stuff of my frock. Who was it, while I slept who loosened the coronet of plaits coiled about my brows like the tresses of a grave young Ceres? I was . . . I was . . . there was a garden . . . a peach-colored sunset sky . . . a shrill childish voice answering the cries of the swallows . . . yes, and that sound like distant water, sometimes powerful and sometimes muffled: the breath of a forest. I had gone back to the beginning of my life. What a journey to catch up with myself again, where I am now! [P. 119]

In this dream Renée begins in hesitant, incomplete sentences to retrieve her inner landscape, to recover the lost myths and memories that link her to herself. Compared with this forsaken but true self, her present adult self now seems remote, unrecognizable; even her own body feels uncannily estranged. The vividness of oneiric reality shows the "reality" of the waking world to be an impoverished, fictionalized construction; rather than a process of growth, her adult life has been an exercise in self-denial.

This repudiated self is a queenly young Ceres with her hair plaited crownlike about her head. Her "shrill childish voice," so like a bird call, is in fact part of nature's own voice, the indistinct, murmuring sound of the surrounding forest. Compared with her muiliated, fragmented, "caged" adult self, the debased queen of the music hall, the Renée preceding that disgrace, the "real" Renée who appears in this dream is a proud goddess in a paradise "garden" at the very heart of the earth's abundant life.

As Colette resuscitates what Renée once was, she emphasizes the essential nature of this lost self by placing her in a mythic context. This is no contingent being, the child of particular circumstances and events, but the unique, original, irreplaceable Renée. This description is not an incident out of history but the recurrent, infinitely repeatable story-dream of the truth.

Nevertheless, part of this story of Renée's original self still lies in mystery. Beyond this myth, uncertain even in this dreamed memory, is another presence, implicit but invisible like the unnamed mother of the mirror's speech. The undefined but implied support of Ceres' truth, this shadowy handmaid-mother-friend thus occupies a place in the lineage of ardent women whose grandiose loves have shaped the world. In her muted presence lies the secret, projected source of Ceres' passionate love for Proserpine, her violated and lost daughter whom she will endlessly grieve and recover.

Through its mythic reference, this brief passage turns out to be the complex *mise en abyme* of *The Vagabond*'s narration, not only Renée's but the text's dream of its own truth. At the literal and figurative center of the book, at once part of the narration and yet participating in another reality, this dream is the symbol and origin of Colette's writing, the place where the world's truth and her mythic account of herself as an author come together. There follows on this passage a grave song to sleep which scans like a Renaissance lyric. Having briefly tasted the bittersweet joy of rediscovering her lost self in Renée's dream, Colette recovers at the same time the solemn rhythmic beauty of poetic language:

O dangerous and too-kindly sleep
That in less than an hour destroys
The memory of myself!
Whence come I, and on what wings,
That it should take me so long,
Humiliated, exiled, to accept that I am myself?

Funeste et trop doux sommeil
Qui abolit en moins d'une heure
Le souvenir de moi-même!
D'où reviens-je et sur quelles ailes
Pour que, si lentement j'accepte,
Humiliée, exilée, d'être moi-même? [Pp. 119–20, TM]

The voyage Renée makes during the second half of the book is a trip into the world revealed through the portal of this dream. By means of this trip Colette explores and elaborates the realizations glimpsed in the fleeting vision of Renée's real self. Her voyage is, then, at once real and symbolic: a trip away from her actual home in Paris, which is a kind of exile, toward a spiritual home within herself. It represents a quest for continuity and wholeness, a search for the center from which she has strayed. If Renée can renew her links with her lost past, she will then be able to repossess and tell her own story instead of acting out the stories of others. With these possibilities before her, Renée's very leaving seems like a release. As she sets out, "reaching out towards [her] new lot with the glorious impulse of a serpent sloughing off its dead skin" (p. 70), she leaves the cage of her dressing room and the confinement of old definitions behind. For those who live in prison, homelessness is a liberation.

Read as the metaphor of Colette's writing, this vagabond life, while it is the very inscription of separation, loss, and rootlessness, nevertheless provides her only hope of healing, of

recuperation. Literal and figurative detachment from the false
selves, false loves, false language enforced by the social structures symbolized by the settled life of the city is a necessary
part of her process of self-definition.

This detachment and its link to female self-discovery are
immediately palpable in the narrator's writing. When Renée
leaves on her tour, the text immediately changes mode: inter-
calated with her previously undefinable private/public discourse are the letters she writes to Max. By setting the letters
off from the narration, Colette sets up a punctual counterpoint
between what Renée says to her male reader and what she
chooses not to say, that is, what she says to and for herself.
Thrown into a defined contrast with the letters, the text of
Renée's musings thus acquires a new status. Emerging from
its earlier ambiguous mode as seduction, with all that seduction implies of anger, self-abnegation, concealment, and dis-
honesty, Renée's extraepistolary discourse now becomes a private, self-centered language. Mirrors no longer speak to Renée,
for her own language has become the reflection of her self.

When Renée is separated from Max and no longer tempted
by his presence to submit to him sexually and emotionally,
what she conceals or reveals becomes a choice rather than a
necessity. Empowered by this new freedom, Renée realizes not
only that she is a text to be read but that she can be a reader as
well. She becomes an astute critic of Max's writing:

> Every day I wait for my love's letter. Every day it consoles me
> and disappoints me at the same time. He writes simply but
> obviously not with ease. His beautiful flowery writing slows up
> the natural impetus of his hand. . . . He associates me with his
> life and calls me his wife. He has no idea that by the time his
> warm solicitude reaches me it has become no more than a beau-
> tifully even writing, all cold on the paper; so far apart, what help
> to us are words? One needs—oh, I don't know—one needs some
> passionate drawing, all glowing with colour.   [Pp. 178–79]

While Max's hand was expressive and moving as it drew its
passionate pictures directly on her body, it does not know how

55

to express passion in writing. Proper, overembellished, "flowery," his handwriting is so slowed by proprieties that the warmth of its sentiments is cooled.

Max does not know how to take distance into account now because he never did. His relationship with Renée has always been for him unmediated by words and their meanings. Renée remarked earlier his indifference to her character, to what she had to say: "Neither does he show any eagerness to find out what I am like, to question me or read my character, and I notice that he pays more attention to the play of light on my hair than to what I am saying" (p. 78). She was astonished to learn that he had fallen in love with her the first time he had seen her dance: "It seems so queer to me that anyone can fall in love with a woman merely by looking at her" (p. 141).

The male reader is thus a false reader, not really a reader at all. His reading of the female text is a pretext, a feint: the words, the meaning of that text are immaterial, a flimsy and annoying covering that he wishes only to dispense with, to remove. As Colette interprets the male reader here through his own imagined writing, she discovers a radical split between language and desire. Because this split is so radical for Max, he has no means of maintaining his relation to Renée's body in his writing. In the male mode recreated here by Colette, that is precisely what cannot be written.

And that is precisely what is lacking not only in his words but in his handwriting as well. The very shape of his writing, the embodiment of his words, is stereotyped, conventional, lacking in passion: Renée desires "some passionate drawing, all glowing with colour." In the literal and figurative sense, writing is the *body* of language, a graphics that includes both its shape and its meaning. What is missing in Max's writing and what Renée longs for is a conjunction of body and meaning, a writing that would be the symbol of that conjunction— precisely its embodiment.

Having gained sufficient perspective to construct an imitation of male writing, Colette is able to engage in a dialogue with it rather than being, as she represented Renée at the beginning of the book, preempted and silenced by male desire, operating within it as its perverse resistance. When she is able to perceive male discourse as a defined shape, when she is thus able to repeat it on her own account, she realizes that the division in her own language originated in a split in male sensibility.

Now that the paramount question becomes not "Does he love me?" but rather "Do I love him?" the fragmentation reflected in and by her writing is revealed as a product of a specific writer-reader relationship and not as a natural state of affairs. Colette again describes here two modes of writing-reading, one a male mode based on power, the desire to possess masquerading as eroticism, the other a female mode based on a true eroticism, a desire for a symbolic union located in words.

Although Renée pleads with Max to be more spontaneous in his letters, to talk about his daily life (p. 187), they become more remote, empty, businesslike as time goes on. When she next receives a letter from him, the thin sheets of his writing paper "rustle like bank notes" (p. 191).

As Max's letters become more and more like public documents, tokens with which he wishes to buy Renée, hers become more disorderly, spontaneous to the point of illegibility: "On the table, four large sheets of paper bear witness to the haste with which I have written, no less than does the untidiness of the manuscript where the writing slopes upwards and downwards, sometimes bigger and sometimes smaller, responsive to my mood. Will he be able to make me out in all this untidiness? No" (pp. 200–201). Max will be unable to read Renée's moods, to follow the ups and downs of her feelings, to follow the disorderly sequence of her meanings. In other words, when Renée expresses herself freely, when her writing truly reflects her life as she experiences it, she loses Max as a reader.

Renée knows now that she would be unrecognizable to Max if she presented herself as she is. She has, symbolically, taken off her makeup. This shedding of adornments destined to make her more pleasing to a man represents for Renée the discovery of a more authentic self that she had lost and now is beginning to find. No longer measuring and molding herself according to Max's desire, she foresees with some bitterness that her natural nakedness—not the contrived, theatrical nakedness that originally seduced him—will be repugnant, incomprehensible to Max:

> "Why did you not know the tall child who used to trail her regal braids here, silent by nature as a wood nymph? . . . And now that it's too late, are not the things you love in me the things which change me and deceive you? What would you say if I were to reappear, if I appeared before you with my heavy straight hair, with my fair lashes cleansed of their mascara, in short with the eyes which my mother gave me, crowned with brief eyebrows quick to frown, grey, narrow, level eyes in the depths of which there shines a stern, swift glance, which I recognize as that of my father?" [P. 176]

The Renée that Max has known is a false one, a staged Renée, made up, seductive, insecure, and angry. The other Renée, the child, the solemn wood nymph that she here reveals to Max, she now recognizes as her real self. And what makes this nymph real, what is uncovered when her makeup comes off, is her resemblance to her parents. That resemblance, that inheritance, that link, is what has been covered up and concealed in her relation to Max, to men, to male readers who have had only a deceptive text to read. To please these readers, she has had to relinquish her identity as the daughter of her parents.

In a male-dominated society, women are denied their links with their own family: the change of names at marriage betokens the radical switch of identity and loyalties routinely expected of them. The price that women pay for this extirpation from their birth families is made vivid in this passage of Renée's letter. Furthermore, the suppression of these natural ties of kinship has tragically included for Renée not only the loss of her meaning but an estrangement from all of nature as well. While she recognizes that she cannot or "would not dare" return to the home of her childhood, tempting and rapturous as it might be to do so (p. 176), Renée can go back to the source of those blood ties, the origin of her own vitality—to nature.

The nature she returns to, rediscovers, is the vibrant, passionate, awakening nature of the southern spring, "which has thrust its way out of the earth and is burning itself up with its own haste" (p. 187). The urgency of this rebirth reflects the impatient spirit of Renée, long buried and now restlessly pushing toward revelation. The long-awaited epiphany takes place in the domesticated nature of a public garden at Nîmes. In a passage heavy with mythological overtones, Colette describes Renée's entrance into the garden, her awakening to life, the beginning of her self-possession: "I want to see again, under this heavy sky, my Elysian refuge, the Gardens of the Fountain" (p. 201).[13]

Renée visits the bath of Diana, "amorously" caresses its stones warm with spring, and gazes into the pool. There, in this new mirror, the world is turned upside down. In this reverse but original nature, old forms dissolve, decompose, and are transmuted into a rich, abundant world of color, silent but for the quiet, insistent sound of itself:

> A whole garden of reflections is spread out upside down below me as it decomposes in the aquamarine water, dark blue, the violet of a bruised peach, and the maroon of dried blood. Oh beautiful garden and beautiful silence, where the only sound is the muted plashing of the green, imperious water, transparent and dark, blue and brilliant as a bright dragon. [P. 201]

13. The pattern of awakening here follows exactly the paradigm proposed by S. J. Rosowski in her essay "The Novel of Awakening," in *The Voyage In: Fictions of Female Development*, ed. Elizabeth Abel, Marianne Hirsch, and Elizabeth Langland (Hanover, N.H.: University Press of New England, 1983). Rosowski identifies a major difference between the male and female *Künstlerroman:* the male novel is most often the story of an apprenticeship, while the female novel recounts an awakening, an awakening that is often also a realization of limitations (p. 49).

As her imagination plunges into Diana's waters, savors their depth and color, Colette travels to the other side of the mirror and takes possession of this new world in her vibrant, descriptive language.

The world is not only inverted in these waters, it is, in a sense, converted as well: Renée's experience here constitutes a baptism, a rebirth to another life. Out of the stones and waters of this pagan bath—the embodiment of the moon goddess, huntress, virgin presider over childbirth—comes a new perception of the world, a new set of values. When she acknowledges her birth of and as a woman, the former structure of the world and her participation in it appear topsy-turvy. Born again of another, symbolic mother, Renée realizes that her search for security in the arms of men, her falsification and abasement of herself to obtain their protective love have all been misguided and illusory efforts. She does not need to be defined through the desire of another because the world and language have always belonged to her.

Identifying and linking up with her own origins, Renée finally finds her place in the world, her home, but in a paradoxical form. The world "belongs" to her in a special way: it is a belonging without possession; a home that is any place:

> The beautiful garden lies spread out below, with open spaces in a geometrical design. The approach of the storm has driven away all intruders, and the hurricane with its hail rises slowly from the horizon, borne along in the billowing flanks of a thick cloud rimmed with white fire.
>
> All this is still my kingdom, a small portion of the splendid riches which God distributes to passers-by, to wanderers and solitaries. The earth belongs to anyone who stops for a moment, gazes and goes on his way; the whole sun belongs to the naked lizard who basks in it. [P. 202]

The spirit that is reborn in Renée is alive, intense, solitary, fierce, serene. A bright dragon, a hail-ridden storm, a basking lizard, she is simultaneously empowered and at peace. She has regained her pride with her inheritance, a strangely self-defining yet anonymous gift from God to the wanderers and solitaries of the earth. It is only those who own nothing, Colette says, who can possess the whole world. The houses men build are citadels of exile. The gift of the earth "to anyone who stops for a moment" is given freely to anyone who does not try to hold on to it. It is a gift that specifically has to do not with mastery and individual property but rather with pleasure and a shared abundance. The new Eden is a public garden.

Colette's vision of this vagabond paradise represents a further development of the mythological paradigm of her writing. Language does not belong to anyone, any more than does the earth. Words are not currency that can buy anyone or anything, nor do they represent a debt: symbols of the gifts of life, they reenact that gift. Misused, words may become, as they had for Renée, the instrument of dispossession; the very effort to own words or to own others through them perverts the nature of language, turning it from a form of expression into a form of oppression. On the other hand, when language is recognized for the gift that it is—public property over which no individual has legitimate control—then it becomes valuable in and of itself; using it becomes its own pleasure and its own end.

Renée's rebirth into being is accompanied, then, by a rebirth into language. Like the words of a child just learning how to speak, her phrases are halting, incomplete: "The whole truth, which I could not tell to Max, I owe to myself. It is not a beautiful truth, and it is still a bit feeble and scared, and slightly perfidious. So far all it can do is whisper to me in short sighs: 'I don't want . . . I musn't . . . I'm afraid'" (p. 202). For the first time her words can express "the whole truth," because they flow directly from their source in herself and are not shunted through a distorting, alien other who claims to control them. Renée's whispered, timorous, incomplete sentences represent the first inscription of her new voice, offered not to anyone in particular, (and) to herself—and they express her fear. What Renée is right now, what she has always been, is afraid. What drove her toward Max and what she covered up in her language was her fear. Now that she can say it, reveal rather than conceal it in her words, Renée is freed from her fear. Finding words for fear domesticates it, makes it part of her, a source of life. Instead of a destructive storm, it becomes sweet-tasting rain: "Now the stormy cloud is passing over my head, letting fall, one by one, sluggish, scented drops of water. A star of rain plops on the corner of my mouth and I drink it, warm and sweetened with a dust that tastes of jonquils" (p. 203).

Renée's discovery of herself and her own language takes place specifically outside her dialogue with Max and as a liberation from it. As she frees herself from her need for him as the "witness," the reader of her life (p. 111), she begins to redefine her nature as a woman. She no longer associates her femininity with the impulse to submit, to seek a master. In fact, the desire for words, for precise, expressive words, displaces her need for Max. The intense but wounding sensuality experienced with him is replaced by another kind of eroticism that makes everything else seem unimportant:

> Sète and the sea! There it was again, running along beside the train, when I had quite forgotten it. The seven o'clock sun, still low on the horizon, had not yet penetrated it; the sea was refusing to let itself be possessed and, hardly awake, still kept its nocturnal color of ink-blue crested with white. . . . Half asleep, like the sea, and yielding to the swaying of the train, I thought I was skimming the waves, so close at hand, with a swallow's cutting flight. And then I experienced one of those perfect moments, the kind of happiness that comes to a sick person, unable to think, when a sudden *memory*, an image, a name, turned me once again into an ordinary creature, the creature of yesterday and the days before. How long had it lasted, that moment when for the first time I had forgotten Max? Yes, forgotten him, as though I had never known his gaze, nor the caress of his mouth, forgotten him as if the one imperious care in my life were to seek for words, words to express how yellow the sun is, how blue the sea, and how brilliant the sail like a fringe of white jet. . . . In that same hour an insidious spirit whispered to me: "And if indeed that were the only urgent thing? If everything save that were merely ashes? . . ." [Pp. 206–7]

Identified at once with the unpossessed sea waking from a long sleep, a child being rocked by the swaying of the train, and the imaginary swallow cutting over the waves, Renée experiences in this moment a totality, a fullness that drives out the fragmented, "sick" being she was with Max. Her need for Max, her thinking about him have been obsessive precisely because her relationship with him was unsatisfying, false, askew. The replete sensuality of her response to the beauty of this scene, her link to it through the metaphors she creates, this is the union that completes her.

Now that she has come back to the sea, homonymic in French with the mother ("There it was again . . . when I had quite forgotten it")—now that she is reconnected, in other words, to the source of her own life and energies—the rift in her that was Max, that "wound" of self-canceling desire, is healed and she becomes a whole person. No longer "sick," in need of protection and care, she rediscovers the roots and wild freedom of her childhood by giving up her childish dependency on a man. At once rocked by the train and swooping with the bird in its cutting flight, she is secure and free at the same time. Her liberation, this *vol tranchant*, both flight and theft, doubles and cuts through the "sombre curtain" of sleep that was both the cloak and doorway of this lost/new world (p. 119). She steals back in effect from Max what was already hers but had been given away under duress: her language, her self had become "alienated" property, as the attorneys say.

Renée recovers her imperious need for expression, her care for words, her pride in choosing the right words to describe the world, not as an "ex-blue-stocking" but as a queenly wanderer. The freedom and power to reunite with the world in her own metaphors, this is the trace of the swallow's flight over the ink-blue sea, the source and shape of Renée's writing that we read.

An "insidious" spirit whispers suggestive questions to Renée, rhetorical questions whose response is an implied yes. Yes, language is all, "the only urgent thing." Yes, all else is ashes. The voice is "insidious" because its suggestions undermine the values the world has set for women, turn them topsy-turvy. Yes, what if women began to care most of all for expressing themselves? Yes, what if the most important thing were not to marry and have children?

Following this episode, Renée indeed decides not to marry Max. Her decision further unleashes her tongue: words come coursing, tumbling out of her, angry, crude, violent words, as if the pressure of all her collected and contained anger were finally released. As before with her fear, this expressed anger connects Renée with herself and her past: in these "fits of coarseness" she finds within her some primitive force, the tongue of a "foul-mouthed ancestor" (p. 211).

Empowered by the release of her anger and indignation, Renée speaks proudly, with a strength and shrewdness that recall the voice of the mirror at the beginning of the book. Speaking now from within Renée rather than without, this voice addresses Max with all the frustration and fury that had before rendered it mute:

> "What are you giving me? Another myself? There is no other myself. You're giving me a friend who is young, ardent, jealous and sincerely in love? I know: that is what is called a master, and I no longer want one. He is good and simple, he admires me and he is straightforward? In that case he is my inferior and I should be making a misalliance. A look of his can rouse me and I cease to belong to myself if he puts his mouth on mine? In that case he is my enemy, he is the thief who steals me from myself. . . . Come back to me, beseeches my love, leave your job and the shabby sadness of the surroundings where you live, come back among your equals. I have no equals, I have only my fellow wayfarers." [Pp. 214–15]

In this imagined dialogue, Renée plays both parts, Max's and her own. And as she, like Colette earlier, imitates male discourse, repeats it faithfully but from her own perspective, it comes undone; the words dissolve into another vocabulary. The claimed objectivity that makes male discourse a mirror of the world is revealed as a false front for seduction, a cover for a power play. Renée translates this distorted language into its precise meaning for her as a woman, and as she does so, the structures of romance and marriage unravel into brutal, immoral ploys. The young, ardent, sincere suitor is in fact a "master." Because his love hides a desire to possess, he is an "enemy," a "thief." The partnership of marriage is in reality always a "misalliance."

When Renée translates male into female vocabulary as it defines the most intimate coming together of a man and a woman, erotic connection and marriage are revealed as an arena, a jousting place, where conflict and power are hidden by false words. "Love," as the word is usually used, is indeed a fiction; the reality is warfare, falseness, and servitude.

In the face of this falsehood, Renée declares her truth: her uniqueness, her wholeness, her strength. Not only is Max not superior to her because he is rich and proper, he is not even her equal. He cannot give her anything because she already has it all. "There is no other myself": this triumphant declaration marks the resolution of Renée's doubts, her conflicts, her dividedness, her fragmentation. Her other scattered selves, fractured off and seeming to speak to her from Max, from the mirror, from the phantoms of her childhood, she now possesses as her own. No longer dispersed in the outside world, they are within her and speak as one.

While these realizations arc truly gained, they are expressed only in an imagined dialogue. Renée never says or writes these words to Max. Since they are not inscribed in her actual relationship with him, as she returns toward Paris she has the impression of slipping backward not only in space but in her emotional state as well. Her return from her trip is another kind of going back. Her sense of wholeness and vitality drifts away from her like the bold landscapes of the South, whose loss she chants in a grave *ubi sunt* motif: "Where are the Pyrenees with their blossoming cherries, the great austere mountain which seemed to follow us. . . ? Where are the narrow valleys, turf-carpeted, and the wild orchids white as gardenias?" (p. 213). The swallow of Sète with its cutting flight is replaced by butterflies that "flutter about with torn wings" (p. 215). The vivid colors of Diana's bath fade into dark hues;

"silvery and twilit like the screech-owl, the silky mouse, the wings of the clothes-moth" (p. 223, TM). The bright dragon has yielded to beautiful but more furtive night creatures. As she returns to her flat unannounced in the first light of dawn, Renée herself has faded so much that she is almost invisible, the color of shadows; she enters noiselessly, "like a thief."

While her triumphant sense of certainty has deserted her, neither does her old place feel like home. The woman who lived there is no more. Truly now she is a vagabond, and as she passes through her former flat she takes care not to disturb anything in this abandoned abode with its "funereal air" (p. 222).

The only trace she leaves of her passing is a letter for Max, a letter of adieu, written slowly and, following Max's pattern, carefully reread for punctuation and spelling. In this letter, she does not speak to him in the full, triumphant voice she had imagined, but rather in soothing, sad tones reminiscent of the old days. In this elegiac letter, she clings to Max even as she takes her leave: "For the last time embrace me as if I were cold, hold me very close, very close, very close . . . Renée" (p. 221). As soon as she seals the envelope, she shivers as if she had "blocked out a luminous opening." If her rejection of Max and all that he stands for is an affirmation of herself, it is also a renunciation of that very human part of her who longed for security, love, and recognition. In a society that classifies and recognizes women only by their marital status, and given the nature of marriage, Renée's only choice if she wishes to be true to herself is a kind of permanent vagabondage. She may be free, but she is also "horribly alone" (p. 124).

In women's lives as presented in *The Vagabond*, self-affirmation and marriage present an either/or alternative. Renée's awakening to herself and the sources of her life, her choice of symbolic creativity, her love of words above all else preclude her participation in more conventional forms of love and creativity. Her decision to search for the whole truth, to choose her own wholeness, imposes, then, dramatic limitations on her. Since women's truth is excluded from male stories of romance, truthful women are therefore banned from playing a role in that story.

Having no other alternatives in a society organized around male power and its justification/concealment in the discourse of "love," Renée's commitment to a language that expresses female being paradoxically and ironically unsexes her. "Look at yourself, my poor girl," she exhorts herself, "look at yourself, you're not an old woman, by a long chalk, but you're already a kind of confirmed bachelor [*un vieux garçon*]" (p. 211). In her last letter to Max she calls herself a *vieille fille*, an old maid: "You will understand that I must not belong to you or to anyone, and that in spite of a first marriage and a second love, I have remained a kind of old maid" (p. 220).

Following Colette's definition of her place as a woman artist, we must then put "woman" in quotation marks or bar it off, for the erotic alliances between woman and man and between woman and children are denied her. In the rules of male-centered social organization, either these alliances come first for a woman or they must be relinquished altogether. Colette's discovery of her place in the world as a writer is the discovery that in the world's (male) definition she has no place, or only the diminished, unsexed place of an old maid. While Renée celebrated the recognition of her true self in the "unsociable look," the "ageless, almost sexless eyes" of the wild wood nymph she had been (p. 92), in the context of her adult life this sexlessness carries with it the necessity of a deprivation. Discovering herself in her fullness as a woman ironically disqualifies her from acting her part in the female role given her by society to play. And so she casts it aside. Unable at this point to imagine a different, more inclusive alternative, she must choose either to be a "woman" or to be herself.

Although Renée continues to assert her independence, this very assertion is now absorbed into a system of destructive alternatives. All choices involve a loss, and the accent here is on what Renée has lost by choosing herself. Although she has unraveled the tangled hypocrisies of male discourse and rewoven a language of her own, Renée's truth neither triumphs nor creates a consolation of its own. Colette never arranges a direct confrontation between the reborn Renée and her "dear adversary." As she has Renée explain, "A heroine who is only human, like myself, is not strong enough to triumph over all the demons" (p. 219).

The message Colette leaves for us, like Renée's letter to Max, is mixed, melancholy, colored with loss. Because Renée's rejection of Max is never registered or recognized in his discourse, she cannot be the "heroine" of her own story or of ours. Even her letter to him remains, as she says, "unfinished" (p. 222), not only because she will never be able to tell a man the whole truth but also because all her writing from now on will be the repetition of her sacrifice. Because the final encounter never took place, because the final words were never exchanged, Renée, in effect, will never totally take leave of Max; she will continue writing and talking to him in her mind until her last word is spoken. The text of The Vagabond, which was a dialogue with herself, now becomes a never-finished message to Max:

In each place where my desires have strayed, I leave thousands and thousands of shadows in my own shape, shed from me: one lies on the warm blue rocks of the ledges of my own country, another in the damp hollow of a sunless valley, and a third follows a bird, a sail, the wind and the wave. You [Max] keep the most enduring of them: a naked, undulating shadow, trembling with pleasure like a plant in the stream. But time will dissolve it like the others, and you will no longer know anything of me until the day when my steps finally halt and there will fly away from me a last small shadow. [P. 223]

In this final passage of the book Colette traces the desires that shape her discourse. While once they put her together, they are now her undoing. No longer conceived as emanating from an infinitely renewable source, her desires-words flow rather from a finite fund that will one day be exhausted. The shadowy ghosts of an already lost vitality, they do not create wholeness but rather betoken separation and death.

At the end of her book Colette slithers away from her own discovery. As she rewrites the epiphany of the bath of Diana in the imagery of this passage, water is no longer a life-giving reflecting pool, a new world, but a fatal, dissolving stream. As if drowning once again in her own fear, like Millais's beautiful but quiescent Ophelia, the queenly Colette is borne to her death by the very element that gave her life. The flow of her words marks the ebbing of her life because, in this version of her writing, they do not connect her to anyone, not even, or perhaps most especially, to herself. Unable to conceive of a reader other than the already rejected Max to receive her writing, Colette imagines her desires-words as isolated fragments of herself which in a continuously depleting process are shed and then dissolved. Her writing is not, therefore, a gift, part of a symbolic exchange, but rather the record of her ultimate solitude.

In this final message, *The Vagabond* seems to repeat "the appeal of the forsaken" with which it began. Returning to the graffiti writing of her initial cage, Colette does indeed seem to have "become again *what [she] was*" (p. 124). Read recursively as flowing from its own ending, *The Vagabond* is the story of a woman going in circles who endlessly meets herself in her solitude. But this vagabond, rather than seeming a drifter, can now be seen as someone who has reluctantly but lucidly chosen the cycle of life and death, triumph and solitude that shapes her journey.

In the tradition of male literature, the once-married woman is often presented as the only available model of a sexually mature, independent woman who can choose for herself. But the Célimènes and the Aramintes of the world, as fantasized by men, are interested only in choosing another man, in marrying again. Colette rewrites this male fantasy of a woman's independence from the woman's point of view; and, of course, the story turns out quite differently. She imagines what a man could not or would not dare—a woman who does not wish to choose another man. Like her predecessor, Mme de Lafayette, Colette portrays this exercise of female will as both triumphant and destructive. But although the end of *The Vagabond* contains echoes of the Princess of Cleves's wasting death, Colette imagines a more vigorous protagonist who reflects both the doubts and the determination with which she herself launched her fledgling career.

Beginning as a narrator with a sense of being overwhelmed, squelched, silenced by the tradition of male accomplishment and betrayal, Colette finds a way of taking a place in that economy of desire by using words seductively. Adapting conventional male military metaphors of the "war" between the sexes to the dynamics of writing-reading, Colette represents the female writer and the male reader as adversaries by nature and necessity. The relationship between writer and readers thus becomes a barely disguised struggle for power in which, to maneuver the advantaged male, Colette uses the traditional female arsenal of manipulation and duplicity: she censors her own language, puts makeup on her discourse, controls her vulnerability by dramatizing it. In order to attract notice, love, and admiration, she travesties herself in her words, purposely splitting appearance and reality.

For women, for Colette, writing for a male audience is theater, a staged event. Using her words the way an actress uses her body, the woman writer may appear to be telling a story, but she is—as Colette insistently demonstrates in the choice of her protagonist's career—essentially silent. A woman writing in the male tradition, that is, maintaining her conventional role as object, can end up only as an alienated, angry, fragmented, seductive, betrayed, duplicitous, childish mime who goes through the motions in someone else's story.

When Colette can imagine distancing herself from this male audience and can conceptualize her writing as writing rather than as show, then the falsity imposed on it by her objectification begins to drop away. No longer constrained to channel her words through the filter of a desire that denies hers, she can reconnect them to her own subjectivity. When her own desires are the subject of her writing, Colette recovers not only her present perceptions but her past as well. She can use her words to reconnect the parts of herself she has had to leave behind in order to fit in a male discourse. Restoring her kinship with her parents and thus establishing her own identity, Colette repossesses a continuity, a history that had been lost: the story of her life told from her own point of view. So glorious is her sense of (re)discovery, so precious are the memories she recovers, that they seem to her a paradise. Feeling reborn into a truer, more natural self, one less subject to the ill-fitting, artificial rules of men, Colette no longer needs to disguise herself in what she says. The colors she was preoccupied with in her makeup resume their original setting in the glorious shades and tints of nature.

This free writing, expressive of female experience and desire, can occur, according to Colette, only outside the circuitry of heterosexual desire, which she interprets as the pervasive paradigm controlling all relationships between men and women, including literary tradition. She exposes the origins of this tradition in the economy of private property and the legal and emotional power of men as the proprietors, the masters of the earth. In place of this system based on the notion of quantifiable, limited resources, Colette proposes another, female economy in which resources are infinitely renewable and therefore freely available to all. In this view, language is a genuinely public artifact, belonging to anyone and everyone. Seen as a gratuitous gift rather than as an instrument of mastery, language is at once a reflection of and a trope for the creation of the female subject.

In *The Vagabond* Colette does not conceive of any actual confrontation or dialogue between these two models of language. The male system is clearly preemptive in her mind. The male-based, heterosexual structures and her own deeply rooted complicity in those structures are "demons" so dangerous and powerful that she dare not meet them head on. Persuaded that the "whole truth" can never be told to a man— and perhaps not to any other being—in the name of realism she rejects the role of heroine and strikes a compromise. Neither speaking out directly nor remaining silent, she slithers

71

away in an inconclusive ending. She finally preserves the integrity of her discoveries, of her text, but as a homeless, vagabond discourse with no defined place in a network of sexual, social, or literary connection.

When it comes to placing her writing as a woman in a new, public structure of desire, Colette's imagination falters, blocked. She fleetingly evokes the possibility of a writing-reading that would be an exchange between women (p. 188), but this model of two women sharing "the bitter happiness of feeling themselves akin, frail, and forgotten" is encapsulated in a depressed helplessness that quickly fades into silence.[14] As though wary of being snared again in the betrayals of possessive love, and knowing she cannot return to the paradise of childhood, Colette remains suspended between these two negative alternatives, never fictionalizing a positive place for her text. Conceptualizing language as a gift, she nevertheless gives it to no one—or indifferently to anyone—and, contrary to all internal evidence, declares her writing unsexed.

This failure, this fading, has the bizarre effect of putting the reader in a perverse relationship with the text. Like a woman who accidentally-on-purpose "forgets" to draw the curtains while she undresses, Colette offers her subjectivity to us, but as a surreptitiously arranged spectacle staged for a denied/desired observer. By thus theatricalizing her discovery of herself in a specious, technically hysterical way, Colette preserves the fragile integrity of her newfound language without making it vulnerable to the power of another's desire.

Although there is some coyness, perhaps even cunning, in this defensive exhibition,[15] it is the dark side of Colette's real

14. We witness here a puzzling discrepancy between the appearances of Colette's life and what she wrote in her books: while Colette was scandalously blatant at this time in her affair with the Marquise de Belbeuf (Missy), she was most discreet in her writing. In the "Nuit blanche," *Les Vrilles de la vigne* (1908), a lyrical expression of love written about Missy, Colette took care to conceal the gender of her lover. Later, in *Le Pur et l'impur* (1932), she wrote openly about lesbianism, but the attitude she expressed seems at times severe, at its most generous ambivalent.

15. Colette was preoccupied all her life with these ambiguities of exhibi-

triumph—her recovered wholeness, her union with herself. It is the triumph of this desire, a woman's desire for herself—grievously feared, distorted, decried, and denied in male tradition—that Colette dares declare in her writing and strives valiantly to protect.

To watch a woman love herself, one need not be a voyeur; to adopt that stance as readers is to drown in the values that turn women's self-love into pornography. Rather, precisely because we live in a world in which Colette has written, we can imagine for ourselves as readers another place that she dared not offer. It is the place of a vagabond but loyal companion who will follow the ups and downs of her moods, the ins and outs of her writing: the tough-talking mirror; or perhaps we can fill the one place left empty by Colette in the book—a shadowy place before myth, before story, an origin unnamed, a companion unimagined, the invisible handmaid-mother-friend who lets down her hair, undoes her plaited crown.

The slyness, hesitancies, fears, unfinishedness of this book may startle coming from a writer who in her life was the image of courage, persistence, and strength. She was a woman who, as Erica Jong says in the poem addressed to her, seemed to have it all.[16] The differences between the fictional and the real stories may be a measure of the very falsity of public stereotypes that Colette herself decried. Or it may be that Colette revealed in her writing the difficulty of being who she was: a writer. She lived another forty-four years after the pub-

---

tionism and concealment in her writing. She seemed to enjoy giving the impression of revealing herself when she was intentionally hiding. At one time she remarked, "Give me the right to hide myself in my novels even if it is in the same way as the 'Purloined Letter.'" At another, she asserted that her most authentic intimacy was a "secret treasure" that she revealed to no one (Sarde, *Colette libre et entravée,* epigraph and p. 262).

That Colette actually felt her story overwhelmed by intimacy with a man at this stage of her life is borne out by the fact that during her marriage to Henri de Jouvenel, which followed by three years the publication of *The Vagabond,* Colette wrote exclusively as a journalist; she did not allow herself the "luxury" of writing any novels until after their divorce (see ibid., p. 293).

16. Erica Jong, "Dear Colette," in *Loveroot* (New York: Holt, Rinehart & Winston, 1975).

lication of *The Vagabond,* and she continued to write for all of those years. But even for Colette, the apparently simple act of writing in her own voice was a task not easily achieved. That the difficulties and dangers involved in that task, that the struggles and compromises scarring her hard-won integrity are audible in her voice is not surprising. By gallantly persevering in her search for her own words, this persistent vagabond domesticated writing for the women who came after her. By insisting on being human, she became a heroine.

2

Simone de Beauvoir:
The Murderer

It is hard to imagine two women more different in temperament and style than Colette and Simone de Beauvoir: Colette,
the Bourguinonne, revering the earth, its plants and animals,
passionate, anti-intellectual, flouting convention but tolerant
of those who did not; Simone de Beauvoir, the Parisienne,
intellectual, reserved, a determined challenger of accepted values. The two women met a year or so before the death of
Colette. Understandably, they did not take to each other. We
have no record of Colette's reaction to this meeting, but Beauvoir recorded her impressions in *The Force of Circumstance*,
part of her autobiography. Colette received her "coldly," Beauvoir says, and she goes on to comment a bit disdainfully on
Colette's "startling make-up."[1] In an interview ten years later,
Beauvoir is even more negative in her attitude toward Colette:
"Colette is after all very taken up with her little stories of
love, of households, of laundry and animals."[2]

This disdain bordering on hostility points up a characteristic
that has troubled many feminist critics: Beauvoir's haugh-
tiness, even toward other women, and her contempt for

1. Simone de Beauvoir, *The Force of Circumstance (La Force des choses)*,
trans. Richard Howard (New York: Putnam, 1964), p. 237.
2. Quoted in Serge Julienne-Caffié, *Simone de Beauvoir* (Paris: Gallimard,
1966), p. 212.

"household" stories.[3] For Colette, writing was not a privileged activity: it was one craft among others. For Simone de Beauvoir, writing was a sacred task, a vocation and a way of salvation: "Through literature, one justifies the world by creating it anew, in the purity of the imaginary, and by the same token, one saves one's own existence."[4] All other activities paled for Simone de Beauvoir in the light of this scriptorial salvation: "I never regretted not having children to the degree that what I wanted to do was to write."[5]

Colette integrated her "household" experiences, including her motherhood, into her writing; Beauvoir regarded those domains as more or less mutually exclusive: one canceled out the other. Writing was the justification of her life; no other justification was necessary. Beauvoir constructed a system of priorities concerning her writing so rigorous that it had the effect of diminishing all other values. Writing justified her life, but as the only means of salvation, it made life itself seem by comparison impure, incomplete, unworthy.

This sense of hollowness explains perhaps Simone de Beauvoir's minute documentation of her life,[6] but it does not explain her almost equally abundant commentary on her writing. Not only was Beauvoir's life doubled by its own chronicle, her writing as well is documented and shadowed by another writing, as if it too were insufficient and incomplete.

3. See "Interview with Madeleine Gobeil," in ibid.; Elaine Marks, *Simone de Beauvoir: Encounters with Death* (New Brunswick, N.J.: Rutgers University Press, 1973); Jean Leighton, *Simone de Beauvoir on Woman* (Rutherford, N.J.: Fairleigh Dickinson University Press, 1975); Carol Ascher, *Simone de Beauvoir: A Life of Freedom* (Boston: Beacon, 1981).

4. Quoted in Anne-Marie Lasocki, *Simone de Beauvoir, ou L'Enterprise d'écrire* (The Hague: Martinus Nijhoff, 1971), p. 24.

5. Quoted in Julienne-Caffié, *Simone de Beauvoir*, p. 215.

6. *Memoirs of a Dutiful Daughter (Mémoires d'une jeune fille rangée)*, trans. James Kirkup (New York: Harper & Row, 1974; first pub. World, 1959); *The Prime of Life*, trans. Peter Green (New York: World, 1962); *Force of Circumstance; All Said and Done (Tout compte fait)*, trans. Patrick O'Brien (New York: Putnam, 1974). Beauvoir has also documented other specific events in her personal life: the death of her mother in *A Very Gentle Death (Une Mort très douce)* and the death of Sartre in *La Cérémonie des adieux*.

I wish to look first at some of Beauvoir's statements about writing and then double back on a primary text, her first published novel, *She Came to Stay.* This technique of holding her writing up to its own mirror will reveal the doubleness (duplicity) of her image of herself as a writer, which ends up making her fiction the endless repetition of a (self-)murder.

Double Writing: Fact and Fiction

Simone de Beauvoir wrote literally thousands of pages of autobiography, in which she chronicles, among other things, the birth of her vocation, the genesis of each of her books, its composition, and its publication. She also provides her interpretation of each book and a commentary on its critics. What we find in her autobiography, then, is a second writing that explains, completes, and justifies the first. Each commentary on her novels in the autobiography becomes a companion text to the original, a nonfiction partner of the work of imagination. The texts form a pair, one the explanation and justification of the other.

In the cases where the primary—in the sense of "first"— text is a fictional work, the relationship Beauvoir establishes between it and its commentary tends to reproduce the original relationship she posited between life and writing. Just as life paled in the sacred light of writing, so fiction begins to seem insufficient in comparison with nonfiction: "It's a little boring to make up stories. So many people think that it's better to be very close to reality and to recount one's life as it is rather than . . . to fictionalize, as they say, that is to transpose, and therefore to cheat."[7] Nonfiction, she believes (or is it only the other "people," the "they"?), is somehow closer to reality than fiction and is therefore a superior mode of expression. In this truly Platonic statement, she envisages fiction as a distortion, as "reality" twisted out of shape. Beauvoir thus sets up a

7. Alice Jardine, "Interview with Simone de Beauvoir," *Signs* 5 (Winter 1979), 234.

hierarchy of kinds of writing, with nonfiction—her auto-biography, essays, and published interviews—at the top, and fiction coming after as a less true, more distorted version of the truth.

At other times she speaks in a more positive mode about fiction and its role. She calls it the "privileged locus of inter-subjectivity," where separation is overcome and people—namely, she and her readers—can come together.[8] Fiction is the arena of feeling and connection, the same domain as that allotted to women in our society. Nonfiction, as she defines it, is the sphere of reason, lucidity, truth, the province assigned to men.

Thus Beauvoir dichotomizes writing into two modes that correspond to the traditional division of human experience according to gender. She goes on to arrange these modes of experience in a hierarchy that also reflects traditional values. While she defines the work of Eros accomplished in fiction as one of her most "comforting" experiences as a writer,[9] she still sees it as inferior to the more direct expression of reality accomplished in nonfiction writing. Nonfiction corresponds finally to what so many "people" value—rigor and veracity—while fiction, comforting as it may be, is messy, distorted, a cheat.

Nonfiction, the male mode associated with reason, instru-mentality, and objectivity, is, according to Beauvoir, the more nearly complete and self-sufficient of the two modes of know-ing. The complementarity of the fiction/nonfiction couple is only apparent. The secondary text—the commentary—is ac-tually primary in importance. The interpretation takes prece-dence over the fiction, not because it fills in its gaps but rather because it presents a more accurate representation of its sub-ject. While appearing to be partners, fiction and nonfiction are in fact unequal: nonfiction supplants its predecessor, whose

8. "My Experience as a Writer" ("Mon expérience d'écrivain"), lecture given in Japan in 1966, reproduced in Claude Francis and Fernande Gontier, *Les Ecrits de Simone de Beauvoir* (Paris: Gallimard, 1979), p. 459.
9. Ibid.

connection with the female mode of intersubjectivity makes it the expression of doubt and distortion. Beauvoir regards fiction as the inscription of fantasy and therefore as a somewhat frivolous stage of development that one abandons as one grows older ("It's a little boring to make up stories"). Fiction is a little juvenile, a little crazy, and it needs to be contained and corrected by good solid commentary, good solid facts.

In spite of its pleasure, fiction (woman) cannot stand on its own two feet; it does not constitute a self-sufficient and complete reality. Even women writers of fiction are tainted by their *genre* (gender): in Beauvoir's view they are in general "inferior to men," good only when they have been pushed and encouraged by their fathers.[10] Literature is an inferior mode of knowledge, and it sinks even lower when it is not animated by male seriousness and ambition.

As we can see, while Simone de Beauvoir had an intense and elevated sense of her vocation as a writer, she had a highly ambivalent and conflicted view of herself as a writer of novels. On the one hand, she regarded fiction as an inferior form of writing, in fact, a form of lying. On the other hand, she also viewed fiction as the place where all the mess and complexity of life could be exposed; the place where her need to be recognized and loved in all her confusion could be met. Furthermore, this ambivalence toward fiction is inextricably linked with Beauvoir's ambivalence toward her own gender. For her the question of writing could not remain neutral, or rather neuter. Like all other activities of life, both for the collectivity and for Beauvoir as an individual, writing is visualized, explained, and justified by means of a mythology of gender. The gender of the writer cannot therefore be a neutral issue: it is called into question by the very writing whose task it is to express it. The explanatory mythology of gender reflexively undoes the fact it is called upon to explain and express.

---

10. "Woman and Creation" ("La Femme et la création"), lecture given in Japan in 1966, reproduced in Francis and Gontier, *Ecrits de Simone de Beauvoir*, pp. 465, 468.

Beauvoir's double ambivalence toward her writing and her gender creates a turbulent but hidden complex of vulnerabilities and defenses which makes her fiction a puzzle of mixed connections. While her ample commentary on her fiction betrays some uneasiness, some attempt to domesticate her fiction's wildness, the net effect of these commentaries is to cover the confusion, to shield or prevent the reader from facing the trouble that is there. This preemptive move by Beauvoir in respect to the interpretation of her fiction turns the task of the critic, whose place has already been taken by the author, into an act of antagonism, even of violation.

Which was perhaps Beauvoir's most hidden but most imperious wish.

The Right to Write

She Came to Stay, Beauvoir's first published novel, is itself a story of love turned into antagonism and violence.[11] Beauvoir tells us that she drew heavily on her own experience for the plot of the novel. In 1933 she and Jean-Paul Sartre formed a trio with one of her students, Olga Kosakievicz, to whom the novel is dedicated. For more than three years they worked on this relationship as an existential enterprise, trying to move beyond the bourgeois notion of love as possession in a generous extension of the couple. This unusual network of attachments proved to be highly unstable and depended for its survival on a certain amount of self-sacrifice on Beauvoir's part. She says, in fact, that she was never happy with the trio but attempted to make it work because she did not want to block Sartre's wishes, as at that time he was highly unstable, on the brink of psychosis.[12]

11. Trans. Yvonne Moyse and Roger Senhouse (London: Martin Secker & Warburg, 1949); first pub. as *L'Invitée* (Paris: Gallimard, 1943). All quotations are from the London edition. Modifications of the translation are indicated by "TM." The title is infelicitously translated, especially in view of what happens to Xavière: the French means simply "the guest."

12. *Prime of Life*, p. 204.

Though their attempt to realize a new kind of intimacy ultimately failed, as Beauvoir tells us in her autobiography, she and Olga continued to be friends. In the fictional transposition of this experience, however, in the messy, female domain of fiction, Beauvoir's counterpart murders the younger woman.

A first published book cannot help having a special standing in the life of its author. For one thing, the enterprise of writing has to justify itself in a more essential way at this time than it does later, when the question becomes whether to write and publish this particular book, not whether to write at all. The very uncertainty of its publication makes the impetus driving the author forward even stronger and more vivid in its definition than it is likely to be later on. In this respect, Beauvoir makes some interesting comments on what her desires and fantasies were as she worked on *She Came to Stay.* She first of all links writing the book with an attempt to separate her being from Sartre's, to feel and express her own autonomy. Strangely, she associates this gesture with the commission of a crime. The murder that ends the book is not only the raison d'être of the novel for her, it is also a fictional reflection of Beauvoir's fantasy of writing: a fantasy of a radical gesture whose very enormity would isolate her in her responsibility for it. She also says that as she worked on *She Came to Stay* she had another fantasy: "I dreamed of splitting off from myself, of becoming a shade [*ombre*] that would pierce the hearts of my readers and would haunt them."[13]

These fantasies share a common element: the linking of writing with a murder. Writing may be a sacred vocation, but it is also a crime, the only means Beauvoir, as a woman, could conceive of to establish herself as a separate, autonomous being; the only way she had of establishing her author-ity.

Even though it is a first novel, *She Came to Stay* is not a *Bildungsroman.* The protagonist, Françoise (she bears the name of Beauvoir's mother), who considers herself a writer, is

13. Ibid., pp. 270–71, 291 (TM).

established in a long-term relationship with Pierre, an actor and director. The conflict between commitment to love and commitment to work, which often plays an important role in female writers' novels, is thus already reconciled in *She Came to Stay*. In fact, both of these elements of Françoise's life—her love for Pierre and her work—are curiously effaced or muted. The novel that Françoise is writing during the course of *She Came to Stay* is rarely mentioned, while Pierre's work in the theater appears constantly in the foreground; and there is essentially no depiction of physical passion or deep erotic connection between Françoise and Pierre. The history of the struggles, passions, conflicts that must mark the life of a woman as unusual as Françoise is simply absent. So although Françoise is presented as a character who has solved the usual conflicts of a professional woman, it is as if she never confronted them at all. She gives the impression of being at a stage before these conflicts had arisen, where love and independence present themselves in more primitive forms than those of adult eroticism and creativity.

This same effacement of eroticism applies to the triangle Pierre-Françoise-Xavière as well. The fact that adult eroticism or passion, although it is stated as a possibility, is never acted on within the trio creates an impression of uncanniness or gratuitousness in this enterprise of triangularity. These people seem to operate in a world predating sexual passion. We find, then, the central characters playing out with extreme intensity a drama that makes sense as a childhood fantasy but not as an adult enterprise. The plot has the air of an acting-out in which all the reasoning and talk seem but rationalization; the energies of the protagonists appear misplaced.

This displacement of energy and the apparent gratuitousness of the situation create the feeling that underneath the rivalries and trivialities of this triangle, something else is going on. We are in a world in which the issues are in fact more primitive than those of erotic connection, in which, to speak the language of psychoanalysis, the problem is not which "object" to love but rather that there are "objects" at all. What looks like an adult erotic trio or even an oedipal triangle turns out to be, rather, a series of superimposed dyadic relationships in which the dynamics of fusion and separation creates a fatal power struggle over the individual's right to survive. The triangle flattens out into a straight line stretched tautly in a tug-of-war between self and other.

Although Simone de Beauvoir always spoke with great serenity about her vocation as a writer, the pseudo triangle of *She Came to Stay* uncovers authorial conflicts of the most fundamental sort: conflicts not between male and female but about the possibility of being female at all; conflicts not between life and death but about the right to live at all. And so this first fiction, *She Came to Stay,* stands at the crossroads between life and writing, the place where Beauvoir's most fundamental conflicts about her right to exist, her right to be female are intimately linked with conflicts about another right: the right to write.

The Imperious "I"

Beauvoir's ambivalence about her relation to her own gender-life-text becomes apparent not only on the level of plot but in her use of language as well, especially in her use of the authorial "I." In the first chapter of *She Came to Stay,* Beauvoir introduces a technique that she continues to use sporadically in her later fictional works as well: the interspersing of the first-person pronoun "I" in an otherwise traditional third-person narrative.

Every now and then an "I" will burst through or into the texture of the narrative, disrupting or displacing the focus of consciousness in the text:

> She turned over a page. Two o'clock has struck a short time ago. Usually, at this hour, there was not a living soul left in the theatre: this night it was alive. The typewriter was clicking, the lamp threw a rosy glow over the papers. And I am here, my heart is beating. Tonight the theatre has a heart and it is beating. [P. 5, TM]

These incursions of the "I" are infrequent and occur principally in the opening sections of the novel. They usually appear at moments such as this, when Françoise ecstatically experiences herself as the living center of the world or as the consciousness that bestows vitality on lifeless objects: she is the beating heart of the otherwise "dead" theater. A godlike source of life, Françoise is situated at the living center of a mass of inert, abandoned silent "things." If she did not bring them to life in her consciousness, if she did not structure and express them, they would remain inanimate forever. The world does not live in and for itself; without the consciousness of the "I," it is dead.

As this center of consciousness in the novel, Françoise plays out the same authorial drama of creation that attaches the novel to its author, Simone de Beauvoir. And, in fact, Beauvoir coincides ambiguously with Françoise as the "I" of the text. Author and character share a personal pronoun, blend into each other, so that a statement of the character is potentially a statement of the author. This ambiguous fusion of author and creation in an "I" foreshadows the future relationship of Françoise with her creation, Xavière. At the outset, Françoise (Beauvoir) expresses the sense of power that accrues to her as the source, the author of the world around her: "And I—here I am at the very heart of the dance-hall—impersonal and free. I am watching all these lives and all these faces. If I were to turn away from them, they would disintegrate at once like a deserted landscape" (p. 26). Not only things but other people as well play the role of objects in her landscape. Without her consciousness of them, they would come undone, lapse back into some original inertness.

This kind of imperialism characterizes the attitude of Françoise during the entire first section of the novel. She deals with other people in a condescending way, talks about them as if they were to be humored, controlled, used—rather like pets. With these existences annexed to hers Françoise creates stories. In fact, she alone knows the whole story:

Xavière's gestures, her face, her very life depended on Françoise for their existence. At this very moment, for herself, Xavière was no more than a taste of coffee, a piercing music, a dance, a light feeling of well-being: but for Françoise, Xavière's childhood, her days of stagnation, her disappointments made up a romantic story as real as the delicate contour of her cheeks. And that story ended up precisely here in this café . . . where Françoise was turning toward Xavière and contemplating her. [Pp. 15–16, TM]

The world, things, other people's lives are inert, disconnected, ungraspable until the consciousness of Françoise, the observer, the writer, tells their story for them. And for Françoise at this point, there is no separation between fact and fiction. Her stories are real; they are, in fact, the only reality.

At the end of everyone else's story, we return, as at the end of this passage, to the gaze of Françoise, the seeing eye, the "I" whose contemplation creates and maintains the world's reality. What she creates never really has a life of its own; she works by a process of annexation and possession.

The Gaze Relayed

The only person Françoise does not possess is Pierre, her lover. But although her relationship with him is ostensibly founded on mutual independence, in fact they operate as if they were fused into one: " 'It's impossible to talk about faithfulness and unfaithfulness where we are concerned,' said Pierre. He drew Françoise to him. 'You and I are one. It's true, you know. Neither of us can be defined without the other' " (p. 21, TM). Pierre and Françoise have one rule: to tell each other everything. There is to be nothing hidden between them, no dark corners, no silences. Their relationship is perfectly transparent and "pure," to use Françoise's word (p. 21), and, as such, it reflects the transparency of the world of male discourse described by Beauvoir in her other writing.

Françoise becomes in effect Pierre's writing. Her rela-

85

tionship with him expresses the clarity of his relationship with reality. So while at first Françoise seems an imperial creator, the center of the world's consciousness, it turns out that her own consciousness is not centered in her. While she believes she owns and controls the story of everyone else, her own story does not belong to her: "As long as she hadn't told Pierre about it, no event was altogether real" (p. 21, TM). Her consciousness is not split, rather it resides altogether in Pierre. Without him and his discourse, his formulations of things, she is empty, or at least just a swirling mass of unstructured impressions. As long as her union with Pierre is perfect, however, as long as the fusion of the two continues, Françoise does not *feel* empty; she suffers no sense of loss from this displacement of self-consciousness.

Françoise's liberty and power do not, therefore, reside in her but in Pierre. This fact makes this apparently iconoclastic couple oddly traditional in the dynamics of relationship. Pierre's wishes, desires, words, work dominate the life of the couple. Pierre speaks with assurance, never doubts himself, dallies with other women to please his vanity, and it is his idea to form the trio with Xavière. Like the female partner in the traditional heterosexual couple, Françoise, without realizing it, is living as a kind of parasite. But there is a payoff in this parasitism which forms an opaque blind spot in this supposedly transparent relationship: that payoff is Françoise's unacknowledged enjoyment of an imperious power for which she does not have to take responsibility. When she does begin to feel her own power openly, it feels to her like an overwhelming rage, and she is terrified.

Françoise's fear of that rage and its violence sustains the myth of transparency that structures her relationship with Pierre, but as a cover for the hidden opacity of their words and the concealed transference of power. Françoise feels like the all-powerful creator, but her power is, in effect, both borrowed and delegated.

As presented on the surface of the text, the male is the possessor of language and creativity. Flowing from this possession, his power at once creates and validates his authority. Although Françoise may make up stories, they do not seem true until she tells them to Pierre. The male is the source of "reality." So although it seems that we are reading a female text, insofar as it is a fictional one, in fact we are facing a divided discourse. The voice of Françoise is a kind of dummy voice, with Pierre playing the role of ventriloquist.[14] Françoise specializes in feeling, in giving support, in mediating, while Pierre is the authority, the consciousness, the voice of the couple. Françoise's words are not validated until they pass through the checkpoint of male discourse.

A Second, Indirect Look

This very traditional connection between Pierre and Françoise operates on the same principles as the relationship Beauvoir establishes with the readers of her novel. To understand this, we will have to take a second look at the author's stance in her own narrative specifically as it is thrown into profile by her use of the first person. These sporadic eruptions of the "I" into the narrative have an uncanny double effect. On the one hand, as we have already noted, they suggest to us an identification of the author with the main character of the novel, and seem to invite us as readers to participate in that identification. On the other hand, their irregularity leads us to question that very identification. Is the implicit identification of author, character, and reader actually present at all times, becoming explicit only at moments? Or is it rather a decoy, a false fusion hiding, like the transparency of the couple, the dark divisiveness of power and aggression?

However important the imperial "I" may be as an ideological and psychological point of fusion bonding author, char-

---

14. In the 1950s Hazel Barnes presented a similar reading of *She Came to Stay*, interpreting it as a kind of defense and illustration of Sartre's *Being and Nothingness*, published the same year as Beauvoir's novel (*The Literature of Possibility* [Lincoln: University of Nebraska Press, 1959], p. 113).

acter, and reader as Pierre and Françoise appear to be linked, this union is far from being a constant in the text. Just as the eruption of the "I" posits the possibility of that fusion, so its constant disappearance puts it into question.

Beauvoir's resumption of the third person creates the effect of a withdrawal from this union, an abandonment. This withdrawal effect makes a neutral use of the third person impossible. Each time the switch is made from first to third person, the distance and difference that separate the character, the author, and the reader are emphasized. The third person takes on, then, a negative aura implying judgment and disapproval. Beauvoir's descriptions of the thoughts and feelings of Françoise, rather than being straightforward expository statements, become instances of the ironic narrative technique used to such advantage by Flaubert: *le style indirect libre.*[15]

The technique of the *style indirect libre* allows the author to identify with the characters of her novel but in an ironic, disrupted way that points up their self-delusions. Every statement the author makes about a character or in that character's name may be either taken at face value or read as an implied criticism of the character's bad faith. When, for instance, at the beginning of the novel, Beauvoir reports Françoise's reflections on her relationship with Pierre, it is difficult for the reader to evaluate the status of these declarations:

> Before, when she found Pierre intimidating, there had been a number of things that she had brushed aside in this way: uncomfortable thoughts and ill-considered gestures. If they were not mentioned, it was almost as if they had not existed at all, and this allowed, underneath her true existence, a shameful, subterranean vegetation to grow up where she felt utterly alone and in

15. English has no equivalent term for this technique, in which an author reports directly the thoughts or words of a character in the third person without indicating specifically that they are the character's. While the *style indirect libre* is sometimes used in traditional fictional discourse as an extension of the omniscient narrator, its ambiguities open up possibilities of irony amply developed and exploited by Flaubert, especially in his novel *The Sentimental Education* (1869).

88

danger of suffocation. And then, little by little, she had yielded everything; she no longer knew solitude, but she was purified of those chaotic swarms.   [Pp. 21–22, TM]

It is important for us as readers to know whether we are meant to take these statements at face value or whether we are intended to read them as ironic signposts pointing to Françoise's ability to fool herself. The tone of this passage hinges on the word "purified"; in order to interpret the text, we have to decide whether this word is used as a transparent purveyor of a message or whether it is meant to emphasize the erroneous belief on Françoise's part that she can ever be pure.

No one instance of the *style indirect libre* can be used as a decisive illustration, for the ironic effects of the device are inevitably cumulative, resulting from subtle but numerous discordances between a character's thoughts and actions. What I would like to point up here is the potential disruption of the author-reader relation created by the textual ambiguities of the *style indirect libre*. It activates a doubly charged connection of author, character, and reader—a relationship that hovers unspecifiably between identification and condemnation.

While on one level the use of the *style indirect libre* creates a connivance or complicity between author and reader as ironic judges of the fictional characters, on another level it creates the possibility of separation and judgment. The seeming transparency of the language is put into question, and we are called on at each moment to judge the degree of clouding that is taking place. When Beauvoir writes that Françoise "was overwhelmed by it. She trembled at the thought of danger, but it attracted her irresistibly. She had never been able to stay within the bounds of prudence" (p. 369, TM), the only way we can decide whether Françoise is deluding herself is to consult our own judgments about her conduct, our own distinction between neurotic foolhardiness and real courage. Since the author's negative judgment of the character is always ironic, indirect, unspecified, it is up to the reader to decide, without guidance from the author at any given moment, what is ironic and what is not. The final effect of the use of the *style indirect libre* is, then, to challenge the values and authenticity not only of the character but of the reader as well.

This kind of ambiguity and suspicion between author and reader characterizes much of modern fiction, but Beauvoir puts it to particular use in *She Came to Stay*. By maintaining the reader in a confused and confusing relation to her discourse, flipping in and out between emotional fusion and moral judgment, Beauvoir as author finally displaces the text as object of desire. The text is so undependable and contradictory that in order to take up a well-defined relation to it we must seek help, guidance, approval from *outside* the text, in the mind and will of its creator.

We are, in other words, in the same relation to Beauvoir outside the text as Françoise is to Pierre inside the text. As the author, Beauvoir is the only one who holds the secret of the "correct" attitudes to take toward her book. The mythology of the all-knowing and all-judging creator suggested here is doubly reinforced by her comments and commentary on the book in her autobiography. If only we can "yield everything," as Françoise did to Pierre, we can be rid of all that "shameful, subterranean vegetation" of doubt and become one with the author, the "purified" consciousness of the text, the only one who knows what is "real" in this fiction.

Beauvoir thus establishes a model of reading based on the dynamics of the traditional heterosexual couple with herself as the dominant male and the reader as the yielding female. Beauvoir's authority as author reposes on her identification of herself as creator with a superior knowledge of reality available only to males. Curiously enough, although Beauvoir later appears to call into question the imperious nature of Pierre's relationship with Françoise (thus apparently calling into question the relationship she has established with the reader), the resolution of this issue is short-circuited by Françoise's murder of Xavière. The belief in the superiority of male knowledge and the prerogative of male authority thus remains unchallenged. Even as the author of a confused and confusing "female" fiction, Beauvoir maintains within the text an ambivalent relation to that fiction and finally projects outside the text the image of herself as the morally pure, unimpeachable, male source of authority.

Woman to Woman

In one area of *She Came to Stay* Beauvoir's confrontation with herself as a female and more particularly as a female author has a chance to surface outside the precincts of male dominance. Although Françoise and Xavière are part of a trio and their relationship is often mediated by Pierre, the two women develop an intense connection that serves as a central focus of the novel. If a model of female writing and reading is developed anywhere in this text, it is likely to be here.

In many respects, Françoise reproduces in her relationship with Xavière the same power structure that has evolved with Pierre, but with the roles reversed. Françoise becomes the powerful authority, the ratifier of mutual experience, while Xavière is the murky, unfinished creation. The fact that the two players in this drama are women, though, makes the dynamics of this relationship somewhat different. Shifting out of the heterosexual paradigm of divided discourse, Beauvoir uses a specifically female interpretive model to characterize this relationship—that of mother and child.

This kind of affiliation is reinforced by the material details introduced by Beauvoir: Xavière is much younger than Françoise; she depends on her for financial support; and while Françoise takes a cool, rational, "mature" approach to life, Xavière is impulsive, spoiled, childlike. From the outset, Françoise enjoys and emphasizes this aspect of her relationship with Xavière. She takes pleasure in Xavière's youth and dependence on her and tends to minimize the emotional strength of the younger woman: "She smiled. She owed to Xavière both this hour and this evening. Why exclude from her life this offering of refreshing richness, a young, completely fresh companion, with her demands, her reticent smiles, her surprising reactions?" (p. 29). Later on in the novel, even after much conflict and jealousy centering on Pierre, Françoise still thinks of Xavière as "this little sleek, golden girl whom she had adopted" (p. 216). And just before she decides to kill her, Françoise sees in her mind's eye Xavière's "pale, childlike face" (p. 430, TM).

The male model of authority slips, then, under the metaphor of maternity. The mutual exclusiveness of writing and having children gives way, and the structural analogy that makes one a substitute for the other surfaces as the major metaphorical vehicle Beauvoir uses to explore her relationship as a woman with her own reproduction in writing. But when Beauvoir replaces the lucid, idealist male language of authority with the messy, biological female language of maternity, something curious happens. Feelings flood in, and what was called the sacredness of a vocation looks more like a grandiose and ferocious attempt to control another being, or perhaps a part of herself:

> Whether she wanted to be or not, Xavière was bound to her by a bond stronger than hatred or love. . . . Françoise was the very substance of her life, and her moments of passion, of pleasure, of covetousness could not have existed without this firm web that supported them. Whatever happened to Xavière happened through Françoise, and whether she wished it or not, Xavière belonged to her. [P. 267, TM]

Reading Xavière as Beauvoir's child-text, we see that "adoption" means total possession. Language "belongs" to her; she sees it as an inert instrument totally malleable to her desires. Since Beauvoir does not conceive language as having a source or life outside her relation to it, neither can she imagine that it would be tricky or pose any obstacles to her expressive needs. This perception of language as a kind of dead letter, the inert simulacrum of a child, contributes no doubt to the flatness of Beauvoir's prose. There is no sense here that, like a naughty child, language might be playful or elusive.

While any resistance must be threatening, nevertheless the logic of this biological metaphor of motherhood inevitably introduces the possibility, the danger, of development and growth. Françoise is indeed troubled by any signs of independence in Xavière, any evidence that her daughter may be growing up: "Françoise looked at her a little uneasily; it seemed sacrilegious to think of this virtuous little austerity as a woman, with the desire of a woman" (p. 196, TM).

Besides raising the troubling possibility of sexual rivalry or even of sexual desire between the two women, Xavière's sexuality represents for Françoise another danger by even greater proportions: a sacrilege, a profanation of her belief system in a possessable, transparent language that, like Pierre's love, will justify and redeem the inadequacies, the distortions, the cheat of female life. Françoise's dream of a symbolic maternity, an adoption in and of language, ends up reflecting (repeating) the dynamics of traditional heterosexual relationships played out in her liaison with Pierre. The coincidence of this heterosexual paradigm with Beauvoir's dream of literary maternity is borne out by Françoise's depictions of Xavière as a conventional heroine of a novel: she calls her a "young angel" (p. 227) and a "young heroine, the sweet sacrificed figure" (p. 420). Like the fading females of Victorian fiction, Xavière is set up as an emptied-out front for Françoise's authority.[16] Xavière's virtue, both as a character and as a text, is to be vacant: she is sweet *because* she is sacrificed, sacred because she is void.

Not only does Françoise balk at attributing any adult sexual desire to Xavière, she blanks totally when she tries to imagine desiring her herself. No alternative to the dominance of male desire seems possible; reciprocity between Françoise and Xavière is literally inconceivable precisely because they are both women. Françoise (Beauvoir?) questions herself: "But what did she desire? Her lips against hers? Her body surrendered in her arms? She could think of nothing" (p. 263).

16. A comment that Beauvoir makes in *The Prime of Life* is particularly relevant here: she states that she had first imagined using Simone Weil as a model for Xavière (pp. 252–53).

The possibility that there is another desire, a specifically female desire not mediated by the secure laws of transparent male language, this possibility overwhelms François with terror, sets her adrift. The difference of no difference threatens to put her directly in touch with that "shameful, subterranean" world of her own desire—the desire of a woman but precisely as a "nothing," unknowable and unpossessable, suffocating and alone; the desire of a woman who is at once her substance and yet not her. The shadow of this desire, Xavière, reveals to Françoise that she is a frightening stranger to herself; she knows for the first time the terror of having to desire herself as another.

Françoise retreats in panic when Xavière puts her face to face with her own desire of and as a woman. The blank she draws becomes a yawning chasm that threatens to engulf her. Although Françoise attempts to circumscribe the danger of confining Xavière in the image of a pure child, Xavière—this part of Françoise that eludes her own possession and control—continues nightmarishly to expand: "Françoise stiffened, but she could no longer simply close her eyes and blot out Xavière. Xavière has been growing steadily all through the evening, she has been weighing on her mind as heavily as the huge cake at the *Pôle Nord*" (p. 68).

Like the unappetizing cake, Xavière grows too big to take in, to engulf, to swallow. And because she represents this unswallowable gob of existence, she seems herself voracious:

> For a second Françoise looked with horror at this delicate but implacable face in which she had not once seen reflected any of her own joys and sorrows. . . . Sobs of revulsion shook her: her anguish, her tears, this night of torture belonged to her and she would not allow Xavière to rob her of them. She would fly to the end of the world to escape the avid tentacles with which she wanted to devour her live.   [P. 313, TM]

As she looks into the implacable face of her own unsentimentalized desire, Françoise sees the little angel as a "witch" (p. 253), a voracious monster ready to eat her up. The encounter with her own hidden, unspeakable desire in the reflection of another woman's being, this difference of no difference, means that Françoise experiences this encounter not as a confrontation but as an implosion. The nonmediated avidity of her own desire sucks her into an infinite wordless emptiness:

> It was like death, a total negation, an eternal absence, and yet, by a staggering contradiction, this abyss of nothingness could make itself present to itself and make itself exist for itself in all its fullness. The entire universe was engulfed in it, and Françoise, forever dispossessed, was herself dissolved in this void whose infinite contour no word, no image could encompass.   [P. 310, TM]

This reflection of herself in her adopted daughter which mirrors the inadequacy of her own words, this unendurable experience of her own femaleness as a simultaneously imperious and uncontrollable desire, is what drives Françoise to murder Xavière.

While Françoise was able to tell (almost) everything to Pierre, here she can say nothing at all. Words fail her, she says. But what has failed her in truth is her ability to imagine a female discourse that would emerge out of her terror as its embodiment. Since language represents for her the purity of an idealized male desire—the fully adequate and transparent correlation between a statement and reality—and because all writing thus ideally approaches nonfiction, anything that intrudes in the purity of that correlation—such as her feelings of confusion, jealousy, and rage—must inevitably seem to her a blotch, a shame. According to Beauvoir, then, a specifically female discourse must, by definition, be morally and philosophically dirty. Wishing to construct a dirty discourse, in the clean world of "Beauvoir," of seeing everything as beautiful, is quite simply absurd.

The murder of Xavière comes as the substitute for, the acting out of, this absurdity. The senseless act fills up the empty place of Beauvoir's female words; it replaces her encounter with language as a sullied, intractable, hungry version of her

95

own desire. Instead of yielding to the maelstrom of that desire, to the frightening meaning of her gender as confusion, Beauvoir simply kills it off.

The banishment of metaphor that this murder represents paradoxically makes the murder itself seem strangely unreal. As Elaine Marks has pointed out, "When at the end of the book, Françoise kills Xavière by turning on the gas . . . , we are conscious neither of a real murder nor of a real death."[17] This is a ritual murder emptied of reality precisely because its meaning lies elsewhere, because it is, finally, a failure of meaning. So although Beauvoir represents the murder as a triumph for Françoise, the affirmation of herself, on another level it seems to be a copout, an abdication of the author's desire to write as a woman.

The Corpse

But something seems wrong here. It has been too easy to prove that Beauvoir is a coward, that she does not like herself as a woman. It occurs to me that I have just killed off Beauvoir the way Françoise kills Xavière, to avoid anxiety, to cut off some meaning. I have been drawn into the confused and confusing position of a dependent female reader who crazily identifies, merges with the characters of a book. Perhaps, like Françoise, I have fallen into the trap of fusing with my double and then having to kill her, to demolish Beauvoir, to protect my identity as an authoritative (male) critic. I have refused an encounter with Beauvoir as a messy, cheating female.

Instead of taking Beauvoir at her word and accepting the priority of her "male" explanation of this text in her autobiography, let us let this female-authored book speak for itself. In spite of Beauvoir's repeated assertions that she put herself in Françoise—in her (the) mother?—that she limited her point of view to that of her characters,[18] we have seen that her

17. Marks, *Simone de Beauvoir*, p. 77.
18. *Prime of Life*, pp. 251, 253, 271.

identification with these fictional intelligences wavers often into irony and moral judgment. What's more, if Françoise as a character in the book experiences a radical dispossession, a failure of language in the face of a female counterpart, the author does not; she puts that failure precisely into words.

In other words, words have *not* failed, and the acting out of hostility in the murder of the threatening fictionality of her femaleness is, contrary to the message of the book, subsumed in and by language. Beauvoir has managed to articulate a tale in the chaotic space of her panic, a tale that distances her from that very panic, that conjures and contains it.

The murder is indeed unreal, a cheat and a lie—and in more ways than one. Not only is it a switch to allegory in a realistic novel, not only does it misproclaim its own message, it is not even really a murder! It is not only not a murder in the sense that it is made up of words, but it is not even a murder in the plot of the story. Françoise has decided to kill Xavière; she has turned on the gas and knows that Xavière will be dead in the morning. But when the novel ends, Xavière is still alive. The "murder"—as everyone, including Beauvoir, calls it—is incomplete. As far as the novel is concerned, it will never be finished. Moving always toward completion outside the book, it is forever frozen in its own process: not a murder but a murdering. Xavière will always be this woman in the process of becoming a corpse; her death, her disposal, her apotheosis are forever deferred.

It is this body on the way to being a corpse, this fake murder moving endlessly toward its completion and definition outside the confines of the words on the page, this expression of a female will always postponed—this is the *abyme* where Beauvoir and her writing come together. At once language and its symbol, hidden and yet crazily blatant, this unfinished murder, this woman becoming a corpse, embodies Beauvoir's writing as a false resolution.

Beauvoir does not confront her vision of her own gender as sullied and dangerous, as contingent, as fictional, as something made up of a woman's own words, but neither does she entirely kill off, silence, her own femininity. She sets up, rather, a protective, negative logic of preserved ambiguity and permanently false resolution. This is not the either/or logic associated with maleness or the both/and logic associated with femaleness, but rather a strange neither/nor logic that simultaneously incorporates and denies both of them.

By neither fully espousing nor fully repudiating her gender, Simone de Beauvoir leaves her writing hovering somewhere between life and death, male and female, never finished, never completed, always in need of being recommenced, restated, rewritten. And as long as her writing is unfinished, Beauvoir's own death, like Xavière's, seems deferred.

Writing does not replace or debase life, and Beauvoir's own statements about the precedence of male lucidity over female distortion are themselves distorted. Her yearning for clarity and repose on the one hand and her ravenous desire to plunge into and possess life on the other remained in an unresolved tension. And as long as that tug-of-war continued, as long as the crime of writing, of self-definition, was not completed, as long as the corpse, the corpus was unfinished, then its author, by definition, could not die.

To write is to assert oneself, one's self. It implies, therefore, authority, a sense of justification. But what if the self one wishes to assert turns out to be confused, guilty, soiled? In that case, writing becomes an exhibition of just those qualities one wishes most to hide. Beauvoir attempted to solve this dilemma she felt as a woman by projecting and enclosing the messy parts of herself in the female characters in her books, thus preserving the "purity" of herself as author. As Henri Peyre points out in his introduction to Jean Leighton's *Simone de Beauvoir on Woman*: "As an imaginative writer, she has not once, strangely enough, presented a female character whom we might admire, or merely remember lastingly as a complex winning, mature, true woman" (p. 7).

Beauvoir's disclaimer of herself goes to the extreme and almost bizarre lengths of total self-denial; this woman who had written thousands of pages of autobiography asserted that she had no self-image: "I am not involved with myself: I have no image of myself . . . , I think about myself very little."[19] The traditional selflessness of women could be carried no further.

This effort on the part of Beauvoir to remove all evidence of moral or emotional taint—that is, all trace of femaleness—from her writing resulted in a style known for its no-frills quality. As one critic put it, Beauvoir maintained a "doctor's outlook on the world," always preserving "her distance, her self-control and an entire lucidity."[20]

This distance from her female self in writing has led many critics to comment on the "virility" of her style.[21] Konrad Bieber, for instance, notes with much relief: "Whatever qualms the male critic might have, Simone de Beauvoir puts his mind at rest: she speaks and writes in such a way that one might forget about the sex of the novelist."[22] Bieber's appraisal is curiously echoed by Beauvoir's own statements about herself: "I don't think very much about my gender, I don't think about the fact that I am a woman writer."[23] In another echo of her own writing, thirty-six years after the publication of *She Came to Stay,* Beauvoir explicitly asserted the impossibility of constructing a specifically female discourse. Language, she said, belongs to the collectivity; but this collectivity was in her eyes exclusively male: "It's hard to imagine that women can invent within the universal language a code that would be all their own. As it happens, they are doing no such thing. They are using men's words, even if they do twist the sense of them."[24]

Paradoxically, this failure of the imagination, this blank she drew when she tried to conceive of a women's language, this "twisting" that femaleness represents, all these things that

19. Interview with Catherine David, *Vogue,* May 1979, p. 296.

20. Jacques Ehrmann, "Simone de Beauvoir and the Related Destinies of Woman and Intellectual," *Yale French Studies,* no. 27 (Spring–Summer 1961), p. 29.

21. See "Interview with Alice Schwarzer," *Ms.,* August 1983, p. 90.

22. Konrad Bieber, *Simone de Beauvoir* (Boston: Twayne, 1979), p. 17.

23. "Interview with Madeleine Chapsal," in Francis and Gontier, *Ecrits de Simone de Beauvoir,* p. 381.

24. David interview, p. 295.

she thought of "very little" and thus concealed, are blatantly revealed in her writing. Like the letters that Françoise wrote to Xavière's lover, Gerbert, revealing her affair with him, like those guilty letters locked up in her desk, the shameful truth hidden behind and in and by her writing comes spilling out for everyone to read. Those locked-up letters reveal Françoise's betrayal of her "daughter," Xavière. The love trio of Françoise, Pierre, and Xavière is uncovered as a false front, a lure substituted for the real lover's triangle of Françoise, Gerbert, and Xavière. While in the "purified" trio Françoise is generous and longsuffering, on the subterranean level of this other triangle Françoise reveals herself to be a guilty, selfish, passionate, erotic woman.

This is precisely the inscription of herself as a writer that Beauvoir seems most eager to lock up in her writing. But this message has left its mark everywhere in the debased and murdered heroines, in the failed sisterhood and the hostile mother-daughter relationships in her novels. Women, Beauvoir said in response to a criticism of her negative presentations of female characters, women are "divided."[25] Herself, it seems, most of all.

In her public behavior, Simone de Beauvoir challenged traditional values and was always a strong champion of the cause of women. But in her writing, the traditional definitions of gender and her own strivings as a female writer remained in conflict. Beauvoir has presented us with a model of female writing haunted by a history of bad faith and denial. The encounter with herself as a confused, erotic, angry, powerful woman who wrote from within those feelings simply never took place. Taking up a position of mastery with respect to her own femaleness, she thus drained her writing of the enriching power of its own vulnerability. The metaphoric language that might have emerged from confusion as its expression and its transcendence was sapped of its vitality and cast aside. To make up stories—that "boring" female activity—seemed to

25. "Interview with Madeleine Gobeil," pp. 213–14.

100

threaten Beauvoir with the possibility of imagining the unimaginable: that she was not only the mother but also the daughter; that she was not only Françoise but also Xavière, that sweet sacrificed figure who was "so hungry to . . . conquer and so eager to sacrifice nothing" (p. 399, TM).

The writing of Simone de Beauvoir, that model of a liberated woman, demonstrates ironically that the mere fact of writing is not necessarily a liberating experience. The prevailing debased models of women and of relationships between men and women may easily become paradigms for reading and writing even in the works of women authors. But when these models are maintained, as they largely are in Beauvoir's work, they have the tragic effect of splitting the author's gender off from the powers of her own creativity. Rather than becoming a free zone of the imagination in which she could create new images of wholeness, Beauvoir's writing is the reinscription of the divisions that separated her from herself.

This inability to construct with pride a female model of writing and reading finally produced the most devastating split of all: the split between Beauvoir and her own writing—the vocation that was to be the sustaining enterprise, the "salvation" of her life. All those millions of words that she aligned with such care and tenacity finally did not belong to her, did not express her, since she shut off significant parts of herself from them. They are, therefore, strangely stiff and empty, severed from their inspiration. Because Beauvoir failed to establish a relationship of reciprocity with her writing as a reflection of her female self, it continually drifted away from her and had to be endlessly recommenced in a second, shadow writing. She was thus caught in a never-ending process of subversion and attempted recuperation of her own texts. Maintaining a traditional heterosexual pattern of relationship with those texts, she continued to perpetuate their powerlessness to stand alone. It seems no accident that Simone de Beauvoir's debut as a writer tells the story of a murder. The most anguishing and criminal aspect of that murder is that it was (almost) a suicide.

3

Violette Leduc:
The Bastard

The shadow of Simone de Beauvoir hangs over the writing of Violette Leduc, both literally and figuratively. Not only did Beauvoir write the preface of her protégée's autobiography, but the same issues of self-rejection and self-justification that play so large a role in Beauvoir's work also dominate the writing of Leduc.

Violette Leduc was born in Arras, France, in 1907. The beginning of her life reads like a novel. Her mother, a servant in a great house, was seduced by the master's son and was sent away as soon as her pregnancy became known. Leduc's father gave some financial support to her and her mother but rarely saw them. Later Leduc's mother made a good marriage, and her daughter was educated at a boarding school.

Leduc then moved to Paris, where, during World War II, she attempted suicide. Encouraged by her friend the writer Maurice Sachs, she published her first book, *L'Asphyxie*, in 1946. It was a slim autobiographical work that described one short period of her life. In 1948 and 1955 Leduc published two more books, *L'Affamée* and *Ravages*, in which she again wrote about discrete episodes in her life.

It was not until 1964, with the publication of *La Bâtarde*,[1]

1. Paris: Gallimard; published in English under the same title, trans.

102

that Violette Leduc, at age fifty-seven, produced the first auto-biographical work that purported to give a complete chrono-logical account of her life. Or almost complete, for *La Bâtarde* ends with the end of the war, on the eve of the publication of her first book, *L'Asphyxie*. This ending with the author's coming to writing recursively structures the book as a kind of artist's novel. Not only is the author of *La Bâtarde* a bastard child, but the book is a bastard of another kind: a mongrel genre, a cross between an autobiography and a *Künstlerroman*. This crossing of genres in *La Bâtarde* highlights one of the main issues presented both in and by the book: the relationship of life and writing.

Autobiography provides a kind of limit case for the study of this relationship, because the writing presents itself as a repetition or a reproduction of the author's own life. She lived it once as a living being, now she is "living" again in writing as an author. The difference between living and writing in this case is thus ideally reduced to the smallest possible interval. The life and the autobiography become a minimal pair. And the difference between living and writing, thus reduced to its minimal aspect, becomes paradoxically glaring; its radicalness emerges.

For unless autobiography is an entirely gratuitous enter-prise, which is possible, it seems to be adding to the author's life something that the that life would otherwise have lacked: an affirmation, a shape, a meaning. Writing comes after living, then, as its supplement, its supplement of meaning. Looked at from this point of view, the difference between living and writing appears to be the difference between presence and ab-sence—presence of life or its absence, presence of meaning of its absence. But it can also be envisioned as an interval of

---

Derek Coltman (New York: Farrar, Strauss & Giroux, 1965). Despite its popular success, *La Bâtarde* has attracted very little critical comment over the years. One could almost say that it has been ignored. The best and most comprehensive study of Violette Leduc's work is in Jacob Stockinger's un-published dissertation, "Violette Leduc: The Legitimations of *La Bâtarde*," University of Wisconsin–Madison, 1979.

deferring, an interval that, Derrida says, implies some impurity in the original.[2] The interval of deferring between living and writing involves, according to Derrida, both a postponement—of meaning, of shape—and a yielding to the priority of writing.

For Violette Leduc, this interval of difference, as minimal as it may be, at first imposes the sense of radical incompatibilities between her life and her autobiography. The writing seems to cancel out the very validity of the life whose meaning it is to complete. In a significant analogical shift, she expresses this sense of incompatibility and devaluation as a difference in gender. Not unsurprisingly, she associates biological birth and life with her female gender, while writing becomes a masculine enterprise. Autobiography appears, then, to be a male affair: a paternal supplement to the maternal process of giving birth. The very act of writing by which Leduc asserts her claim to identity simultaneously invalidates her as a woman. Her wish to authorize herself by her writing entails for Leduc the paradoxical and painful necessity of self-repudiation.

Leduc's attempt to come to terms with her autobiographical project carries with it, then, a simultaneous confrontation with sexual difference. While Simone de Beauvoir, who wrote the preface to *La Bâtarde*, also associated autobiography with maleness, for Leduc the rift between her gender and her writing is even more radical. While Beauvoir's devaluation of herself as a woman was partially muffled in her writing, Leduc's is agonizingly amplified. As she struggles with her overwhelming sense of unworthiness and attempts to discover a model of writing that does not cancel her out as a woman, Leduc returns to the sources of life as mythic representations of her literary creation. Initially Leduc explores the mysteries of gender, like the perplexing relationship between writing and life, by means of godlike parental figures with whom she seeks to identify. But as she tries on these opposing male and female identities, the

2. Jacques Derrida, *L'Ecriture et la différence* (Paris: Seuil, 1967), p. 366.

"purity" of gender as a legitimization or explanation of her self is finally revealed as spurious. Exploring gender through myth, Leduc finds that gender itself is a myth that, located outside her in a system of idealized images, will never give a true account either of her life or her writing. While identifying with these ideal parents initially gives her a sense of power, these traditional definitions of gender in terms of "opposite" sexes and reproductive relationships finally serve only to fragment her further and impoverish the richness and complexity of her desire.

In a glorious awakening to herself as a woman, Leduc discovers in erotic desire and her own body as re-created by another woman's love another definition of gender and another model of writing. Defining her difference as a woman not in relation to an "opposite" sex but rather by the infinitesimal and gloriously gratuitous interval between like and like, Leduc constructs a model of writing based on self-affirmation rather than on self-denial. Just as Hermine's and Isabelle's love creates a transfigured body of desire traced on the very contours of her flesh, so Leduc's words simultaneously repeat and redeem the illegitimacy of her fierce, female vitality.

The Father

From the very beginning of her autobiography, Leduc puzzles over her identity, which she envisions as part of a conflict between her origin in two different, mutually exclusive genders: "Here I am, born in a city-hall register at the point of a city employee's pen. No dirtiness, no placenta: writing, a certificate. Who is Violette Leduc?" (p. 4).[3] Does her identity proceed from her birth—the "dirty affair of women"—or is it created by her civil status—the male domain of writing?

Leduc goes on to emphasize the illegitimacy of the female subject and to express a longing for purity, a purity she associates with art: "I would have liked to be born a statue; I am a

3. All page references are to the New York edition.

slug buried under my own dung" (ibid.). At the very moment she is claiming to be a repulsive creature, Leduc is nevertheless beginning to mold that slug into a statue by writing. She begins to reshape her messy and unjustified female existence in the pure lines of a (male) life history.

Her existence as a female is rendered doubly illegitimate by her father's refusal to recognize her. While she first experiences this lack of recognition as a humiliation, she turns that paternal denial to her advantage. If she can succeed in occupying the empty place of her procreator, she will simultaneously annul the anguish of her abandonment and become the guarantor of her own legitimacy. Her flaunting of her bastard birth thus becomes a way of reversing her abandonment and of disinheriting her father in turn. By proclaiming the absence of her father, she preempts his powers of (pro)creation.

In order to occupy the father's place, Leduc invents a complex and ambiguous game in which the sexuality of both men and women is at once inverted and denied. She plays *le petit bonhomme*, the little man, for Gabriel, the soft and feminine man she eventually marries. She says: "I did not desire Gabriel, and I didn't want him to desire me" (p. 119). Her relationship with the writer Maurice Sachs is inscribed in the same register of muted and blurred sexuality where male heterosexual desire is effaced so that the difference between the sexes will not be manifest. She describes her feelings for Sachs in a depersonalized mode: "She could not imagine him any other than homosexual. His erect sex would have been for her a masquerade" (p. 399). By denying the masculinity of men and declaring it a "masquerade," she disarms her adversaries; she castrates them in order to take their place. If male sexuality is turned into a masquerade, her masquerade as a male will be no less authentic than theirs. By erasing difference, she becomes free to wield male generative power.

Leduc applies this strategy of denial and castration to her literary fathers as well. The opening sentence of the book, "My case is not unique" (p. 4), brashly reverses the prologue of the *Confessions* of Leduc's autobiographical predecessor, Jean-

Jacques Rousseau. It is curious that this literary father of Leduc had such troublesome problems with paternity himself, producing and then abandoning, according to his own claim, not one but five bastard children. Ironically, Rousseau's claim to uniqueness and his assertion of priority in brutal honesty and merciless self-revelation are borne out by the textual exhibition of that same "ridiculous object," his impotent sex, that Leduc desires in Gabriel and Maurice Sachs.[4]

Her choice of male companions and father figures, both literal and literary, is determined by their attractive impotence. Leduc denies their maleness in order to seize for herself the creative power of their "pen." For Leduc, then, literary creation becomes a strategy analogous to her shoplifting (pp. 178ff.). Just as she steals merchandise, she usurps and steals the creative power of men. But, like her shoplifting—which she describes as a capricious adventure—her theft of male power, of writing, in the end is not motivated by a desire for gain but serves as the expression of a gratuitous impulse. As Leduc begins to write, she describes herself as a god creating a new world. Imbued with a sense of Olympian power and independence, she emphasizes nevertheless the arbitrariness of her will to create: "I wanted a tree, I got a tree. I wanted a house, I got a house. I wanted night, rain . . . I could have anything. All I had to do was imagine it" (p. 324).

As the vindication of the primacy of the imaginary over the real, this world engendered solely by the will to create is thus purified of any contamination by the contingency of need. By virtue of its very gratuitousness, writing attains that purity which was symbolized at the beginning of the book by the birth certificate registered by an indifferent scribe: "Light with the lightness of Maurice, my pen was weightless. I continued with the insouciance and the easiness of a boat pushed by the wind. Innocence of a beginning" (p. 418). As she undertakes her autobiography (not *La Bâtarde* but the earlier frag-

---

4. Jean-Jacques Rousseau, *Les Confessions,* in *Oeuvres complètes* (Paris: Gallimard, 1959), 1:5, 344.

mentary version, *L'Asphyxie*, published in 1946), Leduc plays the role of the creator who created her. But this time, conception will be free of the betrayal and humiliation that accompanied her "real" conception. By taking the place of the male—God, the father, Maurice—she redeems her dirty, female birth by recreating it with a stolen male instrument that, in a paradoxical effort to preserve her lost female dignity, she claims she does not need. This writing, which is at once of and for the father, cleanses her female impurities by effacing her identity and needs as a woman. As the careless author of her autobiography, Leduc deifies herself in a mythology of male creation: her identity is synonymous with the presence of the pure Word that is actualized without desire and thus without reference to another gender—the mother's.

But Leduc writes with a borrowed or rather a stolen pen. It is "weightless" precisely because it is propelled by another's desire. The Olympian creator may share his indifference with the city-hall scribe, but he does not share the source of his power. Leduc's unitary experience as a "male" writer is undone by its own contradictions. Her sense of potency is momentary and illusory and dissolves like her sense of adventure when she is caught shoplifting. Her possession of the male pen is not real just as her possession of the objects she steals is a fantasy. Leduc's desire for justification emerging from her self-loathing as a female leads her to seek vindication by illegitimate means, thus tripling her helplessness. Not only has she renounced her identity as a woman, she has yielded the source of her desire to write to an idealized male origin. The comparison of Leduc with the scribe turns out to be profoundly accurate. He writes, inscribes, registers, but as an employee. As a hired pen, he writes what he is told to write, just as Leduc undertakes to write at another's behest. She admits with a mixture of childlike simplicity and puzzlement: "I wrote to obey Maurice" (p. 418).

The Mother

As she undertakes the writing of her first book, *L'Asphyxie*, Leduc's pen, although blown by the wind of male will, falters

and stops. She is overcome by sweet memories and anticipation:

> The birds suddenly stopped singing as I sucked on my pen: the
> pleasure of foreseeing that my grandmother was going to be re-
> born, that I would give birth to her, the pleasure of foreseeing
> that I would be the creator of the person I adored, who adored
> me. Writing . . . That seemed superfluous to me as I remem-
> bered my tenderness for her, her tenderness for me.   [P. 418]

All voices stop as Leduc's pen becomes the source of another
kind of creation. It nourishes the writer with a new kind of
pleasure as she sucks the sweetness of maternity from it, a
sweetness that opens for her a world both of memory and of
anticipation. Past and future blend in the potential of writing
as the arms of Leduc's grandmother opened wide to enclose
and protect her when she was a child.

Just as the real father ceded his place to a mythic creator—
god or scribe—who purified birth by its inscription, so the
troubled and complex relationship between Leduc and her
mother is superseded by the purity of the adoration that linked
her and her grandmother. Not responsible for the shameful
birth of the bastard child, her grandmother, that "angel
Fidéline" (p. 6), represents the return to a pure maternal origin
which simultaneously renders writing superfluous and justifies
the desire for it: "You will become my child . . . I carry you in
my head. Yes, for you, my belly is a volcano of warmth" (p. 4).

The birth of the mythic mother in and by writing recalls the
birth of Athena, who emerged pure and intact from Zeus's
head. But here paternal birth is transmuted by the volcanic
warmth of female love into the maternal loins of the text.
Leduc becomes both the mother of her grandmother and the
mother of the child she herself was in the past. Casting aside
the shirt and tie she wore to be Gabriel's "little fellow," Leduc
dons the sky-blue apron of the angel Fidéline to give birth to
herself in a text untainted by bastardy.

If she is to safeguard the purity of this relationship with an
idealized version of her mother, no father may intervene in

this birth. And so the (male) text of the autobiography is pushed aside as Leduc strives to establish with the reader a direct relationship that will reproduce the dazzling symbiosis of adoration and gentleness she experienced with her grandmother: "June 15, 1961. They're cutting the hay, my children. Summer is in a good mood, the fields are beginning to grow hills" (p. 342). The gentle voice that speaks to us directly and calls us her children emanates from a time and place outside the autobiographical narration. It introduces into the chronological history of the past another dimension where the time is always the present: "8 o'clock in the morning of June 24, 1962. I've changed my place, I'm writing in the woods because of the heat" (p. 4). The coordinates of time and date which always accompany the interventions of the author's maternal voice project at their intersection a second being and a second world that are characterized as more immediate, more "real" than the beings and the world evoked in the autobiographical narration.[5]

Leduc's creation of a model of writing based on the notion of a pure maternal origin takes place in the margins of the autobiography in this mythic extratextual dimension of a perpetually renewed present. Chronology is replaced by cycles of maternal love; generations become interchangeable; birth is reproduced as a gift of writing: "August 22, 1963. This August day, reader, is a rose window glowing with heat. I make you a gift of it, it is yours" (p. 488). Leduc's text is sustained by this myth of an authentic writing of maternal love where difference—between generations, between author and reader, between life and writing—does not exist. By separating herself from her text and by making herself our mother in the present of her writing and the present of our reading, Leduc creates a maternal writing, an arena of love, more authentic, more real,

5. See Philippe Lejeune, *L'Autobiographie en France* (Paris: Armand Colin, 1971), for a commentary on this authorial strategy, which he calls *le pacte autobiographique* (p. 23). Leduc's placement of this intimate pact with her reader in a specifically maternal space represents a significant transposition of this literary convention.

more pure than the official birth certificate of her autobiography.

In the mythical world of female writing introduced by Leduc—in contrast to the male mode of chronologically recorded history, which replaces messy female life with orderly inscription—the story of maternal love is told over and over in a perpetual present. This writing is offered in the form of a gift that will unite the adoring, submissive reader not to the gift but to the giver. It is a writing, then, which, having served its function, must finally be denied, expunged. Rendered superfluous by the immediacy of the love it gives birth to, this maternal writing is, like all traditionally good mothers, self-effacing.

The Mask

This mythical extratextual writing is, however, part of the texture of the text, and the "reality" of the dates and hours depends finally on the connivance of literary convention. The purity of this mythic maternal writing and the love it gives voice to can be maintained only by preservation of the illusion of its freedom from the conventions of male writing which sustain it. In order to establish this independence, Leduc paradoxically emphasizes the mechanics of writing itself. She undermines the apparent reality of her writing in order to establish it as a game she plays at will, behind which, she implies, there is this other "real" desire, this other "real" game of love. Like a magician who slows her hands to reveal the secrets of her tricks, Leduc makes the artifice of her writing an object of observation: "It took me two and a half hours to write that, two and a half pages in my cross-ruled notebook. . . . May 15, 1961, 9:20 in the morning in a village of Vaucluse. I haven't changed; I still haven't overcome my desire to juggle with words so that people will notice me. A new combination, that's my number" (p. 325).

But when the magician reveals the mechanics of her craft, this revelation inevitably merely displaces the trickery to another level of illusion. For the maternal author who wishes to protect her integrity and to possess her reader-children outside the text, the enterprise of writing her life becomes a pretext, a "number." The textual strategy that Leduc uses to preserve the pure maternal origin of writing eventually undermines its own purpose and creates a yet wider zone of contradiction between the immediacies of maternal love and statuesque male writing. In this zone the original paternal values are reversed, and the very fixity of her writing becomes the false purity of a mask. By fictionalizing her writing as a mother, she turns it into a mere artifice where the logic of the lure performs its ambiguous acrobatics: "Drum rolls that I need when I write . . . with you it's the right tone. I'm playing too; I tap dark-toned make-up on my Nordic face . . . a few taps on the left cheek, a few taps on the right cheek since you're supposed to tap it in before you spread it out, that's the secret of a natural base, of a perfect make-up" (p. 201).

Instead of being the domain of transparency and union, writing hardens into a barrier, a disguise, hidden, however, by the naturalness of its own conventions, "a perfect make-up." Leduc's face has become a mask, and she fears that her "real" self will go unnoticed: "I walk on unnoticed. It's horrible, it's unbearable. I am not the center of the world" (p. 203). Caught in the *trompe l'oeil* of her own writing, Leduc is obliged to wish to fool us. She becomes an imitation of herself in a futile effort to make herself recognized, or misrecognized, as the wearer of a mask.

When she tries to tell the story of her life in order to be loved as a woman (mother), Leduc denies the difference between writing and love, the distance between her words and her readers. In this effort to make writing and life coincide, the deferral that writing represents seems momentarily to be swamped by the fierce flood of Leduc's desire. But while the instrument of her expression, with all its rules, conventions, and history, may temporarily fade into feeling, its role as the armature, the vehicle of her love causes it to reappear in all its hard necessity.

Having already polarized writing and life along the fault-lines of gender, Leduc cannot help feeling her writing as a rigid mask containing and concealing the volcanic warmth of her female life and love. In order to express herself, to make herself known, she must accommodate herself to this alien, male medium, and ends up miserably becoming an imitation of herself. In order to translate her life into words, she is forced to betray herself as a woman.

Infuriated by her own artifice, snared in the loathsome tricks she must play, Leduc hurls her autobiography at us like a challenge that registers the feigned contrariness of her enterprise. Her only means of achieving authenticity in her writing is to show us her mendacity, to insist on her betrayals. Emphasizing her own dark baseness—"I tap dark cream on my Nordic face"—in a desperate attempt to break through the contradictions of her travesty, Leduc exhibits, like a terrifying and disgusting Medusa mask, her ugliness, her frailties, her cruelty, even her crimes. Describing herself as an "ugly young lady without religion, without respect for the laws, without principles" (p. 61), as a shoplifter and the successful organizer of a black-market operation, she is placed outside the law by her character and her acts as well as by her bastard birth. Intensifying her illegitimacy is the only way for Leduc to remain true to herself in a situation where self-expression necessitates distortion and betrayal, where writing is the same as lying. Forced into a tragic dilemma by the contradictions of gender and genre, Leduc insults herself to stay honest. Her original self-loathing as a woman is thus irresistibly confirmed.

Caught in the agonizing aporia of self-mimicry, Leduc finally attempts to master the travesty of writing by turning it inside out and changing her clothes into a kind of writing. She becomes obsessed with her wardrobe during her liaison with Hermine and, putting aside the tie and masculine attire she wore for Gabriel, immerses herself in the world of high fashion. Realizing she does not need to be ugly, she buys designer clothes and visits the famous hairdresser Antoine. She emerges from his salon transformed or, perhaps more accurate, unrecognizable.

The Waltz

In the episode following her visit to Antoine's, the mythology supporting the image of the writer as a unified, self-present male or female, defined by the opposition of male and female, is dramatically put into question. The idealized parental definitions of gender are overturned in a catastrophic confrontation. The very fullness and self-sufficiency that seemed to legitimize the parents as origins of language reveal them to be nightmarish figures of death. The function of these godlike prototypes as creators is shown to be a myth in another sense of the word, that is, an illusion.

Leduc makes a special appeal to the reader to accompany her in this initiatory pilgrimage through the trials of despair and death. No longer the benevolent but condescending mother, she becomes a suppliant pleading with the reader to accompany her, to stay with her. This must be a joint venture: "Reader, follow me. Reader, I will fall at your feet begging you to follow. . . . Reader, we will say: we stepped onto the sidewalk, we jumped with our feet together into silence. A long, long scarf of raw silk grasped between thumb and forefinger." Her hands joined in prayer to enjoin us to leap with her into the silence beyond her own writing, Leduc plunges into that formless dimension where "everything is gratuitous" (p. 216).

Leduc and her lover, Hermine, are crossing the Pont de la Concorde when a passerby, whose face, "neither beautiful nor ugly" (p. 217), recalls the anonymous public of readers shadowing the author, shouts an insult at Leduc, an insult that is audible to her alone. The effect of this mysterious word is violent and profound. A metaphoric knife, it cuts through Leduc's newly acquired costume; it unveils her, divests her of her protective mask: "The Schiaperelli suit is falling off me. . . . My stockings are falling down over my ankles" (p. 218).

114

This disrobing proves to be a prologue to an even more radical unveiling. The metaphor of verbal abuse is literalized. Leduc is wounded, and this painful blow reveals to her that not only her clothes but her very body as well had served her as a protective envelope. In a nightmarish experience of helplessness and mutilation, she feels her body flowing out of itself through her wounds: "My wounds wounded the sidewalk. I walk inch after inch on the soft flesh of a butchery" (p. 217). The arbitrary autonomy of her body, now exteriorized by another's word, is represented by the sensation of the uncontrollable growth of her nose. Freudian phallus par excellence and to Leduc the symbol of her ugliness, her nose becomes a huge appendage: "My nose. Sudden and terrifying inflation; I was sweeping the bridge with my elephant's trunk" (p. 218). This hyperbolic, misplaced excrescence of maleness, the result of her own castration, weighs her down with its grotesque size.

The sensation of alienation from this uncontrollably distorted body is repeated on the level of language. Leduc's sense of linguistic helplessness returns her to infancy. Her protective mask of language deserts her and, unable to speak, even to pronounce words, she gurgles primitive sounds: "I tried to make sounds. Nothing came out but the hiccups of a baby being fed. . . . 'You open your mouth, but nothing comes out,' said Hermine. 'AEIOU,' I moaned" (p. 219).

Wounded by the gratuitous word of an anonymous passerby, Leduc is stripped of the defensive disguises that defined her as a consistent self. Her body fragments, disperses, inflates; her language becomes inarticulate. In disarray, reduced to a state of primitive fear and vulnerability, Leduc seeks psychological refuge in the mythological paternal and maternal figures with which she identified as a writer.

But the paternal godhead now takes shape in a bizarre vision: "Calf's head, color of livid flannel, lying languidly on the butcher's parsley bed, give me your sleep, give me the ecstasy of your slashed mouth" (p. 219). As a way of parrying the word-wound of the other's language, this vision of the animal's head represents, like a primitive and macabre god, the fusion of face and mask in death. The power underlying the masculine mask of writing is revealed to be a fatal violence. As the symbol of the recuperation of self-presence in authentic writing, this textual godhead inscribes its smiling wound, that imitation of a mouth, as language that dissolves into the silent ecstasy of self-destruction.

The figure of the mythological mother appears next. A voice speaks sweetly and seductively from the throat-breast (*la gorge*) of the river. This soothing maternal voice promises to enfold Leduc in love and admiration just as she was wrapped in her grandmother's apron and in the admiring looks of her child-readers: "I am at your service, come in, come into the water this throat said to me. I will go in, effortlessly I will part the avenue of men and women, lovers kneeling in approbation of me" (p. 221).

The mouth-wound of the paternal godhead here becomes the throat-breast-womb of the angel mother who promises the easy achievement of wholeness, of centrality, by the nourishment of adoration. The river-writing reproduces this fantasized apotheosis of the maternal author who, like a new Isis, will bathe in the reflection of the worshiping looks of her readers. But like the macabre death-smile of the paternal godhead, this vision too dissolves in the plenitude of its own smothering fullness. Power, death, ecstatic union, these are all ways of seeking oblivion, forgetfulness of the division within her, the illegitimacy of her birth. These refuges from her shame, the panicked sense of her own ugliness, symbolically smother not only the words Leduc sought as a justification but the very life she would redeem.

The narrative changes at this point from hallucination to lyric description. The symbolic shifter between these two modes is Leduc's nose: "No, no, oh no, because my carnival nose will float on the water" (p. 221). This inescapably ugly object obtrudes by its irreducible grotesqueness into the world of the imaginary. The impossibility of integrating this gratuitous piece of flesh into a mythology of the godlike subject has the effect of drawing Leduc back into the world of the real.

She turns to Hermine and finds her sprawled on the river-bank weeping. Although she does not understand the cause of her companion's misery, Leduc's desperation finds expression in and through her lover's tears, and this expression, ignorant of its own meaning, redeems her despair by turning it into an act of generosity. The self-redeeming gift of life and love Leduc sought to generate in her writing comes to her unexpectedly from the outside—like the insult—at the moment she has become empty and thus able to receive it. An abundance of wretchedness unites the two women; their despair becomes a dance:

> We cried entwined together, we turned in place, we turned on the deserted riverbank, Hermine's snot flowed down on my cheek, my snot flowed down on hers. Weeping also with us the wind, the sky, the night. Charity of sex. Our ovaries and clitorises were melting too. She licked my snot, I licked hers. "Mon petit, ma petite." We turned, we cried, she called me, I called her "mon petit, ma petite," to infinity. Tell me what that woman said to you. That woman said, If I had a mug like that, I'd kill myself. Let's waltz, my darling. Let's waltz, my love. [P. 222]

The word-wound of the other has opened Leduc to the presence of a world outside her that she has not created and that dances with her. Blasting the myth of self as plenitude and as origin of speech, the gratuitous insult strikes Leduc like a redemptive coup de grâce. Her very ugliness, physical and moral, which she sought both to hide and to legitimize in her writing, becomes the ground where grace will grow.

Language no longer functions here as a mask or as an instrument of dominance: words are exchanged by the two women like their snot and tears. Dancing in symmetry, alike but not the same, they exchange language as both a gift and an appeal across the indeterminate space that separates their two embracing bodies. The different genders—"mon petit, ma petite"—are named and exchanged without neutralizing each other. Paradoxically coexisting in the same bodies, gender's dance of difference turns and twirls into infinity.

The Muse

This powerfully luminous passage, which appears at the real and figurative center of the book, condenses in one ritual scene the drama of gender and writing played out in Leduc's autobiography. In it she dons, one after the other, the inherited costumes of the male and female creator intended to sacralize the use of language as a justification of the self. The use of language and the traditional notions of gender are thus inextricably linked by their functions as self-explanation.

The inadequacy of these traditional notions is revealed with hallucinatory clarity as Leduc pursues them to their origins (conclusions). Remaining fiercely faithful to the voice of her own feelings as primitive as it may seem—"'AEIOU,' I moaned"—Leduc finally cannot be lulled by the promise of apotheosis held out to her by the ideal of writing as a self-sufficient creation. The images of the male and female authors bringing language out of themselves in an act mimicking God's creation of the world or a mother giving birth reveal themselves to be the opposite of what they appear: they are, in reality, defenses, lures, concealing the grotesque mutilations of the self they promised to forestall.

The very illegitimacy that Leduc associated not only with her lack of a father but also with being a woman and that drove her to recover maleness in her writing becomes a fulcrum of another kind. Betokening the impossibility of ever coinciding with herself in life or in writing, her shame—these unpossessable, unassimilable ugly fragments of reality represented variously in the text by her nose, her aborted child, Maurice's unthinkably erect sex, or the insult of the passerby—no longer threatens her with despair but opens up another zone of difference in which language can resonate. Her words and her (their) truth can never originate in her, any more than life truly

118

originates in fathers or mothers. Language, like life, does not belong to any one person or any one gender: it is as anonymous, uncontrollable, gratuitous as the insult of the passerby or Hermine's tears. Since language emerges from and in the gap between self and truth, difference—between herself and her body, between herself and her gender, between herself and her words—becomes for Leduc a zone of liberty where she and the world can joyously be reconciled.

As a result of this shift in her perception of difference (illegitimacy), Leduc no longer conceptualizes her writing as a contradictory mode of being (gender) that cancels out her life as a woman, but rather sees it as a kind of gap or empty space in which she can meet her own desire and reclaim-rename her life.

Significantly, the model of this other kind of writing appears in the love scenes between Leduc and her first lover, Isabelle:

> The hand moved up again: it was drawing circles, overflowing into the void, spreading its sweet ripples ever wider around my left shoulder, while the other lay abandoned to the darkness streaked by the breathing of the other girls. I was discovering the smoothness of my bones, the flow hidden in my flesh, the infinity of forms I possessed. [P. 83]

Desired by another who is in her own image and who is yet a vexing stranger (as Leduc is to herself), she learns to love herself. Isabelle's desire and her own assumption of that desire reveal to Leduc the vitality of her own flesh, the "infinity of forms" she possesses.

She need not lie, distort, deny herself to share a language with Isabelle: this language of touch which creates the possibility of endless new meaning in and of her body is not the stultifying language of statues but somehow her own language at once intensified and redeemed:

> The hand still seeking to persuade me, was bringing my arm, my armpit, into their real existence. The hand was wandering through whispering snowcapped bushes, over the first buds as

they swell to fullness. The springtime that had been crying its
impatience with the voice of tiny birds under my skin was now
curving and swelling into flower. [P. 84]

Using, like Colette, the symbol of impatient spring to express
her feeling of rebirth, Leduc equates the awakening of erotic
desire with the liberation of the "voices" under her skin. Isabelle's caresses, bringing her body into its "real existence,"
become a trope for Leduc's writing and its relationship to her
life. Leduc calls Isabelle the "muse hidden inside [her]" (p. 75),
and the trace of words left by her hand on Leduc's body is the
very text we are reading.

Given the fact that what was initially in question for Leduc
was her worthiness as a woman, it is not surprising that she
should visualize another woman as her muse. The asymme-
tries of the male and female relations to writing and literary
tradition are perhaps nowhere clearer than in the personae of
this allegory. While the male writer extends himself by desiring his writing as an other, the female writer, in order to
avoid canceling herself by identifying with the male pen, must
desire her writing as her self.

As we noted in our reading of The Vagabond, it is precisely
this affirmation of self expressed in love for other women that
is taboo.[6] Trivialized as vanity in male tradition, this female
"narcissism" is a powerful source of vitality and creativity for
those who have been separated from their own bodies. Contrary to the psychoanalytic model of homosexual desire, this
woman-love is not a sterile enclosure in the self but rather an
opening to the world. The other woman may indeed be a mirror of the self, but of a self who was first loathsome and now
can be loved. By means of these paradoxes of lesbian love,
Leduc discovers a mediating desire that links her at once to

6. It is interesting to note in this regard that these passages were excised
from Leduc's earlier book Ravages; the censored portions were indicated by
ellipses. The source of her writing in her love for another woman was thus
suppressed as being too scandalous to print (Simone de Beauvoir, "Préface,"
in La Bâtarde, Paris ed., p. 16).

herself and to her writing both as self and as other. In this scandalous relationship of one woman with another which demonstrates the very principle of difference, Leduc generates a symbol for the mysterious minimal pair that life and writing represent: "She molded the charity we had around our shoulders. Her careful hand traced lines on my lines, curves on my curves. Under my eyelids, I saw the halo of my shoulder reborn, I listened to the light of her caress" (p. 75).

The apparent sterility of this love creates the conditions of its fruitfulness. Out of this improbable union where procreation is impossible Leduc's artistic self is born. Gratuitous, an expression of charity because there is nothing to be gained, Leduc's writing, like Isabelle's caresses, creates another world blooming with words in the place of the real. It is in the infinitesimal but profound difference created by repetition— "lines on my lines, curves on my curves"—and in the unnaturalness, the gratuitousness of that very wish to repeat that the virtually infinite world of writing opens up.

In the lesbian logic of women's writing-reading proposed here by Leduc, life and art are not in conflict. Setting aside heterosexual paradigms based on notions of opposition or even complementarity, Leduc creates a new model based on the uncanny minimal shift between two women's bodies. Freed from the so-called natural laws of heterosexuality with its parents and inescapable responsibility to deserve love, Leduc proclaims all writing to be unruly like her. Rejecting the myth of language as an inheritance that must be inscribed in the registers of tradition, Leduc perceives in her illegitimacy the illegitimacy of the writing that records her bastardy. It is precisely the break in the line of penmanship which a woman represents that reveals the disquieting, unpredictable freedom of language usually masked by the rigid rules of propriety. In this gap between birth and creation, between the fleshly body and the body of desire, as between the thumb and forefinger of Leduc, shimmers that "long, long scarf of raw silk," the dazzling fabric of her words.

The flowering spring of love passes for Leduc; the searing

heat of summer comes. Inspiration falters, the muse betrays, sluggishness returns; old myths, ghosts of lost parents, dreams of merit come back to haunt her and twirl tantalizingly before her as a temptation in her writing. The gift of a new writing is not a given; like her gender, precisely because it is not self-justified, it must endlessly recreate its meaning.

La Bâtarde ends with the beginning of a book—not itself, but another book, *L'Asphyxie*. Unlike so many *Künstler-romane*, *La Bâtarde* does not explain itself, is not recursive. The structure of this autobiography reproduces, rather, the spiral of its own thematic waltz, in its syncopation paradoxically remaining constant to its own fierce but fragile vision. The ending, which defers its own beginning for another sixteen years, opens a free space where, repeating and transforming each other, Leduc's writing and our reading can come (in)to play. At once excrescence and emptiness, generosity and lack, this space is the painful and glorious zone of bastardy where women and their words can recreate (a) life.

4

Marguerite Duras:
The Whore

Although Marguerite Duras had been publishing novels, plays, and short stories for twenty years, when she wrote and published *The Ravishing of Lol V. Stein* in 1964, something changed.[1] She says she realized that she had reached a turning point in her relation to her writing. She seems to have endured rather than willed this turning point; it was part of a painful process of change and liberation that at the time had its frightening aspects. This is how Duras remembered the writing of *Lol V. Stein* thirteen years afterward: "This had never happened to me before. I was writing, and suddenly I heard myself screaming, because I was afraid . . . I was afraid of losing my head."[2]

There was something about the shift in Duras's writing that made her afraid of losing her head, afraid of going crazy. Something about this book, her own writing, put Duras in a panic. *The Ravishing of Lol V. Stein* is in itself this fear of madness; the writing on the page contains the obbligato of this scream.

---

1. Marguerite Duras, *Le Ravissement de Lol V. Stein* (Paris: Gallimard, 1964); published in English as *The Ravishing of Lol Stein*, trans. Richard Seaver (New York: Grove, 1966). In referring to this book in my text I have restored the middle initial, inexplicably deleted by the American publisher.
2. Marguerite Duras and Michelle Porte, *Les Lieux de Marguerite Duras* (Paris: Minuit, 1977), p. 102.

The threat of insanity that the writer says she felt as she wrote the book is, not surprisingly, one of the book's central themes. A complex and in some ways unanalyzable dynamics is therefore established between book and author. Was it her own madness made visible in the book that caused Marguerite Duras to scream, or was it the madness of the writing that aroused her fear? How do we distinguish between the screams (*les cris*) and the writing (*l'écrit*)? How do we distinguish cause and effect, inside and outside?

The structure of the novel simultaneously emphasizes and puts into question our habitual ways of making these distinctions. In doing so it unveils the power politics implicit in love, language, and the writing of fiction. As Duras lays her craft, herself as writer, bare within the confines of her writing, out of the logical blurring of fact and fiction, before and after, inside and outside emerges a clearly defined and radically new shift in an old definition of women's writing as whoring.

As we have seen, Colette explored the exhibitionism involved in writing and publishing and the anxieties aroused in women in our society by the transgression of the requirement to keep covered. Violette Leduc went a step further and redeemed the illegitimacy of the female writer by proclaiming that illegitimacy as the very condition of all writing. Duras pursues much the same strategy as Leduc: she assumes a socially condoned but transgressive image of women—in this case, the whore. But, rather than defining this condition in respect to the traditional norm, and thus as an instance of defiance or marginalization, she turns transgression inside out. The whore becomes the looker, the chooser, the center of power, and in so doing defines a new logic, a new economy in the exchange of language. In *The Ravishing of Lol V. Stein*, as Duras uncovers and explores the indecency of female writing, she discloses that indecency as a cover for something else: the hidden whoring of all language.

Women as the Object of (Fictional) Desire

The Ravishing of Lol V. Stein is a first-person narrative, although "narrative" is hardly an adequate word to describe this string of words which goes back and forth in time, weaving a web of uneven texture broken by holes and blanks. This web creates, finally, not so much the chronology of a history as the portrait of a madwoman, a woman whose story is characterized precisely by its blanks.

Surprisingly, perhaps, for twentieth-century women's fiction, the first-person narrator of this "story," the apparent creator of Lol's portrait, is not Lol at all, but rather a man, Jacques Hold, a man who eventually becomes Lol's lover in all the conventional senses of that term. Duras uses this male narrator as a kind of front: first to present and explore the characteristics of traditional male narrative and then to dramatize the undoing of that very narrative, an undoing that is, in a sense, the risky unraveling of Duras's own past history as a writer.

At the outset, Duras presents us with a traditional and perhaps all-too-familiar configuration composed of the male subject—the center of knowledge, vision, and language—and the female object—the silent, passive form, there only and precisely to be shaped, understood, and narrated by a man. When Jacques meets Lol, she is twenty-nine years old, married, and the mother of three daughters. What makes her apparently ordinary life extraordinary is the mental breakdown she experienced ten years earlier as the result of a dramatic and public abandonment by her first fiancé, Michael Richardson. This critical event occurred at a summer dance where Michael met another, older woman and, after dancing with her all night, left with her, never to see or speak to Lol again.

The propelling motive of the narrative is Jacques's effort not only to reconstruct Lol's story but also to fathom the madness that seems still to lie beneath the surface of her apparently calm and ordered life. Furthermore, Jacques's curiosity about Lol becomes increasingly fired by love and sexual appetite. Finally his intellectual curiosity and his desire for Lol mingle and fuse until he/we cannot tell one from the other. Erotic and intellectual desire become indistinguishable, expressed in Jacques's single, irresistible drive to possess this perplexingly transparent but enigmatic woman.

Lola Valerie Stein serves, then, as the object of diverse but intertwined strivings: she is at once a woman whose perplexing madness provokes a desire to understand and explain and whose slumberous sensuality seems to call for erotic awakening. As both the arouser and object of desire, the character called Lol V. Stein incarnates the curiously contradictory double role women traditionally play in love and fiction. As the passive provoker of desire, she is simultaneously the cause and effect of a man's love, the cause and effect of a man's writing.

Although Lol appears at first to be a kind of pale ribbon that Jacques can follow to its source, her simplicity and blandness turn out to be deceptive: Lol is rather a kind of maddening Moebius strip, joining inside and outside, beginning and ending in a seamless continuum. Her function as confounder, as the one who makes distinctions impossible, and therefore as lure, calls to mind the banal but fascinating figure of woman as deceiver. At once possessable fiction and perpetually receding reality, Lol symbolizes, in this imitation of a traditional male narrative, the mysterious Other, the dark continent, the chaos to be plumbed and curbed by the male conquistador, the knower, the One.

From Quest to Inquest

As male narrative, *The Ravishing of Lol V. Stein* appears to be a conventional, modern, antiheroic story: the story of a man in quest of the knowledge/love of a woman and of the progressive uncertainty that accompanies the quest. From the beginning Duras posits both the traditional heroic values of quest fiction and the equally conventional modern subversion of those values. The old heroic quest is thus brought low, transformed into its ironic version—the inquest.[3] "Lol V.

3. The investigative structure of Duras's novels has been noted by many critics, among them Jacques Guicharnaud, "The Terrorist Marivaudage of Marguerite Duras," *Yale French Studies* 46 (1971), 113–24; and Erica Eisinger, "Crime and Detection in the Novels of Marguerite Duras," *Contemporary Literature* 15 (1974), 503–20.

Stein was born here in S. Tahla, and she spent a good part of her youth in this town. Her father was a professor at the university. Lol has a brother nine years older than she—I have never seen him—they say he lives in Paris. Her parents are dead" (p. 1).

The book opens with these words: a presentation of Lol, the object of investigation, and the relevant background information, her family history. The sparseness of her history differentiates this presentation from the opulent creation of detail in "realistic" novels. It also introduces the play of doubt and subjectivity into the presentation of "facts." The existence of Lol's brother is, against all rationality, put into question by the narrator's parenthetical expression, "I have never seen him," while the weight of rumor called in as a resolution at the end of the sentence seems a sparse and unreliable corroboration of the brother's existence and whereabouts.

This pattern of objective presentation followed by the introduction of doubt and multiple points of view is repeated and intensified as the novel continues. The narrator calls in several people as witnesses in his effort to piece together Lol's past. One of these people is Lol's school chum Tatiana Karl (who, we find out later, is Jacques's mistress). Tatiana was with Lol the night Michael Richardson betrayed her; in fact, she stood beside her, holding her hand, as Lol watched her fiancé and her rival dancing together. As an actual observer of this dramatic event, as the only available witness besides Lol, Tatiana is ostensibly an important source of information. But even her judgments and observations are soon undercut by the narrator's spectacular repudiation: "I no longer believe a word Tatiana says. I'm convinced of absolutely nothing" (p. 4).

Even the comments of Lol's husband, Jean Bedford, whose proposal of marriage to the severely disturbed young woman occurred in bizarre circumstances, are distorted and tainted by self-interest:

> Jean Bedford claimed that he loved his wife. He said that he loved her still, the way she was, the way she had always been,

both before and since their marriage, that he did not believe he
had changed her so much as chosen her wisely and well. He
loved this woman, this Lola Valerie Stein, this calm presence by
his side, this sleeping beauty who never offered a word of com-
plaint, this upright sleeping beauty, this constant self-effacement . . . which he called her gentleness, the gentleness of his
wife. [Pp. 23–24]

In this passage the narrator uses two simultaneous but conflicting levels of discourse to put into question the comments
of the speaker. The language Jean Bedford uses to describe his
wife and his relation to her—"love," "calm presence," "gentleness"—is translated by the narrator into another set of
terms—"self-effacement," "upright sleeping beauty." What
the husband depicts as feminine fragility and passivity the
narrator calls the somnambulistic silence of a zombie. By this
means of translation, the husband's view of Lol as a model
wife and mother is made to appear a drastic distortion and
denial of her real state. By retrospective implication, all of his
statements about her are therefore subverted, and the subversion is intensified by the narrator's use of indirect discourse:
"Jean Bedford claimed that . . . , said that . . ." The very re-
porting of the claim by indirection suggests that there is another, more accurate view of the situation.

Although the novel presents itself at the beginning as a
modern version of a quest, an investigative effort to reconstruct the story of Lol V. Stein and to fathom the mystery of
her madness, this project appears more and more futile as the
novel progresses. As we have just seen, the narrator continually undercuts and puts into doubt the reliability of the
witnesses to Lol's life by emphasizing the self-interest that
dictates and distorts their language.

This difficulty of reconstructing a complete and accurate
account of Lol and her life is underscored by the narrator's
revelation of his own activity as interpreter and inventor. At
times his reminders of the particularity of his point of view
glide into a radically different register: "This I invent, I see";
or quite simply, "I invent" (p. 46). Quite different from the

cautious statements above, these announcements of the narrator's invention act to reverse or at least to change the structural expectations engaged by the investigative mode proposed at the beginning of the novel. As these moments of invention are multiplied, the authority of the narrative as an imitation of an inquest, as an imitation of history, is dismantled. Another level of fictionality is introduced into the surface of the discourse, making of the narrative a confusing patchwork of differently constituted segments.

The readers already know that *The Ravishing of Lol V. Stein* is a novel, if only because the book so describes itself on the title page. But the opening sections, which recall traditional forms of novelistic discourse, ask us to suspend our disbelief, to "pretend" that Lol Stein is a real woman with a real history, which the narrator will attempt to reconstruct for us. The narrator plays the role not of omniscient narrator but of a subjective individual motivated by curiosity and love to find out the "truth" about this woman. The narrator maintains or at least alludes to all the conventions of evidence and direct observation.

But here the reader's expectation of fair play is foiled. The conventional structure of the novel is exploded from within. Whereas we have been asked to believe in the narrative provisionally as if it were true, we are now asked to believe in it as if it were false, or at least to accept it as pure invention. The status of the narrator as a reliable actor in a dramatization of the way we deal with a world we don't completely understand topples from its place of authority. He no longer can play the role of heroic model as the observer, the searcher for the truth, because, as he himself tells us, he is making a lot of the story up.

By this means Duras creates an image of the writer who, by calling attention to his craft, undoes its authority. The reader's comfortable relation to the narrative is disrupted and the status of fiction itself is put into question. The reader is kept perpetually off balance by this oscillation between what is "real" and what is "fictional" in the text. Indeed, these two categories, which traditionally define two polarities of our discourse, collapse into each other. The reader must therefore remain vigilant, in a perpetual state of doubt, forced by the antiheroic posture of the narrator to adopt a stance of suspicion as the receiver of this discourse.[4]

Subverting Subversion: The Secret Hero

This undoing of the novelist's position as a teller of essential, if not actual, truth had become conventional at the time Marguerite Duras wrote this novel. What is original and truly subversive in *The Ravishing of Lol V. Stein* is Duras's revelation of the superficiality of these antiheroic narrative strategies. The doubt, the tentativeness, the undecidability of this male narrative are only apparent, for, on another level, the narrator implicitly appeals to the extratextual authority of traditional values shared with the readers, thus reestablishing the authority of his discourse. By "honestly" emphasizing the very subjectivity of his writing, the male narrator does not in fact deconstruct the reliability of his narrative, but merely recasts it on another, less obvious but also less vulnerable level of credibility and authority.

While Jacques Hold undercuts the reliability of the other witnesses in this inquest by retroactively casting doubt on their statements, he enhances his own trustworthiness by a shift in this same method. He habitually prefaces his observations with a demurral: "Here is my opinion" (p. 35); "This is what I see" (p. 43); "This is what I surmise" (p. 62). If such reminders of the particularity of the narrator's point of view were to come *after* a description of events or an interpretation of a state of mind, they would have the same effect as the similar remarks applied to the other characters: they would undercut or ironize his discourse. But coming *before* a passage

---

4. This process exactly duplicates the one proposed earlier as a model for the *nouveau roman* by Nathalie Sarraute in *L'Ere du soupçon* (Paris: Gallimard, 1956).

of description or interpretation, they produce the opposite effect: they increase our confidence in the narrator's reliability.
Here is a man who knows his own limitations, who knows
how to separate opinion from fact. The shift to antecedent
turns these phrases into the cautionary statements of a judi-
cious observer whose very modesty enhances his claim to
authority.

The truth function of this narrative is thus diverted from its
base in objectively grounded language onto a more unstable
but finally less assailable terrain: the trustworthiness of the
narrator. What he seems to give away with one hand he takes
back with the other. His appeals to his own fallibility are a
lure, a con, which encourages the reader to trust him even if
what he says is not wholly reliable: he may make mistakes,
but he's a nice, honest guy who doesn't want to hurt or mis-
lead anybody.

As Duras imitates male discourse, she thus reveals its self-
subversion as merely a ploy. The antihero is really a hero of
another kind. If reality is no longer attainable and if the narrator cannot, therefore, guarantee the truth of his statements,
he can vouch for his good intentions. If he "invents," he does
so not gratuitously but according to principles of consistency
and fair play:

> To level the terrain, to dig down into it, to open the tombs in
> which Lol is feigning death, seems to me fairer—given the ne-
> cessity to fill in [*inventer*] the missing links of Lol Stein's story
> [*histoire*]—than to fabricate mountains, create obstacles, rely on
> chance. And knowing this woman, I believe she would prefer
> that I compensate in this way for the lack of facts about her life.
> Moreover, in doing so I am always relying on hypotheses which
> are not gratuitous, but which, in my opinion, have at least some
> foundation in fact. [Pp. 27–28]

Although on one level the narrator creates confusion and
doubt by emphasizing the subjectivity of his witnesses and by
thrusting a second level of fiction into the surface of his discourse, he reinstates the credibility of his discourse on another

level by asserting his personal trustworthiness. He is not frivolous or unpredictable, and his discourse is anchored in a judi-
cious appraisal of probabilities. His invention or fabrication of
history is strictly limited, he says, to the filling in of gaps, and
even this filling in of gaps is accomplished according to carefully defined standards of reliability. And so the reader need
not worry, for if the narrator undermines objectivity and emphasizes plurality of point of view, this subversion is limited
and contained. Doubt and uncertainty are part of a game that
can be played safely because the boundaries of the playing field
are clearly marked. Although first appearing in the guise of an
antihero, Jacques Hold reemerges in the traditional role of the
male I/eye who can see the truth—even if he has to level, dig,
and penetrate—of women's history.

The passage above in which the narrator pursues an elabo-
rate self-justification is at once a replication and a parody of
traditional male authoritative discourse and its (ab)use of the
woman-object. Its unctuous reference to fair play only partially conceals the assumption that the woman-object cannot
think and speak for herself. The paternal narrator must therefore fill in for her in all senses of the term.

Though anxious and free-floating in one sense, Jacques
Hold's narrative is actually firmly anchored in the very traditional assertion that he, the male narrator, has sole access to
knowledge of the woman-object. If he allows himself to invent, to fill in gaps, it is only because he "knows" Lol in the
same way he "knows" facts. These two kinds of knowing—
about things and events on the one hand and about the inner
lives of human beings on the other—he assumes to be identical. "Woman" and "object" are indeed synonymous in this
discourse; Lol can be known—that is, possessed—the same
way an object can be possessed. If the truth be known, it is a
woman.

The object of the quest, the narrator's knowing Lol, is thus
reported recursively as successfully accomplished. Jacques
Hold is able to write this book about his getting to know Lol
V. Stein precisely because he has succeeded in his mission.

Duras later uses this setting up of his quest as a success story in an ironic treatment of Jacques's narrative, which we will explore further on. For the moment, operating at the level of the narrator's assertions, we will examine the way in which these assertions about "knowing" as the foundation of truth in language uncover a frightening will to destroy as the motive of male writing. Behind the quest for knowledge in *The Ravishing of Lol V. Stein* lies the story of a rape.

Getting to Know You

The reason that Lol V. Stein cannot or will not tell her own story is that she is crazy. Because he loves her and wants to understand her, Jacques Hold sets out to reconstruct her story for her. The narrator's wish to know, his need to write, and his desire to possess sexually are all fused, then, into one gesture—getting into Lol's place. Jacques's progress in this direction defines the major narrative line of the novel.

There are, of course, various ways of getting into another's place: open struggle, usurpation, fusion, identification—techniques in which, as the vocabulary suggests, the ingredients of power, persuasion, and seduction vary. Jacques chooses what looks at the outset like a gentle mode of knowing: empathy. He attempts to understand Lol by getting inside her world, seeing what she sees, feeling what she feels. He imposes on himself an intense discipline of perception as he follows Lol on her walks through S. Tahla, trying to understand the principle of her seemingly unpredictable movements. As he yields to the rambling rhythm of these aimless walks, the narrator's language becomes full of cautious questions and conjectural statements: "Lol must have given herself credit for passing unperceived"; "She must have felt all the more reassured" (p. 31); "Did she, Lol, recognize anyone in S. Tahla? . . . I doubt it" (p. 32).

But doubt yields quickly to certitude as Jacques succeeds in imaginatively taking Lol's place. By the end of the chapter, his language has shifted from conjecture to the expression of certainties:

> She recognized S. Tahla . . . but without there being any proof reflected by S. Tahla to reinforce her own, each time that she recognized something, a bullet whose impact was always the same. All by herself, she began to recognize less, and then, in a different way, she began to return day after day, step by step, toward her non-knowledge of S. Tahla. [P. 33]

His empathic imagination, Jacques believes, enables him to experience the world as Lol experiences it. The rhetorical strategies of the sentence shift as they follow Jacques's progress into Lol's mind and feelings. What is lost in this progress, though, is an awareness of the conditional mode of Jacques's knowledge. As the conjectural sentence gives way to simple predication, the separateness of Lol is suppressed or denied. Her interior—her thoughts and feelings—seems perfectly permeable, knowable, offers no resistance. In fact, the very inscrutability of her madness turns out to be this imagined emptiness. Lol, the woman-object, is a void sucking in the fullness of the male knower; she is an empty page calling for the traces of his pen.

In the passage just quoted, Jacques Hold reenacts this traditional model of male writing. But the ambiguity of the processes of empathic imagination, seen as a dynamic interchange between two subjectivities, still remains. In one sense, the narrator has triumphed in the attainment of his desire to understand Lol: his knowledge of Lol has indeed taken the place of her unknowing. But, paradoxically, the very conditions of his knowing, founded as they are on replacement and denial of otherness, preempt the possibility of Jacques's ever knowing Lol's madness as it "knows" itself. Caught in the same paradoxical position as Heisenberg's uncertain scientist, the writer seems snared in an inescapably solipsistic medium. Tragically unable to reproduce in reality the heroic gesture his writing purports to accomplish, he is doomed to write only about himself in a language that looks like an ideal instrument of knowledge but is actually the trace of annihilation.

Those Little White Lies

Paradoxically, then, the narrator's position is not unlike that of Lol, who does not know what she knows. As Jacques continues on his quest, the negativity inherent in his project becomes clearer and clearer to him; the further he proceeds, the less he seems to know: "Now I alone of all these perverters of the truth know this: that I know nothing. That was my initial discovery about her: to know nothing about Lol Stein was already to know her. One could, it seemed to me, know even less about her, less and less about Lol Stein" (p. 72). The narrator's movement toward the subject/object of his writing, toward Lol Stein, ironically reproduces the movement of Lol herself in S. Tahla. The more she walks, the less she knows.

In a surprising reversal, the writer's project becomes a voyage not into light but into darkness and ignorance, into madness perhaps. The other characters in the book, the other witnesses to Lol's life, become "perverters of the truth" precisely because they claim to know something about her. The only way to the real truth, the narrator claims, is to know that one knows nothing.

Lol's very appearance seems to reproduce the "nothing" that she represents. She habitually dresses in dull, anonymous colors, or in that no-color, white. Her eyes, her hair are bleached out, her body seems barely inhabited: "Her hair had the same odor as her hand, the odor of some long-unused object. She was beautiful, but there was a sadness about her, as though the blood were slow to circulate in her veins, a grayish pallor. Her features were already beginning to fade into that pallor" (p. 19). Like the faded echo of an already fading nineteenth-century heroine, Lol seems barely able to maintain herself at the center of this fictional enterprise. It is as if, by its very emptiness, the traditional subject of fiction, its field of reference, were about to disappear into nothingness, taking with it the robust life of the writing intended to inscribe it.

But Lol's transparency, her self-effacement, her yielding are deceptive, for if they represent the featurelessness of anonymity on the one hand, they are, on the other, a deception:

> Whenever she speaks, whenever she moves, when she looks or is lost in thought, I have the feeling that I am witnessing with my own eyes some personal and capital manner of lying, an immense yet strongly defended field of lies. For us, this woman is lying about T. Beach, about S. Tahla . . . she is lying about herself too, because the divorce between us . . . she alone announced it—but in silence—in a dream so compelling that it escaped her, and she is unaware that she ever had it. [P. 97]

Like centuries of male creators of fictional females before him, the narrator associates fragility and passivity with a gift for prevarication, simulation. Everything Lol says is a lie, her whole appearance is a deceptive construct. What has been regarded, from Eve onward, as one of the characteristic traits of women has advanced in Lol to the state of pathology. Although there exists in her an intention to deceive, the reasons for that intention have been effaced. The Great Female Hoax becomes something even more sinister: a gratuitous, inexplicable, senseless will to deceive.

While Jacques came to acknowledge his claim to knowledge as illusory, he was mistaken both in the certainty of his ignorance and in the mode of his unknowing. Appearances were deceiving. Lol's transparency turns out to be the opaque limit of a lie. Her emptiness foils knowledge not as its undoing but rather as its contradiction. Hers is not a silence that would finally support and delimit the meaning of Jacques's language: it is a counterdiction, an antilanguage of lies.

When appearance is substituted for being, as it is in Lol's universe, language is set adrift in a chaotic and limitless space. When fiction has no reality, even a conventional one, to measure itself against, but only a counterfiction, all hierarchy, all order, all appeal to meaning disappear. No accommodation is possible between these two uses of language: there is no mediating word.

In confronting Lol's architecture of prevarication, Jacques comes face to face with radical otherness. Although once her lies operated as a defense, the thing defended—her self—has already been obliterated, so that the defense is senseless. And yet the structure remains, the reverse of a memory; not an empty citadel into whose quiet center one may penetrate but rather an endless facade. There is no inside to this surface of lies; that secret has disappeared irretrievably into nonexistence just as surely as a forgotten dream.

The Ritual of Rape

While some anxiety of the unknown tinged or even propelled Jacques's original quest to understand Lol and to tell her story, he nevertheless operated in an ostensibly generous mode of empathic imagination. However, when the object of his quest proves to be recalcitrant, not just in the ordinary way that reality foils and eludes its fictional reproduction, but in a more positive and definitive way, Jacques's generosity falters. When Lol's appearance of fragility and transparency turns out to be fallacious, Jacques perceives the unknowableness of Lol's inner life as resistance to him.

Jacques's desire to write Lol's story presupposed a hierarchy of reality in which his language would subsume her silence. His apparent yielding to Lol in an effort to understand her is revealed now as a provisional act based on the actual possession of power. Through Jacques's disarray and his consequent behavior, Duras shows that the authority to speak assumed in the male quest for knowledge is based on a radical power drive to conquer and to possess. Faced with the perceived resistant otherness of the female object, the male narrator's quest becomes a war: "My hands are becoming the trap wherewith to ensnare her, immobilize her, keep her from constantly moving to and fro from one end of time to another" (p. 97).

Without relinquishing the heroic vocabulary of the (in)quest,

Jacques pursues his relationship with Lol on another, more primitive level. Lodged within the narrative movement blending the thirst for truth, the need to write, and the hunger for love is the narrator's struggle for power, a struggle fueled by a need to dominate, possess, and destroy whatever is not-self. What is most revealing about this apparent shift in the narrator's motivation is that his violent, primitive wishes do not contradict or enter into conflict with the so-called higher desires for love, truth, and creation. This accommodation in Jacques's discourse of the rhetoric of love to the rhetoric of domination suggests that the two must somehow have been related from the beginning, that the violent instincts of domination and destruction have indeed always been implicit in the search for truth and love.

Whether our cultural and romantic pursuits can be reduced to clashes for survival is not decided in this novel. But what is asserted through the allegory of Jacques Hold's narrative is that these two levels of motivation are inextricably related to each other. The narrator's construction of a text will involve, then, the ritual, if not real, destruction of its object. Like a scientist dissecting a body, Jacques Hold must destroy the very life he seeks to understand.

This destruction of the object of fiction by the author and origin of that fiction is carried out at the end of the book in a scene that demonstrates its title. Jacques and Lol have gone to T. Beach to visit the scene of Lol's abandonment. They return to the ballroom of the casino as if to the scene of a crime, looking for clues to the cause of the disaster. But there are, of course, none: "A monumental calm reigns over everything, engulfs everything. One trace remains, one. A single, indelible trace, at first you don't know where. What? You don't know? No trace, none, all has been buried, and Lol with it" (p. 171). At this moment Jacques realizes that Lol has left no trace of her own, contains no trace, is not a trace. His adversary has already been defeated: Lol's lie is itself a lie. In Jacques's eyes there can no longer be a contest between him and Lol because Lol has already been destroyed. He perceives, however, that her obliteration does not after all signal a triumph for him because she has been the author of her own destruction.

Jacques cannot abide this discomfiture; with a grisly inertia, his need to dominate and possess Lol, to be her author, persists even after her self-destruction is exposed. Jacques and Lol's love scene in the hotel following their visit to the casino is a barely masked ritual of rape. Love, reduced to a drama of possession, has come too late. One of the partner-adversaries is already not there.

> I am obliged to undress her. She won't do it herself. Now she is naked. . . . Stretched out on the bed, she does not move a muscle. . . . She is motionless, remains there where I have placed her. Her eyes follow me across the room as I undress, as though I were a stranger. . . . She doesn't recognize me, hasn't the faintest idea who I am anymore. [Pp. 177–78]

Jacques's penetration of Lol reveals simultaneously a truth about writing and a truth about rape: at the very moment that possession of the object seems to occur, what is revealed most blatantly is that the object is no longer there to be possessed. The woman-object protects her subjectivity by the ultimate gesture of self-erasure. She makes herself indeed an object, thereby apparently fulfilling but actually foiling the (false) quest of the male narrator-rapist. For hidden underneath his fusion of female and object in his search for the truth is his desire that the woman-object wish to yield, wish to be undone and possessed by him. This imputed desire-to-be-an-object will, of course, soothe the male's anxieties and justify his conflation of quest and conquest.

But since neither Lol nor any other independently existing being can be possessed in this way, both the rape and the writing become grisly, empty rituals that, always belated and having no meaning in themselves, must be endlessly repeated. The author-rapist is ultimately left, therefore, not with a glorious sense of triumph but rather with the emptiness of helpless rage.

Is this why Marguerite Duras screamed as she wrote this book? Is her cry a shriek of horror in response to this vision of the realities of her craft? What the male narrator, Jacques Hold, has demonstrated is that writing is founded on a fearful power play; that, inevitably, it must result in a violent exploitation, a destruction of otherness, a sadistic delight in domination and possession, at best a solipsistic and delusional ritual always excluded from its own meaning.

If that is true, if writing is rape, this novel does indeed represent the ravishing of Lol Stein—the rape of a silent, estranged subject—and by extension, all fiction, all writing reenacts this rape of its object.

Duras affirms this model of writing and reading in an eerie allegory toward the end of the book: "On that section of the beach where the swimmers are . . . there is some commotion, a crowd gathering around something, perhaps a dead dog" (p. 174). Like a dead animal washed up on the shore, Lol lies inert at the center of our fascinated attention, the remains of some repeated and unknowable story of disaster. The readers circle around her, like the characters in the book, like the author, seeking to repair our sense of vulnerability by reconstructing her destruction in the language of our desires.

An Other Look

There is, though, a difference between the narrator, Jacques Hold, and the author who has signed her name to this novel. Jacques Hold's narration embodies the principles and values of male literary tradition, a tradition that includes a territorial, if not proprietary, notion of language, an authoritarian concept of authorship. Jacques states at the outset, "I shall relate *my own* story of Lol Stein" (p. 4; italics mine). And his story drives out Lol's story, replaces it in a finally violent move of attempted domination, which, Duras implies, is a product of the simultaneous polarization of male and female, subject and object. Because difference is seen as opposition, because otherness is seen as resistance, the male author must of necessity

140

seek to replace and destroy the female subject. Duras states elsewhere more explicitly her view of this male drive to dominate: "They [men] all live with a nostalgia or longing for violence. . . . There's a Marine in every man."[5]

But to the extent that there is a difference between the narrator and the author, between Jacques Hold and Marguerite Duras, between male and female, the narrator becomes a character in his own narration. His relation to his own project, rather than the investigation itself, becomes the subject of the novel. Jacques's story of Lol becomes a story for someone else to tell, the pretext of Duras's own project of writing. The male narrator becomes, then, the other in relation to the female author of the book, and *The Ravishing of Lol V. Stein* emerges as Duras's critique of a male literary tradition in the name of another story written from the point of view of the female object of male fiction.

This female writing may also be a replacement of Lol's story, but a replacement of a different kind; not a preemption or destruction, as was Jacques's, but rather a repositioning, a placement somewhere else. As we look at the book from this other perspective, not from beyond but rather from the nearer side of the narrator's discourse, we see that Lol's story is a story of replacement. The event that caused Lol's breakdown was her replacement by another woman in the affections of her fiancé. The fact that this sad but finally banal event is traumatic for Lol requires us to look at it from another point of view. For while this scenario has been romanticized in the long tradition of the love story, that tradition now appears—in the light of Lol's madness—as a neutralization of a meaning even more radically disturbing than that of betrayal and abandonment.

For Lol, the pathogenic element in this scenario is precisely the act of replacement, the possibility of one person taking another's place, or, more precisely, one woman being put by a man in another woman's place. Lol's sanity stumbles on this

5. Marguerite Duras and Xavière Gauthier, *Les Parleuses* (Paris: Minuit, 1974), p. 33.

simple truth: she is exchangeable. How could a love that singled her out as unique be transferred to someone else? She
cries out plaintively in her puzzlement: "I don't understand
who is in my place" (p. 127).

The irony of the situation is that, although mad, Lol has
survived this exchange. This kind of replacement is part of a
dynamics different from the aggressive replacement we identified in the duel between Jacques and Lol. In the present model,
one person need not destroy the other to take her place. "Perhaps she will die" (p. 95), Lol heard the new lovers say as they
passed by her on their way out of the casino. But Lol does not
die, although who this "she" is who still lives is the un-
answered question that forms the core of Lol's insanity.

With a need to find the answer to this question, to understand who she has now become, Lol is driven ceaselessly in
her imagination to that moment of transfer when she was
replaced by another woman. She tries in her fantasy to slow
and deconstruct that moment in order to locate the precise
gesture of exchange, the exact second when "love had changed
hands, identity, when one error had been exchanged for another" (p. 92):

> For Lol, it is unthinkable that she not be present at the place
> where this gesture occurred. This gesture would not have oc-
> curred without her: she is with it flesh to flesh, form to form, her
> eyes riveted on its corpse. . . . The tall, thin body of the other
> woman would have appeared little by little. And in a strictly
> parallel and reverse progression, Lol would have been replaced
> by her in the affection of the man from T. Beach. [P. 40]

But like the arrow in Zeno's paradox, this gesture never arrives
at completion. Lol simply cannot think through the punctual
moments of her replacement: "Lol had never been able to
carry this divesting of Anne Marie Stretter's dress in slow
motion, this velvet annihilation of her own person, to its con-
clusion" (p. 40).

Lol attempts to reconstruct another triangle with Jacques
and Tatiana in order to try in another way to master the princi-

ple of transfer. And this reenactment of the triangle, an active reversal of the first, is the place within Jacques's story where Lol writes the script, does the casting: "I picked you out" she says to Jacques (p. 102).

Jacques believes he has been chosen by Lol for a special reason: he believes she has singled him out because he is singular, just as she believed Michael Richardson had singled her out. Jacques believes her actions, her feelings are dedicated to him: "The pink of her cheeks is for me, she smiles for me, her ironic comments are meant for me" (p. 75). And he is right in a way. Her feelings are directed toward him, but not because he is special; on the contrary, she has chosen Jacques precisely because he is like everyone else, like all the men of S. Tahla— inane: "'Jacques Hold.' Lol's virginity uttering that name! Who except her, Lol Stein, the so-called Lol Stein, had noticed the inconsistency in the person so named. A dazzling discovery of the name that others have abandoned, have failed to recognize, which was invisible, an inanity shared by all the men of S. Tahla" (p. 103).

In this passage Jacques becomes aware of the absurdity, of the arbitrariness of names. They imply, he says, some consistency of character; they are the sign of a supposed identity. At the outset, the irony for Jacques derives from the mistaken application of a singular identity to Lol, with her inconsistent, multiple, changing personality. But as he continues, the irony changes levels. The absurdity in using names is not that people differ so much from themselves but that they are not at all different from each other. We use names precisely because otherwise we would not be able to tell each other apart.

Contrary to what Jacques first believed, Lol's choice of him was arbitrary, gratuitous: "Her choice implies no preference. I am the man from S. Tahla she has decided to follow" (p. 103). The paradoxical possibility of a choice without preference shreds the entire fabric of our belief in love and individuality. The individual identity bestowed on us as discrete objects of desire is illusory. This recognition, which is both the cause and the effect of Lol's madness, turns our sanity into fiction:

our "sane" belief in a particularized identity, in a speaking subject who can desire—or write—in her own name is revealed as a system of prevarication. It is a massive hoax designed to keep the nightmarish recognition of our namelessness at bay.

"What is it you want?" Jacques asks Lol. The incompleteness of her answer is only apparent: " 'I want' she says" (p. 102). Actually, her silence is more truthful than any object she might name. Desire has no direct object, not because there is nothing in that place but because everything is in that place. The direct object of desire is an infinite chain of interchangeable nouns and names.

As a character in Lol's scenario, Jacques is depersonalized; he becomes a stranger to himself. It is not clear where his actions originate, in Lol's desires or his own. In fact, the attempt to define either the origins or the objects of desire becomes meaningless, for desire circulates indiscriminately as a kind of impersonal force.

Jacques acts out this anonymity of desire as he makes love to Tatiana, describing himself in the third person: "He hides Tatiana Karl's face beneath the sheets, and thus has her headless body at his disposal, at his entire disposal. He turns the body this way and that, raises it, does with it whatever he desires, spreads the limbs or draws them in close, stares fixedly at its irreversible beauty" (pp. 123–24). Jacques makes love to a headless body, he makes love to any-body. The truth both hidden and revealed by Lol's replacement emerges from under the sheets. As Jacques makes love to the faceless Tatiana, she calls out Lol's name.

Narrative and Prostitution

Marguerite Duras screams at the moment when, like the decapitated Tatiana or the mad Lol, she is seized by the fear of losing her head, of entering into the madness of no-place, nobody, no-name. For if Lol's madness is the truth—if we are all faceless bodies to be exchanged, married, made love to—then

Duras has no name, no identity; she is not the author of her book. Her language does not belong to her; her writing could be anybody's.

The real meaning of Lol's replacement, usually obscured by the romanticization of the love story, surfaces as a truth that turns our sanity into a deception: individual identity and therefore love and heroism as we know them are part of a delusional system. As Duras writes *The Ravishing of Lol V. Stein,* she too is ravished. A radical destitution not only of her own author-ity but of all authority takes place. And suddenly from everywhere—from the casino dance, from Lol's marriage, from the hotel room at T. Beach, from under the sheets, from Duras's headless body—the truth comes at us. The real economy of desire is anonymous and indiscriminate, a system of prostitution.[6]

Our social system, they tell us, is based on the exchange of women.[7] As it is commonly conceptualized, this exchange is the basic social transaction and consists in the trade of a woman between two men. But what if this exchange hid another, more fundamental principle? What if the exchange of women implied another (denied) and more universal exchangeability of persons? Then the system of barter as currently defined could be seen as a skewed and defensive version of the essential exchange: one man's switching of one woman for another; or the replacement of one man for another by a woman. This exchangeability of women—as acted out by Michael Richardson and Jacques Hold—and the exchangeability of men—as acted out by Lol Stein—then be-

6. Ten years before the publication of *Lol V. Stein* Duras had depicted prostitution as one of the central institutions of our society. In the short story "Le Boa," in *Des Journées entières dans les arbres* (Paris: Gallimard, 1954), she fancifully imagines bordellos as a kind of initiation-place where young women who can't otherwise find partners go to "discover their bodies." She speaks of the "sacred anonymity" of the institution and emphasizes the visual aspect of prostitution, which we will discuss later, defining the bordello as "the place where one goes to give oneself to be seen" (p. 114).

7. Claude Lévi-Strauss, *Structural Anthropology,* trans. Claire Jacobsen and Brooke Grundfest Schoepf (New York: Basic Books, 1963).

comes the fundamental truth at once announced and denied by our system of property and propriety. While it purports to be a respecter of persons and individual rights, this system is in fact delusionary, and hides within it, as a kind of clandestine memory of its origins, the formally illicit but universally condoned institution of prostitution. While prostitution appears to be localized in our society, contained in *les maisons closes* as the contradiction of its laws, it is really out on the streets, everywhere, even at the very source of the laws it seems to transgress. The principle of indiscriminate replacement or exchange underlying prostitution permeates our entire society as the repressed but universal dynamics in all relationships of desire.

The elements of Lol's story that differentiate it from Jacques's narrative emphasize this randomness of human desire not only in the "mad" behavior of Lol but in the "sane" behavior of the others as well. Duras emphasizes the fortuity of meetings between lovers, husbands, and wives, and carefully uncovers the element of chance in what we call "choice." Jean Bedford meets Lol quite by accident and asks her to marry him after knowing her for only a few hours simply because she falls into a general category of "young girls, girls not completely grown into adults" (p. 20), which arouses his passion. Another girl would have done just as well.

Jacques and Tatiana's liaison, too, has this indiscriminate quality: "Their union is constructed upon indifference, in a way which is general and which they apprehend moment by moment, a union from which all preference is excluded" (p. 51). Duras emphasizes the resemblance of their relationship to whoring not just in its general structure but in its details as well. Jacques and Tatiana rendezvous in a hotel "of doubtful reputation . . . the only place in town where couples can meet in complete confidence" (p. 52). Once inside the hotel, the lovers abandon themselves to their passion with a lawlessness and violence that eerily recall the theater of other hired beds. Jacques manipulates Tatiana's body, as he later will manipulate Lol's, "turns the body this way and that, raises it, does with it whatever he desires" (p. 123). Tatiana is indeed "a marvelous whore, the best of all" (p. 106).

It is in the relationship of Jacques and Lol, the narrator and "his" character, that the dynamics of prostitution are played out in its most complex and developed form. What is most curious about the lines of force in their relationship is that it is hard to tell who is whose whore. At the outset, it seems clear that Lol, the fragile madwoman, has not only been chosen by Jacques but is being exploited by him as well. We have already discussed Jacques's domination and rape of Lol both as a character in his narrative and as the object of his "heroic" quest for truth.

But although Jacques's role as seeing I/eye in the narrative gives him an initial advantage of power, the positions reverse when Lol takes over the center of vision. She becomes the seer, while he, in turns, becomes the seen. This reversal of the conventions of male and female as seer and seen has the effect of uncovering the politics of vision as it is usually practiced/denied. Specifically, it demonstrates that the assertion of power inherent in claiming the role of seer links, improbably, traditional narrative and prostitution. The same principle is at work in both.

Jacques's actions literalize this relationship of narration and prostitution as he stands in the hotel window to show himself to Lol, who has choreographed the scene and is watching from outside (pp. 109–10). He displays himself like a whore in a brothel window, presents himself as an object in Lol's field of vision as she lies, a dark blotch, in the rye field below. Prostitution has to do, then, not only with the randomness of choice, the exchangeability of objects of desire, but also, and perhaps more important, with the power of vision: who sees whom. The etymology of the word confirms this link: "prostitution" derives from the Latin *prostituere,* "to stand forth, to show oneself, to become an object of sight."

Played out in the realm of the imaginary in Jacques's narrative, this power of vision is a radical duel between two opposing points of view, two centers of consciousness; a duel

147

that, like Hegel's encounter, must of necessity end with one the master and one the slave. As if to corroborate this duel for mastery implied in vision, Jacques describes how undone he feels by Lol's look: "I did not move from the window, my worst fear confirmed, fighting back the tears" (p. 110).

But there is a sense, both metaphorical and real, in which Lol does not see Jacques. At the level of metaphor, Lol sees not Jacques but the man whose place he has taken, Michael Richardson. Or beyond him, the inane Everyman of S. Tahla whom they represent. At this level, Lol's seeing undoes the imaginary grounds of Jacques's duel of looks, for no such duel can take place unless two centers of consciousness, two I's, are present. If one of those two centers of consciousness is mad—that is, radically decentered—and the other is an Everyman, the duel fails to take place for lack of combatants. Lol's look does not denote, as Jacques believes, a possession, a domination, a penetration of the other, since her "seeing" takes place at another level.

Lol's seeing occurs precisely at the place where she does not see, where her power of vision falters: "I have no way of knowing what went on in that room between Tatiana and you," she says to Jacques. "I'll never know. When you tell me, it's something else" (p. 125). Lol realizes and enunciates what Jacques, as the explicit narrator, does not: the absolute impossibility of constructing a narrative based on the power politics of sight, a narrative that would be a transparent window through which the reader could see the "facts." Lol knows that she does not know, as Jacques recognized his ignorance, but she also realizes that the narrative is "something else." Most intense precisely at the place of its failure, Lol's vision "sees" what Jacques's cannot: that seeing and the power it appears to bestow are both a mirage.

To emphasize this paradox, Duras describes Lol as sleeping at her observation post outside the hotel. She sleeps not only because she is overtaken by drowsiness but because it is in a deep sense irrelevant whether she is actually watching or not. She cannot in any case, as she says, possibly know what goes on in the room between Tatiana and Jacques. This woman dressed in white becomes, then, a dark place in the rye field of vision where seeing folds into itself; her consciousness forms a blotch not of blindness but of indifference.

The Fiction of the I/Eye

The trip Lol and Jacques make back to T. Beach, back to the ballroom of the casino, dramatizes definitively the default of vision. Lol goes back to see at T. Beach what she couldn't see before. Throughout the entire episode, Duras uses vision symbolically, as Jacques Hold used it, to represent both self-consciousness and knowledge of the truth. For this process to be completed in the usual way, looking must be followed by sight, revelation.

Lol works hard at looking as she and Jacques near T. Beach on the train: "She is completely preoccupied by what she is trying to see. This is the first time she has deserted me so completely" (p. 164). But when they arrive at the casino, Lol of course does not see what she is looking for. At first, this failure produces a sense of relief that Lol turns into a game. She plays at seeing: "Lol sticks her head into every opening and laughs, and is enjoying this game of seeing things again. . . . She is laughing because she is looking for something she thought was here, something she therefore ought to find but doesn't. . . . In the muted light of the corridor, her eyes are shining, bright, clear" (p. 169).

The game of not seeing turns into a graver rite when they enter the ballroom. Here Lol is quieter, concentrating, looking for the truth of the dance that took place there as for the last missing piece of a puzzle. But while Jacques has a rich fantasy of Lol's memories, Lol's mind is a blank. The more she looks, the less she sees: "She cannot keep her eyes fixed for more than a moment on one thing, has trouble seeing, closes her eyes to see better, opens them again. Her expression is set, conscientious. She could spend the rest of her life here looking, looking stupidly at what cannot be seen again" (p. 171).

Like twin scanners, Lol's eyes pass over the scene, waiting for a signal, looking for a trace; but there is none. While Jacques imagines he can see the ball, the events leading to Lol's breakdown, Lol cannot. And in a sense, her look, though stymied in its search, is more acute than her companion's. He "sees" what is not there, while she sees what is.

The room does not tell her about herself, it is not full of her private drama: it is a public room in a public building. Significantly, Lol's inability to find what she was seeking, to see what she wanted to see, is not finally a failure. This episode, although critical, does not represent for Lol some ultimate impossibility of self-knowledge, of self-possession. Or rather it does, but that self-knowledge becomes at this moment irrelevant, for something else takes its place—something having to do with the publicness of the place, its unrelatedness to Lol, its anonymity.

Earlier Lol had recognized and articulated the limits of her vision. She saw that she did not see. Now her failure to see goes by, as it were, unnoticed. Once outside the casino, Lol smiles, yawns, says she is sleepy. She and Jacques go to the beach and she does indeed fall asleep, "completely oblivious." Jacques continues, "I make no effort to fight the deadly monotony of Lol's memory. I fall asleep" (p. 173).

This event, which we expected to be critical, is in fact so boring that it puts everyone to sleep. But this very obliviousness points us in the direction of a meaning as we, too, scan the scene for knowledge. Lol's failure to find herself in the ballroom is superseded by another seeing that is not a discovery but a recognition. The absence of Lol's past in the ballroom, which blocks the completion of her story and from the individual's point of view is a tragic obstacle, on another level reveals an obvious and banal truth. And that truth is that this story has never been Lol's, any more than it could be Jacques's. For nobody has a story that belongs to him or her. And the effort to possess one's story, to stake out a territory in language, represents the ultimate disorder of sight: hallucination.

Lol's madness, her depersonalization, ironically embodies this universal and therefore monotonous truth. And to see that, to see that Lol has no story of her own, any more than anyone else, is to see her as she is, as she has been from the beginning—anonymous, exchangeable, the best whore of all.

Sleeping Beauty Is a Whore

The very odorless, tasteless quality of Lol's body, the color-lessness of her dress, the transparency of her gaze, all make of her a living nonentity, a cipher, an allegory of anonymity. And what makes Lol's madness so troubling, so threatening to those around her is precisely this absence of individuation, for she bodies forth the anonymity that threatens them all from within. She embodies the secret truth that their lives have been constructed to hide and that they must keep from becoming visible or audible in the outside world:

> People are a shade more solicitous with her than they need be, than their remarks or replies require. In everyone's gentle amiability—which is also the attitude of her husband when dealing with her—I detect the sign of anxiety, both past and present, which is the constant concern of those around her. They speak to her because it would be awkward not to, but they are afraid of what she might reply. [P. 132]

The "sane" people around Lol are disquieted by her presence and try to contain her madness by a smothering politeness. They never know what she will say. And this potential randomness is menacing to them precisely because their rules of conduct and conversation are constructed to hide (from) this frightening and potentially omnipresent unpredictability. Lol is indeed like everybody else except in her refusal or inability to conceal her embarrassing anonymity.

Paradoxically, the reverse side of the anonymity that Lol wears like a white dress surfaces in the high colors of the prostitute: "Tonight she is wearing make-up which is a little too heavy . . . and carelessly applied" (p. 136). The model wife and mother is the streetwalker of S. Tahla. She married a man without loving him, allowing herself to be passed on to him like a piece of merchandise. She picks out Jacques Hold on the street not because of personal preference but because any man would do. The Sleeping Beauty is a whore.

Lol makes love with Jacques in a hotel room and, although from the individualized point of view it is a rape, this event reconstitutes her at another level. While Lol loses her "identity"—at least in the way we usually use that term—she does not lose her knowledge, her know-how: "But now at last she begins to doubt that identity, the only identity familiar to her, the only one she has used at least as long as I have known her. At the end of my strength, I ask her to help me. She helps me. She knew, Who was it before me? I shall never know, I don't care" (pp. 178–79). Lol's erotic technique denotes experience, but a kind of experience that cannot be compiled and integrated into a history. Who came before him, who will come after, Jacques will never know; he is one in a chain of exchangeable men whose names are forgotten because they make no difference.

Lol returns to S. Tahla, posts herself in the rye field outside the hotel of public love, and, waiting for Jacques and Tatiana to appear, falls asleep. With that obliviousness, that indifference, the book ends.

The Shift

As Duras initially takes up the pen in the persona of a male narrator, she explores and pursues traditional (male) models of writing: writing as a quest for knowledge, for truth, for understanding; writing as a way of constructing and possessing a story; writing as a way, therefore, of establishing a relation to and a position in the outside world. All of these functions of writing presuppose a heroic model of the writer—a unique individual on a quest that includes benefits (or failures) for the whole community.

As the narrator of *Lol V. Stein* pursues these ends, Duras

demonstrates that the assumptions underlying his quest are fallacious or inadequate. The assumptions that support his narrative—that the outside world, including other people, exists in the mode of fact, that language can reflect that fact if only obliquely, that a coherent account of human personality is possible, that the writing subject has a definable and unique point of view—all of these assumptions falter in Jacques's confrontation with an object that does not meet his criteria.

When Jacques begins to sense the inadequacy of the principles that support his narrative, he falls back on a more primitive mode of relating to the content and aim of his writing. His resort to the assertion of power through domination, penetration, and possession has the effect of revealing his original appeal to truth as an artifice designed to camouflage violent and destructive urges. Duras's use of Jacques as the pseudo-author of her book allows her to identify the essential congruence of cultural and military heroism: both are based on violent models that mask and justify primal territorial and aggressive urges by a rhetoric of nobility. Her structuring of Jacques's narration suggests that all male self-definition is propelled by these (barely) disguised drives to violate and destroy whatever resists the domination of the self.

While Duras's repetition of male narrative strategies permits her to deconstruct those strategies from within, it also allows her to dramatize the relationship between male tradition and the writing she produces as a woman. The shift from one to the other in *The Ravishing of Lol V. Stein* serves as a model for the strategies a woman may use to redefine her place in writing.

First of all, Duras identifies her original function in male tradition as a passive object whose will and personality have been ravished from her by males in their efforts to control, manipulate, and resolve the anxieties they experience in the face of a perplexing and alien world. Like the "mad" Lol, all women are drained of their color so as to serve as anonymous automatons in the narration of male desire.

But when Duras shifts from male writing to another, female

mode, she does not, surprisingly, replace the specific desire of the male writer with another specific (female) desire. Male language is not a mask hiding female authenticity, nor is it even a reversed version of it. When Duras replaces male with female narrative there is no duel, no debate, no confrontation. It is paradoxically Lol's maddening availability that both foils Jacques and makes coming to terms with her impossible. There is no word to mediate the difference between the sexes because the difference is one of indifference. There is no way rationally to structure the shift from male to female narrative because they bear no logical relation to each other. This assymetry of male and female desire which Duras defines in terms of oblivion and indifference makes it impossible to grasp anything across the gap. There is nothing to hold on to, and so the shift from one to the other is a voyage into madness. Duras makes it screaming, afraid of losing her head, her identity, her sanity, in this no-place between male and female.

The shift between male and female does not take place, then, at the level of structural difference. It is a change of position, or rather a change from position to positionlessness. Duras does not undertake this undoing of position or place, like her contemporaries, in the name of some principle of subjectivity or indeterminacy—which she shows to be a cover for another sort of certainty or self-justification—but rather to undo altogether the notions of place and self.

By making this crazy shift, Duras both accepts and redefines the most obvious of truths: women are indeed selfless and therefore have no place of their own. They are bought, sold, traded, given away; they circulate. But when this object of trade refuses the currency that makes the transaction look like a symmetrical and fair exchange, when the whore refuses her pay and takes on exchangeable men simply because she wants to, then everything changes. The fictions that rationalize, justify, and moralize the exchange of women fall away, and the indecency of that exchange, indeed of exchangeability itself, becomes obvious. Love, people, language, truth, desire cannot be retained, possessed, or controlled by anyone. There can be no private property since there are no private individuals. Everyone is exchangeable; the no-place of women is everywhere.

Besides the writing of males which emerges from and expresses the (false) belief in an individual self, there is another writing, the writing of the selfless female, the true woman, the whore; a writing that, like desire itself, does not originate with Duras but passes through her, that she passes on, that belongs to anyone who wants it. Hers is indeed the *voix (voie) publique* and her writing therefore does not define but rather destitutes her of herself. In this infinite chain of exchanges, the book takes Duras's place: "I write to replace myself with the book. To relieve me of my importance. So that the book can take my place. To destroy myself, spoil, ruin myself in the birth of the book. To become vulgar, public, to lie down in the street."[8]

Duras underscores the promiscuity inherent not only in writing but in all public-ation. Her substitute, the book, is literally passed around just as the character Lol V. Stein was exchanged by men and exchanges them in turn:

> It is after all a book that has been translated everywhere. It has passed through many hands. Lol V. Stein is already a prostitution . . . she is yours; Lol V. Stein belongs to everybody . . . and when she goes back toward the dance at S. Tahla [*sic*], toward her birth, she is already worn out as a whore; I can see her covered with make-up, jewels, collapsing under all that make-up, all that jewelry. I think I just said something important about her—it reminds me of something—yes . . . Yes, it's my prostitution.[9]

Like Lol V. Stein, the whore, retracing her steps back to the moment of her madness—that is, of her birth—Marguerite Duras goes back to that turning point, her coming of age, when, after twenty-one years of writing, she suddenly became a woman. And although Duras's sex came second to her, it

8. Interview with Marguerite Duras in Alain Vircondelet, *Marguerite Duras, ou Le Temps de détruire* (Paris: Seghers, 1972), p. 179.
9. Duras and Porte, *Lieux de Duras*, pp. 100–101.

reveals a primary truth: that women writers are indeed prostitutes standing forth with the indecent truth that we are all whores.

This female writing that flows from no-place or the everywhere of in-difference, though it is anonymous, is not an empty, white, no-color writing. If Duras has lost her head like the ravished Lol, she has gained the body of the world. Possessed by life's own shameless promiscuity, Duras speaks a new language whose words and silences can say for the first time the madness of a woman's love.

5

Hélène Cixous:
The Hysteric

Marguerite Duras was a kind of silent partner in the production of Hélène Cixous's play *Portrait of Dora*, performed at the Quai d'Orsay Theatre in Paris in 1976:[1] she executed the filmed sequences used throughout this play about silence and speech, madness and sanity. The themes Duras developed in her work, particularly in *The Ravishing of Lol V. Stein*, glide into the play of her younger colleague and enrich it as a kind of living backdrop.

Like Duras, Cixous was in the midst of a prolific publishing career when *Portrait of Dora* appeared, but it was the first play she had written. As such, it marks a new beginning for her, the place where the various currents of her literary, critical, and political writing come together and take a new direction. Interestingly, Cixous published two major commentaries on the play before the play itself was produced.[2] This unusual reversal of critical and creative chronology made the author's own

1. Hélène Cixous, *Portrait de Dora* (Paris: des femmes, 1976); published in English as *Portrait of Dora*, trans. Sarah Burd in, *Diacritics*, Spring 1983, pp. 2–32. References are to the English text. Modifications of the translation are indicated by "TM."
2. Hélène Cixous, "The Laugh of the Medusa," in *New French Feminisms*, ed. Elaine Marks and Isabelle de Courtivron (Amherst: University of Massachusetts Press, 1980), pp. 245–64; and, with Catherine Clément, *La Jeune née* (Paris: Collection 10/18, 1975).

commentary available to audiences before they had an opportunity to see the play.

But the play is already a kind of critical commentary of another work that presents the problematics of the relationship of subjective and objective discourse and that was itself caught up in a complicated web of delayed publication. Marguerite Duras is not the only predecessor present in this play: another author, this one male, is even more amply represented, for *Portrait of Dora* is a woman's revision of Freud's well-known case history *Fragment of an Analysis of a Case of Hysteria* (1905), popularly called "The Dora Case."[3]

Freud initially envisioned this case history, which he first called *Dreams and Hysteria*, as the place where two main streams of his work on hysteria and dreams would come together and confirm each other. But in a quite remarkable and oft-repeated lapse of memory, Freud mistakenly asserted that Dora had come to him a year earlier than she actually had, making her analysis appear to precede rather than follow the publication of *The Interpretation of Dreams*.[4] Although the final meaning of this slip must lie buried with its author, one of its undeniable effects was to assert fallaciously that theory grew out of experience.[5]

---

3. *Standard Edition of the Complete Psychological Works of Sigmund Freud*, trans. James Strachey et al., 24 vols. (London: Hogarth Press, 1953–74), 7:1–122. The excellent commentaries on this case are too numerous to list here. Two of the most recent essays on *Dora* are Jane Gallop, "Keys to Dora," in *The Daughter's Seduction* (Ithaca: Cornell University Press, 1982), and Madelon Sprengnether, "Enforcing Oedipus: Freud and Dora," in *The (M)other Tongue: Essays in Feminist Psychoanalytic Interpretation*, ed. Shirley Nelson Garner, Claire Kahane, and Madelon Sprengnether (Ithaca: Cornell University Press, 1985). A good bibliography of *Dora* commentary may be found in *Diacritics*, Spring 1983–the issue in which the translation of *Portrait of Dora* also appears. This chapter owes a great deal to Gallop's work in particular.

4. Introduction to the case history by James Strachey, in *Standard Editions*, 7:3. Even stranger, Cixous repeats this mistake in *Portrait of Dora*, pp. 30–32.

5. One of the ironies of the story is that while Freud was writing up the Dora case, he was also working on *The Psychopathology of Everyday Life*, a work in which he first presented his interpretation of what we now call "Freudian slips."

Hélène Cixous: **The Hysteric**

The Pretext: Freud's Case History

The relation of theorizing to a specific, lived situation—a critical issue in all of psychoanalysis—is a particularly sensitive question in this case history, and Freud's management of it with respect to Dora has drawn criticism from many commentators. Cixous was one of the first to emphasize the component of gender in these two rival discourses, although the implication of gender is already clearly present in Freud's presentation of the case. Before looking at Cixous's recasting of Freud's writing, let us review the case that serves as the pretext for the play.

Dora—whose fictitious name was borrowed, Freud tells us, from his sister's maid—was brought to Freud by her father when she was eighteen, not so much in an effort to cure her of her numerous hysterical symptoms—which, after all, had plagued her for a decade—as in the hope that Freud could "bring her to reason" (p. 26). This young woman who suffered from attacks of hysterical aphonia, or inability to speak, was in fact becoming unmanageably vocal about her father's long-term affair with a family friend, called Frau K by Freud. As Freud's case history unfolds, a sordid network of illicit sexual activity is uncovered, involving not only Dora's father and Frau K but Herr K and numerous governesses as well.

Dora, described by Freud as "in the first bloom of youth—a girl of intelligent and engaging looks . . . [who] employed herself . . . with attending lectures for women and with carrying on more or less serious studies" (p. 23), was drawn into this network of adult subterfuge and seduction in a complicated way. In the early days of the affair between her father and Frau K, she seemed to countenance the liaison, indeed to add her young complicity by taking care of Frau K's children while their mother was off with her father. Dora also adored Frau K and developed a close and intimate relationship with her.

At the same time Herr K, who was at least twenty-five years Dora's senior, was very attentive to her, sending her flowers and little presents. His attentions seemed less than innocent when one day, four years before she was brought to Freud, Herr

159

K arranged to be alone with Dora and embraced and kissed her passionately. Although shocked and disgusted by this experience, Dora said nothing of it to anyone. Two years later, as Herr K and Dora walked together by a lake, he made another—this time verbal—attempt at seduction. Dora slapped his face and fled, and later told her parents of the incident. Herr K denied the scene; Frau K claimed that Dora had always been preoccupied with sex anyway; and Dora's parents insisted that the event was all a product of Dora's imagination.

Blocked by this refusal to believe her or to take her allegations seriously, Dora engaged in the confrontive and hysterical behavior that led to her being "handed over" (p. 19) to Freud in October 1900.

Most commentators on the case agree that Freud handled it badly, faulting him, among other things, for his "authoritarian and didactic attitude."[6] Indeed, Freud's depiction of Dora and his description of his own behavior make it clear that the two never got on well. Dora was an intelligent, vulnerable, and rebellious teenager brought to a specialist against her will. She resisted treatment and challenged Freud's interpretations. Freud, for his part, clearly was not only baffled but exasperated by Dora. He has nothing positive to say about her and notes "her really remarkable achievements in the direction of intolerable behavior" (p. 91).

In view of the fairly open hostility between the two, it is perhaps no surprise that Dora abruptly broke off treatment after only three months, thus leaving her story but a "fragment" of a case history.

Freud as Narrator

In his prefatory remarks, Freud specifically addresses the question of his writing, and, as if anticipating an attack, justi-

6. Isidor Bernstein, "Integrative Summary: On the Re-Viewings of the Dora Case," in *Freud and His Patients,* ed. Mark Kanzer and Jules Glenn (New York: Aronson, 1980), p. 289.

fies his publication of the case history. He asserts very strongly that what he is writing is *not* literature: it is not "a *roman à clef* designed for [the] private delectation" of his readers (p. 9). Later he states that he has avoided "the temptation of writing a satire" on the Viennese gentry (p. 49). It seems that the literary character of this case history was tempting not only to his prurient potential readers but to Freud as well. And the temptation to view it as literature stems specifically from the possibility that it appeals to the passions of both author and reader. Freud, then, experiences and defines literature as a temptation, a temptation to yield to intense personal desires, both erotic and hostile. He also associates it with the "delectation" that may accompany the satisfaction of those desires.

Freud contrasts the writing that flows from personal desire and aims at the production of pleasure with another kind of writing that eschews the pleasure principle, that must in fact sacrifice pleasure in order to attain the higher realm of scientific truth: "But in my opinion the physician has taken upon himself duties not only towards the individual patient but towards science as well: . . . thus it becomes the physician's duty to publish what he believes he knows" (p. 8). Here Freud describes a conflict involved in his decision to publish: a conflict between his duty toward the individual patient and the duty he feels toward science. He knows, he says, that if he had asked Dora's permission to publish her case, she would have refused (p. 8).

By his own representation, Freud's writing and publication of this case history already represent a violation of the patient's wishes, which have been subordinated to a more pressing duty to an abstract "science." Freud's duty to science, to knowledge, is set up, then, in conflict with the individual, the personal, and a hierarchy is established which claims the priority of theoretical knowledge over individual pleasure or moral commitments. Knowledge is seen not as flowing from individual and personal desire but rather as conflicting with that desire. The writing of this case history is thus the product of a duel between two conflicting allegiances in which Freud's commitment to science triumphs over the wishes of his patient and his desire to protect her. It seems to be no accident that the individual to be sacrificed in this case, as in Duras's novel, is a woman, and that the voice whose duty it is to publish what "he believes he knows" belongs to a man. The domain of the personal, the literary, is assigned to women, while men claim the superior realm of knowledge and science.

As Freud sets up the narrative of Dora's case history, his duties and values have already supplanted hers. His voice has already recursively seeped into Dora's; his interpretations have already canceled her understanding. This putting of himself in the patient's place contravenes the maieutic ideal of psychoanalysis set up by Freud himself and is a move fraught with ambiguities. But for the moment, Freud "believes he knows" what he is doing.

According to Freud's description, the hysteric's own story is full of gaps, inconsistencies, and faulty connections anyway. In fact, such incoherence is one of the primary symptoms of hysteria: "The connections—even the ostensible ones—are for the most part incoherent, and the sequence of different events is uncertain" (pp. 16–17). By definition, then, hysterics' stories are incomplete and unreliable: one of the major effects of a successful treatment will be to "repair all the damages to the patient's memory" (p. 18).

But, as we have just noted, in the completion of this repair job, the spare parts seem to be coming from Freud's model rather than from the patient's. Freud is aware in some instances that he is displacing the patient, but he justifies this activity by applying the law of consistency:

> In the face of the incompleteness of my analytic results, I had no choice but to follow the example of those discoveries whose good fortune it is to bring to the light of day after their long burial the priceless though mutilated relics of antiquity. I have restored what is missing, taking the best models known to me from other analyses; but, like a conscientious archeologist, I have not omitted to mention in each case where the authentic parts end and my constructions begin. [P. 12]

162

Freud fills in the gaps in the female narrative by borrowing from other women's stories, or more usually by constructing new fragments himself. Patients, in this case women patients, are exchangeable: parts of one story can fill in the gaps in another, and when no parts that fit are available, he will devise some himself. Freud is careful, he says, to let us know when he is substituting his "constructions" for "authentic parts"— that is, he is pretending to be Dora—but his conscientiousness in specific instances hides the fact that he has already taken her place entirely.

Ironically, Freud has already presented some of his spare parts to Dora and she has rejected them as unsuitable. The subject of the narrative has already, within the narrative itself, rejected the narrator's description of her, but then, as we all know, hysterics are unreliable and incapable of reasonable judgment:

> The 'No' uttered by a patient after a repressed thought has been presented . . . does no more than register the existence of a repression and its severity. . . . If this 'No', instead of being regarded as the expression of an impartial judgment (of which, indeed, the patient is incapable), is ignored, and if work is continued, the first evidence soon begins to appear that in such a case 'No' signifies the desired 'Yes'. [Pp. 58–59]

Everyone knows that when a woman says no, she really means yes. Significantly, Freud places his personal judgment here in parentheses—"(of which, indeed, the patient is incapable)"— offering it as an aside to his male colleagues, who presumably agree that hysterics are indeed incapable of making objective judgments.

By way of defending his interpolations in Dora's discourse, Freud goes on to contrast himself as a "medical man" with the "man of letters." As a man of science, he aims to depict "the world of reality" (p. 60). Freud seems here to have no doubts about his ability to achieve a full and complete depiction of reality. Recognizing that the present case is only a fragment completed by his own construction, Freud nevertheless asserts that, had the treatment been continued, had Dora not abandoned him, a complete restoration of "her" story would have been possible: "If the work had been continued, we should no doubt have obtained the fullest possible enlightenment upon every particular of the case" (p. 12).

Freud depicts himself as the heroic scientific torchbearer, shedding light into every nook and cranny where Dora's "mutilated remnants" are buried. But he is not working alone in this enterprise: "*we* would no doubt have obtained the fullest possible enlightenment upon every particular of the case." What is intended by "we"? Is it the editorial "we," which in a paradoxical gesture of self-effacement actually multiplies the self? Or is it the unlikely partnership of doctor and patient, who up to now have been antagonists? Or is it the implied collective that has operated steadily through the case history, Freud and his fellow men of science? Men, "we," talk to each other about women. The inside of the scientific discourse is defined by a shared language, enterprise, and value system. Furthermore, Freud has contrasted its character and boundaries with those of literary discourse, which he equates with a hysterical structure.

But if male scientific discourse is characterized as the obverse of hysterical discourse, Freud and his colleagues are left in an unexpectedly strange position. Just after Freud expresses the temptation he felt to write a satire, he introduces a new hypothesis: that the perversions are the obverse or the negative of neuroses, such as hysteria. He goes on to state that the queen of the perversions, so to speak, is "the sensual love of a man for a man" (p. 50). If Freud's scientific discourse is the negative of literary or hysterical discourse, it falls, then, by Freud's own definition into the category of the perverse, a perversity enthroned in male homosexuality.

In attempting to defend himself against the temptation of his own femininity, implicitly equated in this fragment of an analysis with an inferior, undependable, mutilated state, Freud has paradoxically stepped back into an even more primitive structure. His "scientific" discourse represents an anxious reaction to female gaps and holes and is an attempt to repair or deny those gaps by filling them up with superior spare parts taken from the male. Refusing to yield to the base temptation of personal feeling that might link him to his female patient and her desires, Freud instead constructs a circuitry of supposedly impersonal striving that connects him with an exclusively male community.

Having projected onto the outside what he feels on the inside as a temptation, Freud can feel safe. It is Dora that is incoherent and unreliable; it is she that desires him and is hostile to him, and not the other way around; at least that is the way Freud sees it. He establishes his scientific narrative as a defense against his own pleasures, which he feels as debasing. It represents a contrast to and a mastery of his literary impulses, which he equates with female hysteria. That narrative is, according to the man of medicine, partial, incoherent, mutilated, outlining by its gaps a story of forbidden pleasures. Freud's scientific narrative triumphs over this messy, selfish story by suppressing the pleasure principle in the name of reality. But Freud masters literature-hysteria by constructing a perverse male wholeness on the mutilated remnants of females.

Dora Reviewed

Portrait of Dora is the flip side of Freud's scientific-perverse-male presentation of the Dora "case." As it turns out, though, the reverse of perversity is not as symmetrical as Freud would have foreseen. Cixous's repetition of a male narrative from the other side, her actual quotations of Freud in her own text, have the effect of setting Freud's writing loose from its origin in the supposed author "Freud" and demonstrating that "his" words might belong to anybody—even to a woman.

Cixous might have yielded to the "temptation of writing a satire" on Freud. He would have made as easy a mark as the "respectable gentry" Freud himself disdained to attack. But to yield to such a temptation would have been to make a comic figure of Freud, to dismiss him as he finally dismissed Dora when she returned a year and a half later to ask Freud to treat her.[7] Cixous does not merely turn the tables on Freud; she does not reverse his discourse against him, as he reversed Dora's against her.[8] Nor, surprisingly, does Cixous write from the "real" Dora's point of view, since her sickness lay precisely in a failure of speech. This is the writing of a deferred Dora: a second, symbolic Dora. It is the writing of a hysteric whose world includes both Dora and Freud, whose language has been shaped both by the preemptive filter of male discourse and by female silence.

Cixous speaks in the void created by Dora's aphonia, in the space of meaning vacated by her body's symptoms. But although Cixous's reparation of Dora's speech appears to resemble Freud's "constructions," it differs in two important respects: first, she attempts to recover the worlds of both Dora and Freud by experiencing them specifically in a hysterical mode; second, Cixous's writing is not a strategy of opposition or mastery with respect either to Freud or to Dora.

This case history and its publication, so marked with gaps and lapses, is now punctuated by the greatest lapse of all: a period of seventy-five years between its representation in a text written by a man and its reliving in a text written by a woman. Cixous writes, then, in a double gap: the one between Dora and herself and the one between male and female writing.

The Hysterical Discourse of the Theater

This multiply determined opening into which Cixous's writing flows is characteristic of the hysterical mode of experience that shapes the play itself. "Protean," "seductive," "his-

---

7. When Freud relates Dora's request for treatment, he comments, "One glance at her face, however, was enough to tell me that she was not in earnest over the request" (p. 121).

8. By interpreting her reproaches against others as if they applied to herself, for instance, thus turning her speech into a self-indictment (pp. 36ff.).

trionic," "theatrical," "given to multiple identifications"—all of these terms have been used to describe hysterics over the years.[9] Since hysteria is by definition "theatrical," "given to multiple identifications," it is altogether fitting that Cixous should use a play to dramatize the hysterical way of experiencing the world, to dramatize, in other words, her own hysteria as a writer. Her voice is no longer hers, or no longer just hers: it is at the same time the voice of Dora or of Freud or of the Ks. Her feelings become the feelings of others—or vice versa—and her body becomes the bodies of others—or vice versa. The undecidability that first led psychiatrists to call hysteria "theatrical" is used here to figure forth what might be called hysterical discourse.

The dispersal or multiplication of the subject can be shown in the theater, where actions speak for themselves, and so can the body language that is uniquely characteristic of hysteria. Alone among the literary genres, the theater permits bodies to be immediately expressive, as they are in hysterical syndromes, without first circulating their messages through language (although that operation is always finally implicit). Even more significantly, Cixous uses the modern technology of the theater to dramatize the disruption between body and language which is one of the stranger characteristics of hysteria, producing that insensitivity to physical pain or restriction called by Jean Charcot *la belle indifférence.* The sequences filmed by Duras separate the real from the imagined body. Voice-overs make speech emanate from outside the bodies of the actors; voices, in fact, can be exchanged.

The chronology of events as it is represented in Freud's case history is also jumbled in a way characteristic of hysterical discourse as Freud describes it. The play is an intricate collage of events, memories, fantasies, and dreams, different levels of consciousness melting together, their boundaries often indiscernible.

9. Alan Krohn, *Hysteria: The Elusive Neurosis* (New York: International University Press, 1977), *passim.*

But Cixous's play is an instance of hysterical multiplicity or fragmentation in an even more profound sense than the mode and arrangement of its contents. For the drama is played out at two levels of presentation simultaneously—as an actual performance and as a written text published by *des femmes*, "some women." The play as immediate action and its printed version are thus cut off from each other, each in a sense independent of the other, ignorant of the other's existence, beautifully indifferent, just as the hysteric's symptoms are dissociated from their meaning without her awareness of any gap between them.

Not having seen the performance, most of us are constrained to fill in the gaps, to frame conjectures about the relationship of performance and text. We may in fact, be in a position similar to Freud's as he attempted to bridge the gap between Dora's text and the events in her life which he had, in a sense, missed. Or perhaps like Dora's literary predecessor, Lol V. Stein, we may come to realize that that scene we cannot see is indeed "something else," the pretext for another writing.

Dora's Portrait

Portrait of Dora stands not only at the juncture of dreams and hysteria but also at the point where the discursive logic of written language and the recursive logic of speech (fail to) meet in a play text. The very title of the play emphasizes the doubleness of its project: it is a portrait, a line drawing of written language. It is not, however, *a* portrait or *the* portrait, but simply "portrait"—undefined, unpositioned—a drawing forth into the immediacy of presence.

The portrait of Dora is drawn in word pictures, in Dora's own speech and in the speech of the people who surround her. But we notice immediately that these speech portraits are conflicting and contradictory. "Dora is still a child," her father says, "and Herr K treats her as a child" (p. 3). "Dora is no longer a child" (p. 3), Herr K asserts initially, but later, when

168

accused of trying to seduce her, he reverses himself: "Dora is only a child to me. You know how I respect you and your daughter" (p. 10).

On one level these contradictory judgments are the products of cynical attempts on the part of these adults to protect themselves from exposure and condemnation. They manipulate language in order to hide their own desires; they turn the real ambiguities of the situation to their own profit, setting up now one, now the other aspect of Dora's identity as a screen for what is unacceptable in their own behavior.

But what makes this deception and exploitation possible is the real ambiguity of Dora's situation. On another level, one that they do not of course acknowledge, Dora is in fact both still a child and no longer a child. She is in the limbo of adolescence, loving, desiring, adoring, both as a child and as an adult. She takes care of the Ks' children, is a mother to them, and at the same time is ignorant of what she needs to know to be a mother. She pleads with Frau K, the mother of the children whose mother she has become, "Tell me, tell me all, everything. All the things that women know" (p. 12).

Knowing at once not enough and too much, Dora perceives her own feelings and those of others as confusingly contradictory. She disagrees with her father at the opening of the play when he says he doesn't understand her: "You do understand me, but you are not honest." But then she immediately reverses herself: "You don't understand. I am not honest" (p. 3, TM).[10] Both versions of the statement, though apparently conflicting, are accurate. But what is even more important to notice here is that although the second statement is a negation of the first, it is not in strict contradiction to it. In the process of reversal, of turning a statement around on itself, symmetry of reference and perspective is lost.

The symmetry of the shifters around which this shift takes place—the "I" and the "me"—itself shifts. Subjective and objective discourse are not in a relationship of opposition; they

10. The translation omits the first sentence.

do not cancel each other out. The "me" who is viewed and the "I" who is viewing are not negatives of each other; they are not even in the same place. This uncanny lack of coincidence between opposites, this shift in symmetry between the "I" and "me," opens up a vast space of multiple and paradoxical relationships.

From Proposition to Preposition

One effect of this asymmetrical relationship is that objective discourse cannot master subjective discourse by filling in the gaps. Indeed, the gaps are not gaps at all, but remnants, spillovers that keep escaping oppositional modes of thought. In this hysterical world portrayed by Cixous, opposites do not oppose each other at all but slide off each other without either taking priority.

It is this question of priority that perhaps most clearly disinguishes the hysterical logic of Dora from the logic of the "sane." For Dora the principal modes of relationship are juxtaposition and substitution; there is no subordination. This paratactical mode of relationship operates and becomes vivid on a purely grammatical level in Dora's discourse. Here, for instance, is the way she describes her viewing of a painting in a Dresden gallery: "I lingered for a long time. In front of the painting. It was the *Sistine Madonna*, I stood, alone, immersed. In the painting. For two hours. In its [her] aura. A soft smile" (pp. 10–11, TM). In this passage we hear fragments of phrases that might be joined to form a single sentence but whose grammatical relationship is unstructured, unspoken. We might fill in the gaps, but to do so would be to interpret the statement, to fix on one meaning among the many that are possible. Even predication dims here: the subject, the "I," no longer identifies itself with the seeing eye seeing itself seeing from a single perspective. Dora is both "in front of" and "in" the painting. Objectivity is impossible.

If the places of the seer and the seen are thus blurred, how can we tell the difference between the spectator and the painting? between our reading and the text? In *Portrait of Dora* these questions are unanswerable; they are, in a sense, false questions, since we too (two) are simultaneously in front of and in the text. Just as Cixous has dispersed herself in this theatrical production–text, so we as readers-spectators are divested of a possible critical metanarrative that might put the two together. The logic of meaning cannot emerge here from predication since the places of the subject and object are shifting, undecidable.

As prepositions perform the grammatical function of indicating relational location, they take on preeminent importance in this hysterical discourse. Furthermore, just as the verb "to be" is the foundation of all analytical discourse, linking subject to object, so the preposition "to" stands as the foundation of the synthetic discourse of the hysteric. Dora cries out to Frau K:

> You've killed me! You've betrayed me! You've deceived me!
> . . . Did I not write you unnumerable letters?
> Did I not worship your every step?
> Did I not open my doors? . . .
> And now, to whom do I send this letter?
> To whom my silence? To whom my death?
>
> [P. 13]

Actions are not conceived here as being complete in themselves, as emanating from a self-defining, autonomous subject. They are defined rather by their relation to another subject to whom they are addressed. Actions are not finished statements of identity whose meaning can be referred to the intention of the actor. Nor can their meaning be defined solely by reference to the interpretation given them by the receiver. Feelings and actions, like language, are not subordinate to a ruling core— whether that core be the subject or the object, the conscious or the unconscious—but are linked by their direction toward the potential receiver of their message. Meaning is both suspended and repercussional: the identity of the subject is not definable in *a* position, since it is positionality itself: Dora remains silent *to* someone; she thinks of killing herself *to* someone.

171

These directional intentions, expressed by the preposition "to," represent the vectors of desire that link nouns one to the other, people one to the other, and create finally the possibility of meaning, but in a potential, suspended, anaclitic mode. Meaning in Dora's hysterical system is therefore ambiguous, and in the deeply etymological sense of the word: it literally wanders around looking for its destination, never sure of reaching it, never sure of what or whom it will find when it gets there. "*Who* is abandoning me?" "Who was it?" "Who is betraying whom in this affair?" "Who is in whose place?" These questions pertaining to individual identity are repeated endlessly in this play. And the reason they are asked so often is that there is never an answer.

Interrogative Pronouns: When Everybody Is Anybody

All of the characters in *Portrait of Dora* are caught up in a network of transactions in which each one is being replaced in the mind of the other by another person or persons. This network of substitutions precludes the attribution of a single meaning to each interaction. As the adults in the play behave in a duplicitous fashion, cynically protecting themselves by taking multiple points of view, their duplicity is shadowed by another doubleness in their actions. Dora is her father's daughter, but he also treats her as a substitute for his wife, who he feels has failed him. Herr K treats Dora as a little girl, but she is also a substitute for his wife, who he feels has failed him. She is also a substitute for the governess who was his lover and whom he abandoned. For Frau K, Dora is a substitute for her children, whom she has betrayed. Freud is a substitute for both Herr and Frau K for Dora, as well as for her father. For Freud, Dora is a substitute for his wife and daughter and governess.

There is no point in prolonging the list of standins; the important thing is that these replacements are never exactly coincident, just as the logical reversals of Dora were never symmetrical. They occur somewhere between the modes of substitution and juxtaposition, in the mode of both/and rather than either/or. For all the characters in the play, the answer to the question "Who is in whose place?" is multiple, indefinite. And yet this final unanswerability does not mean that all distinctions are blurred, that the question is unaskable. Indeed, it is the fact that the question is askable that is important.

In *Portrait of Dora* all personal pronouns eventually become questions, become interrogative. Emphasizing the indefinite references, especially of French indirect-object and possessive pronouns, Cixous highlights the question of substitution, not only on the human level but on a grammatical level as well. In French the indirect-object pronoun *lui* stands for either a masculine or a feminine noun. The gender of a possessive pronoun is determined by the thing possessed, not by the possessor. As a result, it is impossible to know whether the person to whom a speech or an action is directed is a man or a woman. It is impossible to know who is possessing whom.

Substituting a pronoun for a noun according to rules of gender and number is an automatic process for the native speakers of any language, but Cixous demonstrates in this play that this process of grammatical substitution reflecting identities may be more problematic than we imagine. Because of this swirl and eddy of replacements, even the referents of subject pronouns become indefinite. When Dora cries out, "Do you hear me?" (p. 6), she appears to be speaking to her father, and yet she is also addressing Freud. Or again, when she imagines writing a letter beginning "You've killed me. . . . You wanted it this way" (p. 9), the reference of the "you" is multiple, undecidable.

Since the identity of the sender is already in some sense dependent on the identity of the receiver, this indefiniteness of reference and address creates a maelstrom of confusion. Contrary to Lacan's celebrated dictum "A letter always arrives at its destination,"[11] in the hysterical world created by Cixous

11. Jacques Lacan, "Le Séminaire sur 'La Lettre volée,'" in *Ecrits* (Paris: Seuil, 1966), p. 41.

in *Portrait of Dora*, neither the sending nor the recieving of messages is ever sure. Since it is impossible to tell precisely to whom a message is sent, the question of whether it arrived or not makes no sense.

The Language of the Sane

In this swirl of revolving and indefinite identities, multiple meanings, and relationships freighted both with tenderness and betrayal, human identity and the language expressing it are dispersed in a synthetic, open, multivalent logic that swamps the logic of tautology supporting what we call sanity. Put in contrast with the wild eddies and chaotic displacements of desire in hysterical discourse, the language of the sane soon appears inadequate to the situation, if not positively deceitful. When Herr K denies (to whom?) that he had any sexual intentions toward Dora, Cixous unveils the spurious objectivity of his language:

> There is nothing in my conduct that might have deserved such an interpretation. I sent her flowers for a year, I treated her as if she were my own daughter. Herr B [Dora's father], whose delicacy with regard to women is well known, is aware of the extent to which my concern for Dora was disinterested. [P. 4, TM]

This statement bears the form of a categorical and unequivocal denial, an official statement of innocence. Like all objective language, it is addressed to anyone, the implication being that all auditors of this statement would interpret it identically. Like hysterical discourse, objective language is addressed to everyone, but this is a different "everyone." This is not the multiple everyone of hysterical address, but rather a unilocal, anonymous crowd. To no one in particular.

Not only is objective discourse directed to no one, it emanates from no one as well. Its field of reference is treated as being empty of any personal meaning. Herr K talks as if what he were saying did not refer to him, and guarantees the authenticity of his assertions by reference to an outside authority. Any personal reference, any particularized meaning would immediately make the statement relative, open to question, interested. One might be led to ask, for instance, what "delicacy with regard to women" may mean in reference to a man who has betrayed his wife for years, given her a venereal disease, and is turning his daughter over to a doctor now that she has started to make trouble for him.

But if objective discourse originates in no one and is addressed to no one, it says nothing at all worth listening to. Isolated against the rich backdrop of hysterical language in Cixous's play, these "sane" statements have the flimsiness of a cover; their emptiness is indeed transparent.

The character of Freud is, foreseeably enough, the leading spokesman of this objective discourse of the sane. He repeatedly asserts commonly held beliefs about the orderly progression of events, the self-coincidence of objects, and the consistency of language and its referents. Cixous appropriately concentrates Freud's expressions of the hierarchical logic we call common sense in his repetitions of proverbs and maxims, the epitome of society's traditional, anonymous wisdom. While Cixous quotes Freud, putting his own words in his mouth, Freud's use of these proverbs is already a quotation of another kind from a public, nonpersonal source. In his and then Cixous's use of these proverbs, the objectivity of conventional wisdom and the authority of scientific discourse merge. "Where there's smoke there's fire," Freud asserts repeatedly, appealing to the general belief that when an effect is observed, it of necessity has a proximate and predictable cause. As he observes Dora absentmindedly snapping her purse open and closed, Freud offers another proverb that expresses a variation of the law of the conservation of energy: "He whose lips are silent chatters with his fingertips" (p. 16). Underlying his use of the expression "I call a spade a spade" is the notion that objective language can have a direct, tautological relationship to its referents.

But these assertions of identity and consistency are themselves, as we shall see, a kind of double-talk, for the words that make them up drip with double meanings. The very science that Freud appeals to as a guarantee of univocal meaning, for instance, has given the name "lips" to more than one part of the female body. And the proverb translated in English as "I call a spade a spade" appears in French both in the case history and in the play as "J'appelle un chat un chat," an expression that, as Jane Gallop points out in *The Daughter's Seduction*, can also be translated "I call a pussy a pussy" (p. 140).

The very definition of identity and appeals to a public common-sense logic are undone by their own double-entendre. And what keeps intruding in this system of tautologous identity and linear causation, what keeps chattering in these proverbs, is what Diderot so discreetly called *les bijoux indiscrets*, those "indiscreet jewels," gossipy female genitals.

This reference to the insistent "speech" of female genitals and their double logic in the letter of the law brings us to the central image of the play and one that reveals the final phenomenological incongruence of the hysterical world and the sane world—the image of the door.

"Don't Close Yourself"

The word "door," interestingly enough, inhabits the title of the play both in French and in English: *porte-portrait*, door-Dora.[12] And doors are everywhere in the play, opening and closing, in reality, in metaphors, and in dreams. "There is a door in Vienna," Dora reports in a dream, "through which everyone can go but me" (p. 4). "There is a door," she says again, recounting Herr K's first attempt to seduce her when she was fourteen, "there is a door leading from the store to their apartment, but instead of going out through the open door, he grasped me, he held me against him and kissed me on the mouth" (p. 5, TM). "There is someone behind the door?

12. Another discussion of doors in Dora may be found in Gallop, *Daughter's Seduction*, p. 146.

You never know. . . . He's going to force the door open and I lean against it" (p. 7). "Didn't I open my doors?" Dora cries to Frau K (p. 13). "Don't close yourself," Herr K pleads seductively to Dora (p. 13, TM).

We can see that the opening and closing of doors is a metaphor for both emotional receptiveness and sexual availability. It soon becomes clear, however, that doors have a different significance for men than for women, and that for the men all other references of this metaphor are subordinated to the expression of the sexual availability of women. In their parlance, doors are female genitals, and according to the logical law of the exclusion of opposites, doors must be either open or closed. Freud leads in the expression of this law as he says to Dora, Cixous again quoting Freud's own words in the case history, "Naturally it cannot be a matter of indifference whether a girl is 'opened' or 'closed'" (p. 15, TM). This "naturally" of the natural law carries with it, of course, a hidden imperative: "naturally" girls ought to be "opened."

This open-door policy of the male characters in the play, while ostensibly one of petition and negotiation, is in fact a strategy of aggression and domination that necessarily leads to the capitulation and defeat of one of the participants. In this logical system based on either/or alternatives, it is necessary that one member of a couple be dominant and the other subordinate. The power politics inherent in male sexual grammar is revealed in one of Dora's dreams: "I have no doubt that he intends to force open the door. . . . How simple and deadly everything is. It is Him or Me. . . . That's a law" (p. 7).

While male discourse purportedly makes reference to a law, to a system of truth outside itself, "naturally" the law men refer to enforces a hierarchical relation of the sexes in which the individual male penis and its symbolic phallic reference are blurred into one. Hidden within the natural law and its disinterested statements is, then, a very interested seizure of power. Recognition of the law requires submission to the powerful phallus-penis: "We all know," Freud continues, "what key opens the door in this case" (p. 15). Dora's reaction to that key is considered by Freud to be the nucleus of her hysteria. Her feeling of repulsion is a neurotic defense against her "natural" erotic drives.

But Dora sees that to be subject to that law, to be opened by that key, is to be annihilated, to be made into nothing. "My wife is nothing to me," Dora's father says to Freud (p. 6, TM). "My wife is nothing to me," Herr K asserts in his seductive pleas to a governess (p. 26). "My wife means nothing to me," he repeats for similar reasons to Dora (p. 27). In the male view, once the female door is opened, she becomes nothing. Once a woman is possessed sexually, once she observes the law, she is annulled by that very law. The void thus created by the opening of one woman creates an empty place where another woman can be placed and so on ad infinitum. The male open-door policy is therefore a method of establishing trade routes for the exchange of women. Dora points out to Freud: "Papa takes advantage of the opportunities Herr K gives him. Herr K takes advantage of the opportunities Papa gives him. Everyone knows how to be accommodating" (p. 21, TM).

Dora's Doors

Since this system of replacement in the discourse of sanity depends on equating male language with the statement of an impersonal truth, reversibility is impossible. It is an either/or code, a one-way affair. Hierarchical substitutions work from the top; reciprocity is unthinkable because the objects of exchange are just that—objects.

Not only are women not permitted to tell their own stories—when Dora starts to tell hers, it is so disruptive that she is sent to Freud to be "brought to reason," that is, to have her story translated into scientific discourse; women are not permitted to be objective, either, since that prerogative belongs by definition to males. When Dora tries to turn one of Freud's maxims around to apply to him, she is sharply upbraided for her presumption:

Dora: Yes, yes, I know. And he who chatters with his fingertips?

178

Cixous

Why do you spin your pen seven times in your hand before
speaking? Why?
Freud: You must respect the rules!

[P. 19, TM]

In order to maintain the system of exchange and substitution
which preserves male discourse as the only truth, women
must, then, be defined as hysterical. Their inability to construct a coherent narrative and their capacity to identify
with—to blur into—others are precisely what is required to
keep the male game going. The first attribute (symptom) justifies male preemptive discourse and the second permits the
easy substitution of one woman for another.

But what if this malady of hysteria were not a disorder at all
but rather another order founding a valid way of being? What if
hysteria represented another truth? In other words, what if
being a woman were not a disease? These questions, inconceivable in male logic, are posed rhetorically in *Portrait of
Dora.* And to answer them we must ask yet another question
that can be formulated only within the hysterical possibility
of multiple identifications: What does it feel like to be the
door?

In contrast to the view of doors as passive objects that must
be either opened or closed, Dora's doors are part of an active
framework of desire and open both in and out. As such they
become the central figures of the logical reversibility and undecidability inherent in the hysterical system. "What is open
may not be open," Dora states. "What happened can not have
happened" (p. 7).

Here again the questions are ones of reciprocal relationship
and multiple possibility. As Cixous presents hysteria in *Portrait of Dora,* no logically dominant point of view is defined as
"objective," founded on the enterprise of making objects out
of people. This objective point of view, this unipositional system, depends, where gender is concerned, on a hierarchical
system in which male genitals are defined as the foundation of
natural law. They turn up everywhere as the "key" to the
system while female genitals are "nothing."

In the plurivalent logic of hysteria, genitals are not privileged by the fig leaf of the law but are themselves a cover to be
thrown off. Once liberated from the unitary logic of the phallus, which pens the truth as it opens the empty hole of the
female genital story, the entire body is free to circulate in a
new system of erotic exchange. "There's more than one way.
A body has all kinds of ways" (p. 11), Frau K says to Dora,
indicating that keys are not the only means of opening doors,
and that in fact a body contains not one door but many.

In this polymorphous world, not just genitals but mouths,
fingers, eyes may be portals of desire. "Look at me," Dora says
to Frau K, "I would like to go into your eyes. I would like you
to close your eyes" (p. 12, TM). And the closing of these double door-eyes may be an opening of another kind: an opening
not just to another person but to, in, and of oneself. As Frau K
draws the curtains across the windows, Dora murmurs: "It's
like a grotto. Where are you? It's like a grotto; it's me! Me in
myself, in the shadow. In you. Now empty, now full. . . . Time
opens and closes like fluttering eyes" (p. 12, TM).

The doors of Dora's desire flutter not in a discursive linear
chronology but in a rhythmic pulsation or flux, always in the
process of being both opened and closed. For her, opposites are
not negations of one another but part of a continuous movement of double linking: "Me in myself. In you."

Dora is both a child and an adult, and she desires both as a
child and as an adult, and these two desires neither entirely
replace one another nor blend into synthesis. She desires also
both as a man and as a woman, and these two desires neither
entirely replace one another nor blend into synthesis. Dora
desires both Frau K and Herr K; she loves Freud both as a man
and as a woman.

These double desires are not alternate versions of each
other—one person or mode never entirely supplants another—
nor are they part of a dialectical process of synthesis presided
over by a ruling concept. Dora is not duplicitous, as the others
are, but double, and her doubleness is doubled. And although
this doubling represents in one sense a painful process of split-

ting and fragmentation, it is at the same time a process of redoubling, of filling up, of moving not toward wholeness but toward fullness—a fullness that includes rending but never excludes any experience as unworthy, never closes itself in, sets its boundaries.

At the end of the play, Dora realizes that the portrait of her constructed by the others within the play is but the scribblings of their denied needs on her body. And she refuses to let herself be confined, silenced, and immobilized by them; she refuses the interpretation of her hysteria as an illness; she refuses to let herself be framed by their conjectures. "No," she says (p. 31), sending back to them the echo of their law. She leaves Freud's consulting room and closes the door behind her.

From Freud's point of view, Dora has, by going out through this one-way door, shut herself out of sanity's frame of reference, destining herself to become in the hierarchy of psychoanalysis, as another analyst later put it, "the most repulsive hysteric" anyone had yet seen.[13] But from Dora's point of view, she has let herself in as well as out—out of that closed system and into a world undefined and unimagined in the play, a world both of potential emptiness and of potential fullness.

Freud the Hysteric

But Dora's leaving is not the end of the play; there is more of the story to tell. In the hysterical logic of asymmetrical reversal, Dora's turning the tables on Freud leaves a remnant, a residue, something that overflows the frame and opens the system to another('s) truth.

As she rewrites this case history, Cixous does not repeat the authoritative strategy of the author, but lets him speak for himself in the voice that was silenced in his own writing. Engaging again the principle of revolving identity, she puts the

13. Felix Deutsch, "A Footnote to Freud's 'Fragment of an Analysis of a Case of Hysteria,'" *Psychoanalytic Quarterly* 26 (1957), 167.

audience in the place of Dora while emerging herself as the "Voice of the Play," which is also Freud's voice. At once inside and outside the play, on the threshold of the text, this voice nostalgically gives expression to the desire that Freud attempted to conceal but finally revealed so blatantly in the case history—his desire for Dora. While the audience becomes increasingly aware that they must, like Dora, get up, leave the theater, and close the doors behind them, Freud remains center stage, the lingering voice repressed but implicit in his own system, the hysterical voice liberated by Cixous, telling of his desire for his daughter, his desire for his own femininity.

Writing as Violence: Cutting into Language

Write: OS *writan,* to cut
—*Oxford English Dictionary*

A door closed on Freud is an opening of another kind. As Dora leaves his office at the end of the play, he says to her, making a significant slip: "I'd like to hear from me. Write me." And Dora answers, "Write? . . . That's none of my business" (p. 32). Dora could not write because, in the closed society she left Freud's office to join, her language could only have been the echo of his story.

Cixous is able to write; she is able to write because Freud's Dora and the world she lived in have become a memory. If hysteria is, as Freud said, a malady of memory, then the "healing," or realization, of Cixous's hysteria—as a move toward fullness and not as a translation into scientific discourse—will be achieved precisely by the process of remembering, of giving voice to the silent, stifled Dora who inhabits her and all women. As Cixous says in *La Jeune née,* it is the memory of the impaired but "sumptuous body" of this symptom-ridden hysteric that compels her to write, that *is* the voice of her writing (p. 76).

Dora is not, then, a real person whom Cixous attempts to master as Freud did, but rather the memory of her own silence.

182

Cixous does not preempt Dora, replace her. It is precisely because she and Dora do not coincide that Cixous is able to speak; it is precisely because there is a difference between Dora's silence as an illness and Cixous's silence as a threshold of possibility that writing can be her business.

Dora refused to reflect Freud back to himself lest she be absorbed once more into the sound of his words. But Cixous's writing sends Freud back another echo of himself—a deferred echo, an echo with a difference. Cixous's hysterical identification with Dora and Freud, her identification with Dora and Freud as hysterics, is not the kind of smothering, sick fusion Freud defined and feared, and whose model is finally the fake objectivity of scientific discourse. It is rather an asymmetrical union that leaves an opening for language, that creates a new mouth.

Symbolizing the noncoincidence of the objectified voice of women in traditional male discourse and the hysterical voice of women who speak urgently for themselves, this new mouth represents a violent cut into and out of the closed body of male language. Cixous imagines a new dream for Dora, a dream that is not in Freud's case history. In the dream, a man is pressing on a door behind which Dora is hiding. He tries to force it open; he wishes to possess her and that possession would be death:

> This man who is behind the door . . . has a familiar look, the look of a ladies' man. *He has a somewhat deceitful look.* His eyes are a little troubled, which doesn't at all go with his mouth. *I must get at his neck.* That motion demands the greatest energy. At the risk of death, I give it all my strength. *I embrace him, I take him in my arms, I lean over him.* Seen close up, his face is unknown; it is not terrifying, as if I knew him well. . . . *I hold him tight and I cut his throat.* My hand becomes the knife. [P. 8, TM][14]

This familiar but anonymous face, this double-dealing face of the ladies' man whose eyes say one thing and whose mouth

14. The translation omits portions of this passage.

says another, is the face of Freud, of Herr K, of Dora's father, the face of all men who force the door of women's desire. Their violence begets another. In an ambivalent gesture expressing both her love and her hate, Dora embraces this figure and cuts his throat, not with a phallic knife but with and by her own hand. This dream of cutting is also a dream of writing, leaving one's mark, for to write in the world of men is also to cut through and into the language that one first loved and that then seduced and smothered.

Both a murder and a healing of old wounds, this slitting of a throat is not a castration but the cutting of another mouth, of other lips out of which the story of women's desire can flow. Cixous creates a cunt in the body of male writing where a new writing, itself an opening, can come to be.

This new mouth is not a hole but a border marking, like Dora's doors, the threshold, the linking place between silence and speech, love and hate, tenderness and betrayal, the world and language: the opening where hysteria—women's desire—and words come together. Like Dora's double doors, this new mouth opens both out of and into male discourse, now transformed by its own opening. It swings between violence, indignation, aggression on the one hand and desire, tenderness, and love on the other.

While Freud's text shut out women's desire in its homosexual appeal to other men, this mouth opens a new space in language undreamed of by men, a space where women, rather than canceling each other out, can love and dance together as they do in Dora's dream, where they can begin to feel "an overwhelming tenderness" (p. 21). This new mouth speaking from the midst of Freud's text tells the story of all the silent, abandoned patients, daughters, governesses, wives moving in a new rhythm, shedding the numbness of their symptoms as they don the fullness of their own sumptuous feelings.

Cixous's writing is this hysteric's dream.

184

6

Monique Wittig:
The Lesbian

In *Portrait of Dora*, Hélène Cixous takes apart traditional narrative in order to open a space for herself in writing. In order to open this space, Cixous identifies with the hysteric and reveals her craziness to be the negative reflection of women's presence in discourse. While fragmentation and violence are part of the dangerous necessities of Cixous's cutting into writing, she presupposes a fullness of female desire that will give a new kind of coherence to the forms she creates. The "sumptuous body" of the hysteric, while numbed and crippled by the law of male desire, has nevertheless remained virtually, if not actually, intact.

In *The Lesbian Body*, Monique Wittig also takes apart male narrative. But her deconstruction involves a riskier enterprise, for she discovers that as male traditions are undone, so also is the female self constructed by and in those traditions. To pursue the metaphor introduced by Colette and Leduc, one might say that the mask of male discourse adheres to the female body; when that mask is dismantled, the body parts come with it. As Wittig pursues her desire to write, she experiences at the same time the ripping and tearing in herself which the history of her desire entails.

But just as the negative implications of their status as women writers are transformed into creative possibilities by the other writers we have read, so, for Wittig, fragmentation becomes at once not only a painful necessity but also the origin of new values. Like the others, Wittig does not master the Master; she does not create a female narrative that is the reverse version of his. Rather, in a more radical gesture, she valorizes fragmentation itself, refusing the mastery that literary and critical narrative presuppose in favor of a disjointed and perpetually changeable confluence of parts.

In *The Lesbian Body* Wittig specifically takes apart teleological readings that create false and therefore oppressive order. She operates regressively, undoing in order to identify, name, play with, and savor all the parts—of women, of language—that have been falsely fused in exclusively male structures. What was, then, an anxious requirement to master and unify thus turns into a game that everyone can play.

The History of the Book

When Monique Wittig published *The Lesbian Body* in 1973,[1] it created quite a stir. Her first book, *L'Opoponox* (1964), had been awarded the prestigious Prix Médecis, and the French press hailed Wittig, then twenty-eight years old, as a promising young talent. But when *The Lesbian Body* appeared, the critical tune changed. The same critics who had praised *L'Opoponox* began to wonder in print what had ruined that beautiful young talent. One called it "a rabid and monotonous book," another "a bloodthirsty . . . bore," and still another said it represented "the phoney heavings of a modish subculture." Even French feminists who had rallied to Wittig's vision of an Amazon society in her second book, *Les Guerrillères* (1969), were appalled by *The Lesbian Body*.[2]

1. Monique Wittig, *Le Corps lesbien* (Paris: Minuit, 1973); published in English as *The Lesbian Body*, trans. David Le Vay (London: Peter Owen, 1975). All references are to the London edition. Modifications of the translation are indicated by "TM" except in the case of italicized *I*, which is silently rendered as "*I*."

2. The references, in order, are to "Butch Telegraph," *Times Literary Sup-*

186

The Lesbian Body, like *Les Guerrillères*, depicts a society made up solely of women. Written in the first person and in the present tense, the book describes a society that is an unidentifiable mix of archaic Amazon-lesbian customs and utopian visions of an indefinite future. Also like the book that preceded it, *The Lesbian Body* does not present us with a narrative; here we find a series of lyrical prose poems.

So far, so good. What makes this book such a shocker is probably not so much that it talks about intense emotional and physical relationships between women but that these relationships are (appear to be) extremely violent and brutal. Dismemberment, flaying, evisceration are all part of the "lovemaking" that takes place between the two nameless protagonists. Body parts are everywhere. It is disgusting. Everyone expects men to be brutal and sadistic, but women? and to each other? The book cuts across the sentimentalized stereotypes of women that are prevalent in our society, not only among the general population but among feminists as well. We see ourselves as peacelovers and peacemakers, even the revolutionaries. Wittig rips open this stereotypical woman and rubs our noses in her guts.

The Voyage Under, In, and Back

The Lesbian Body does not explain itself much as a text. Addressed to a female companion, it hovers somewhere between speaking and writing. Where is it? Where is this writing taking place? But even though we don't know where the text is, we do know we are in it because we live at the same grammatical address as the companion of the speaker-writer. Since as readers we are mingled indiscriminately with the intimate

---

plement, January 4, 1974, p. 5; John Sturrock, "The Lesbian Body," *New York Times Book Review*, November 23, 1975, p. 20; Valentine Cunningham, "Oh m/e, oh m/y," *Times Literary Supplement*, August 15, 1975, p. 913; C. J. Rawson, "Cannibalism and Fiction," *Genre* 11, no. 2 (Summer 1978), 310; H. V. Wenzel, "Resistance, Revolution, and Recuperation: Monique Wittig in Text and Context," unpublished manuscript.

tu to whom these passionate words are directed, every letter of *The Lesbian Body* potentially includes us. Everything done to the companion is potentially done to us; every intestine torn out is one of ours; every touch touches us.

The text is, in a sense, nowhere because it is itself a movement. From the opening sentence it describes itself as a voyage—a voyage that involves a radical break precisely with the place where we are: "In this dark adored gehenna say your farewells m/y very beautiful one m/y very strong one m/y very indominatable one m/y very learned one m/y very ferocious one m/y very gentle one m/y best beloved to what they [*elles*] call affection tenderness or gracious abandon" (p. 15, TM). This voyage is a journey to an underworld, to hell, but to a hell of a distinctive sort. Wittig's use of the word "gehenna"—*une géhenne*—signals from the beginning the mode of displacement and recuperation that will operate constantly in the text. Instead of using the more current masculine word for "hell"—*un enfer*—Wittig puts the more unusual, somewhat archaic feminine word in its place. The underworld is female not only in its population but in the very gender of the word that names it. Possible associations with the heroic male tradition of initiatory voyages are immediately deflected and replaced by a female field of reference.

The grammatical replacement of a common, masculine-gendered word by an older, less common feminine one suggests the uncanny possibility of another substitution that it reverses: not only the masculine word for "hell" but the entire male heroic initiatory tradition was itself a replacement of a more ancient female rite. Pursuing the classical context, we arrive in the mysterious cave of Eleusis.

That we have no precise record of the Eleusinian mysteries is significant. We can have no direct historical knowledge of this ritual initiation into the female secrets of birth, death, and rebirth, only the oblique, partial understanding that references in male texts give us. What appears to be at first glance a translation of a male tradition into female terms is in reality a

188

restoration of an original female structure suppressed in male language and thus erased from memory.

All of the transliterations that we will meet later—Ulyssea for Ulysses, Zeyna for Zeus, Christa for Christ—have the same implication. While appearing to be simple(minded) replacements of female for male figures, they carry with them the strong assertion that these male names and stories were themselves the products of usurpation, an erasure of an older female history.

From the outset *The Lesbian Body* is structured as a journey to this lost, hidden underworld of a female collective past, a past that has been largely unrecorded and has reached us only in bits and pieces as references in male texts. Gehenna represents, therefore, the resurrected female subtext of male cultural tradition. But to descend into this underworld, to recreate this suppressed subtext is not an easy matter. More is required than the mere changing of words and names; more is required even than the strenuous reconstruction of lost and forgotten memories, for we—the voyagers, the searchers—are ourselves the suppressed products of a partial male tradition. Just as our rituals and historical traditions have been uprooted from their original source in female experience and desire, so have we, the female actors in these stories, been remade into distorted male likenesses of a female original.

The Opening

What we are leaving behind, going underneath, as readers of this book, is not only the world of male cultural tradition but also the apparently bright, idealized images of females as that tradition defines them: "what they call affection tenderness or gracious abandon." Wittig warns her companion that she must abandon the male stereotypes of feminity which idealize women and which women then internalize.

The uprooting of these internalized images is represented in the text in a literal and brutal way as a process of evisceration:

189

> But you know that not one will be able to bear seeing you with eyes turned up lids cut off your yellow smoking intestines spread in the hollow of your hands your tongue spat from your mouth long green strings of bile flowing over your breasts, not one will be able to bear your low frenetic insistent laughter.   [P. 15]

Although the opening words—"in this gilded, adored, dark gehenna"—have suggested a *symbolic* journey as the central structuring mechanism of the text, the particularity of these guts makes it hard to believe that they are only metaphorical. As C. J. Rawson put it: "Wittig's protracted elaboration of details of mutilation and death . . . cannot be thought of as a series of images of something else . . . ; the sheer elaboration of particulars both limits the scope of analogy and draws insistent attention to the details themselves in their own right."[3]

But if we look at "the details themselves in their own right," what we see is a curious combination of actual physical horror and total unreality: the "victim" is not only not dead but alive and feeling no pain: she is, in fact, laughing. What can this mean?

It is very hard not to react viscerally to Wittig's depiction of viscera. As Robert Rogers notes in his work on the nature of metaphor, "poets instinctively turn to images of the body when they mean to disturb the reader most."[4] We are indeed disturbed and perhaps shocked by this evisceration, even more so than we might otherwise be because we know the book was written by a woman, and because such a scene blatantly transgresses conventional norms of female sensibility and its literary expression. We have indeed left behind, and in a very distressing way, "affection tenderness or gracious abandon."

In addition, Wittig parries any potential defensive critical gesture that might master the disturbance she creates by loading the passage with contradictions. While, on the one hand, the literalness of the physical details is insisted upon, on the

---

3. Rawson, "Cannibalism and Fiction," p. 287.
4. Robert Rogers, *Metaphor: A Psychoanalytic View* (Berkeley: University of California Press, 1978), p. 90.

other, that very literalness is denied. By scrambling the signals, she prevents us from categorizing this passage along the usual lines of literary genre. We are left as readers in what Wittig herself calls at the end of the same passage an "unbearable" position. Simultaneously provoked and kept at bay, we have to leave behind a "gracious" relationship to the text, a position that depends, as we can now vividly see, on the very sentimentalized stereotypes of women which *The Lesbian Body* decries.

If we emerge from the defensive (male) stereotypes inside us and agree to be unsettled, we discover that there is no unitary "place" we can take as readers of this book. Just as the text itself is a movement, so our reading of it as insiders traces a motion: the dizzy swing between the literal and the allegorical. And our swinging back and forth, the vertigo of that movement, produces finally a crazy but somehow valid smear of guts and meaning coming together. While Wittig allegorically brings to the surface what has been hidden, she also insists that that rupture, that opening, takes place simultaneously outside and inside of us. The symbolic representations of women in our culture have really shaped our very bodies, and to break with the one is to break (up) the other.

The curious thing about this passage is that it is also funny. In its hyperbole, it reads like a parody of Baudelaire and Lautréamont. It is also an obvious pun on "opening," like the slashed eye at the beginning of Luis Buñuel's surrealist film *The Andalusian Dog.* Along with all the other mixed signals produced by this passage, the serious and the comic collapse into each other. Opening up bodies is repulsive, but it is also funny as hell.

Cutting Up the "I"

As Wittig opens up the "affection tenderness or gracious abandon" that might define the way a female reader would expect to approach the text of a female writer, she reveals beneath the flayed surface of sentimentalized connection a horrible dismemberment. The process of bringing hidden mutilation to the surface of the text, of literalizing symbolic violence, dominates this book on all levels of writing and reading. Everything seems to be coming to pieces. Even the writer.

In *The Lesbian Body* Wittig employs a tactic that is literally lost in some parts of the English translation: she splits all forms of the first-person pronoun with a slash. The English translator has chosen to represent Wittig's gesture by italicizing all the *I*'s. But italics produce, of course, an entirely different effect, perhaps even the opposite one, from the slashed "j/e."

Wittig comments on her treatment of pronouns in the "Author's Note" included in the English edition:

> *Je* as a generic feminine subject can *only* enter by force into a language which is foreign to it, for all that is human (masculine) is foreign to it, the human not being feminine grammatically speaking but he (*il*) or they (*ils*). . . . The 'I' (je) who writes is alien to her own writing at every word because this 'I' (je) uses a language alien to her. . . . J/e is the symbol of the lived, rending experience which is m/y writing, of this cutting in two which throughout literature is the exercise of a language which does not constitute m/e as subject. [P. 10]

At the beginning of the book, the speaker-writer takes apart the "you" as part of her initiation to the underworld. But we perceive now, by means of the slashed pronouns, that her dismemberment is also a repetition of something already experienced by the writer. Split, slashed up, one part of herself divided from the other, she has already suffered the dismantling she describes.

The split subject in *The Lesbian Body* is specifically not an instance of the divided self-consciousness of the artist expressed in Rimbaud's famous phrase "Je est un autre." Nor is it an instance of the psychologically decentered subject graphically depicted in Lacanian discourse by the barred "$\emptyset$." The splitting of the subject here has specifically to do with gender and is the precise representation of a female's relation to language. As Wittig suggests, control of language has been the domain of males, and as a result, language has become their domain. Although language and the voice that says "I" within it have been taken to represent all of humankind, in fact they speak of and for men.

As a result of women's exclusion from first-person authority in language, the female "I" who speaks in writing is already a split and alienated subject. Denied as the subject of her own experience, a female has no place as an origin of enunciation. Her own "mother tongue" is, in fact, a foreign language. As a result of this alienation, Wittig asserts, the relationship of women to language in our culture is of necessity violent. Since women have been cut out of language ("excluded" would be the "gracious" word), their tongues cut off, their hysterical bodies speaking the sole crippled and crippling language left to them, the only way for women to resume their place is to cut their way back in.

The slash dividing the subject cuts two ways, then: it splits the subject and it also slashes up the writing. The two-edged sword cutting up the subject of the writing and the writing itself presents in a literally graphic way the very painful necessity women face as authors operating in a tradition that denies them. How can a woman identify herself as a "writer" or an "author" when those words universally connote a male person if they are not, as they are in French, already grammatically masculine? How can Monique Wittig, or any other woman for that matter, be *un écrivain*?

Wittig's answer to this question is to restructure the very order of the written language to make her exclusion as a woman visible. Almost every sentence of *The Lesbian Body* is slashed by the split *j/e, m/on, m/a, m/es, m/oi.* In refusing to abandon herself graciously to a hostile medium that subsumes the female in the male subject, the writer has had to cut herself up; but she has also irrevocably cut up language also. Just like her own body and the body of her companion, discourse is dismembered; it becomes discontinuous, or rather its former continuity is revealed as fallacious, a cover-up. Wittig is not so much disrupting language as she is calling attention to the wounds that are already there but have been concealed by women's silent assent to their own erasure.

The wounds of the language are also the writer's wounds and vice versa. Since the body of the author, her sense of herself, her desire, exist as functions of the text, the dismemberment of one signals the fragmentation of the other. Wittig's text attests to the undeniable connection between the cutting up of language and the cutting up of women.

Who Is "You"?

Wittig writes in *The Lesbian body* from a fragmented self. She is divided not only within herself but from herself as well. And this separation from herself is at the same time a separation from other women. If the speaker-writer cannot relate to herself as a whole being, her relationship with other women will also be disrupted. The fragmentation of the individual woman shatters the community of women at the same time. The discourse the speaker-writer addresses to her companion-reader therefore constitutes an attempt to establish connection simultaneously with herself and with the larger community of women. By the very structuring of the text, Wittig asserts the necessary relationship between the psychological experience of the individual and the political experience of the group. There is no personal salvation or damnation in the gehenna of separation.

If the speaker-writer is to achieve some kind of wholeness, some status as origin of her own experience, her discourse must be structured as an address, an appeal to other female selves who are at the same time parts of herself. Breaking radically with the mythology of gender that has dominated Western culture at least since Socrates, Wittig does not envision the original rupture of experience as taking place between the genders but rather within them. The two genders are not the split halves of an original bisexual or hermaphroditic whole; rather each gender is conceived as a potential whole in

194

and of itself. The lost parts of the female writer's self are not, therefore, male but female.

Seeking a voice, her own voice, in the language that is called "native," the female *I* of the text speaks, then, of and to the fragmented parts of women—herself and others. There is no need to decide whether the "you" in the text represents a real other person, the reader, or the author's ideal self.[5] In fact, the effort to separate out those instances of address is futile, as they are all inextricably linked with each other by their common erasure from and in language.

The bodies of the "*I*" and the "you" as defined by a female who seeks to be a subject in language are therefore lesbian bodies: bodies that can come to be only in a discourse shared with other women. The text of *The Lesbian Body* begins with the mutilated, dismembered bodies-discourse of women as they have existed in a system of heterosexual exchange, and moves toward the shaping of another body-discourse that can become whole only when women love themselves and each other.

Where Have All the Men Gone?

The Lesbian Body creates and operates in a totally female community, including the imaginary reader. No man is even mentioned in the text. And yet, contrary to Wittig's own assertions, references to a former male history and literature abound in this book, The entire work is rich with memories of other (male) texts. The writing-reading established by Wittig in *The Lesbian Body* assumes, then, if only obliquely, the context of traditional male-dominated culture.

On its most blatant level of reference to male history, *The Lesbian Body* provocatively transposes male mythological, religious, and historical figures into women. At times the transposition of gender takes place merely on the level of the femi-

5. Lynn Higgins, "Nouvelle Nouvelle Autobiographie: Monique Wittig's *Le Corps Lesbien*," *SubStance*, no. 14 (1976), p. 162.

nizing of male names: Achillea for Achilles, Patroclea for Patrocles, and so on. This kind of translation seems at first to be only a rather foolish game, but Wittig's technique has the effect of calling to our attention the fact that our history is not the history of all humankind, that it is, rather, profoundly genderized and partial. By respelling these names and thus reversing the process of the exclusion and silencing of women, Wittig suggests that behind these male figures lies a lost female past that can be retrieved.

The reclaiming by women of what has been theirs all along shapes a new relation to male traditions of history, literature, and language. Departing radically from past female and feminist strategies, Wittig positions herself in a novel way with respect to male tradition. At every juncture in *The Lesbian Body* she pursues the assertion implied in the opening section: what appears to be male tradition, male discourse, male history and literature is, in essence, a remembering and a re-creation of its female origins and sources.

But when male history is relived in and as a female structure, something happens beyond a simple grammatical shift of gender or a reversal of power. In her retroactive remembering of a lost female history in the place of the male history passed down to us as universal, Wittig replaces women in areas of experience that have been reserved for males: scientific discovery, heroism, divine authority, anger:

> Am *I* not Zeyna the all-powerful she who shakes her mane and grasps lightning in her hand? . . . the fire of m/y lightning bolts expands in m/y chest ravaging m/y lungs m/y ribs m/y shoulderblades m/y breasts, m/y hands seizing them to thunder from the height of m/y anger . . . a growling rises in m/y throat, a rumbling develops in the cloudless sky, m/y thunderbolts shaken forth strike you in the belly the pubis so that you turn your face to the ground . . . crying to m/e for mercy in such wise that ultimately *I* can lift you at arm's length to m/y mouth, that *I* can laugh in your ears, that ultimately *I* can turn you round and bite you in the hollow of your loins m/y goddess m/y so callipygous one m/y adored. [Pp. 42–43, TM]

Wittig imagines in this passage the towering anger of an all-powerful diety, the female origin of Zeus. She describes the rising rhythms of this anger as it spreads from her body to the universe, and then as it is directed to her companion-reader. But as this formerly male anger is assumed and reenacted by a woman, it resolves into something else. The switch from Zeus to Zeyna shifts the entire spectrum of emotions. Anger and the power it confers become the subject of an amorous game; Zeyna eventually plays at being angry. The repetition of male authoritarian structures by a female undoes that very authority and the prerogatives of the males who wore it as a right.

Repetition, parody, reclamation, and wit all flow together here in a unified gesture fusing Eros and aggression. Wittig displaces males in order to reclaim a usurped female history, but this gesture of displacement is not accompanied by anger or revenge. Like the anger of Zeyna or the evisceration of the opening section, her reclamation is deadly serious, but it is also playful, joyous, part of a loving liberation. By means of these transpositions of history, women's vitality enters into and reclaims dead spots in female history, numb areas of their bodies and feelings.

In a way similar to her imaginative re-creation of female versions of male historical and mythological figures, Wittig also relives male literary texts. Like Cixous, Wittig directly quotes male authors in her own text. But in contrast to Cixous, Wittig does not engage in a dialogue with those texts. Indeed, only brief fragments are quoted or referred to, and the name of the author is not mentioned. The male texts that are quoted are even recast in contexts that entirely change the original meaning.

Readers who are familiar with French literature will find snatches of lines from Du Bellay, Pascal, and Verlaine at various moments in *The Lesbian Body*. Wittig begins one of the early passages in the book with a slightly transposed version of the opening line of one of Du Bellay's sonnets. "Happy if like Ulyssea I might return from a long voyage" (p. 23). At another

197

point she incorporates a familiar line from a Verlaine poem into her text in order to negate it: "It is not the gentle sound of the rain that *I* hear just now, but your blood falling on the metal" (p. 90).

The effect of these transliterations of male texts is similar to that of the twice-told tales of history and mythology. First, they remind us of the genderization of literature and therefore of the falsity of its claim to universality. Second, they actualize the possibility of reclaiming the suppressed expression of female empowerment and creativity.

The "Author's Note" claims that *The Lesbian Body* exists "in a context of total rupture with masculine culture" (p. 9), but we can see that this is not entirely true. The integrity of her drive both to enunciate and to repair the fragmentation of women in our culture has led Wittig to integrate the very forces of fragmentation into her text. Rather than ignoring or expunging the cultural traditions that have ignored or expunged women, rather than scorning them as women have been scorned, she repossesses these past male traditions as part of the retroactive creation of a female past in the present of her text.

This process of repossession is accomplished, then, not by means of usurpation but rather by a kind of transformation that resembles—well, eating. Wittig does not set out aggressively to destroy or obliterate the heterosexual structures of the past; as we have seen, references to male history, male texts, pervade *The Lesbian Body*. What she does, rather, is eat them up, transforming them by the alchemy of digestion into the stuff of her own being. In this underworld of guts, the alien traditions of the past become the fuel of the writer's own energy and growth. Even as the forms of male discourse are broken down on one level, their continuity with female history is restored.

Rotting, Mutilation, and Dismemberment

Early on in *The Lesbian Body*, Wittig recalls the Orpheus and Eurydice story. It is another version of a visit to an under-

198

world, and when relived from the point of view of Eurydice, it takes on a new, harrowing character:

> We traverse the length of the galleries the underground tunnels the crypts the caves the catacombs you singing with victorious voice the joy of m/y recovery. M/y kneecaps appear at m/y knees from which shreds of flesh fall. M/y armpits are musty. M/y breasts are eaten away. *I* have a hole in m/y throat. The smell that escapes from m/e is noisome. You do not stop your nostrils. . . . Not once do you turn around, not even when *I* begin to howl in despair the tears trickling down m/y gnawed cheeks to beg you to leave m/e in m/y tomb. [Pp. 19–20]

Wittig relives here in a gruesome way the entombment of women in a male-dominated world. This entombment, again, is at once symbolic and real. The death is real, the rotting of the flesh is real, the horror. It also becomes a powerful allegory of the action of the entire book. The voyage down into gehenna is also a voyage up to a sunlit surface. The one retraces the other. In order to salvage her mutilated and rotting body, in order to move toward wholeness, the speaker, and with her all women, must first be willing to remember precisely the painful process of dismemberment. For it is the gracious denial of it that allows mutilation to be perpetuated.

The process of dismembering in *The Lesbian Body* is thus a necessary part of the act of re-membering. The excruciating fragmentation of women's bodies and discourse must be relived, brought to the surface, literalized, before that body can become a female text. Each fragment, each severed part of the speaker-writer's own and her companion-reader's body-discourse must be encountered, touched, experienced as a fragment before healing can begin. Indeed, that ferocious remembering of mutilation is itself the beginning of healing.

As we noted at the beginning of the chapter, it is hard not to react viscerally to these scenes of flaying and fragmentation. But why should we resist reacting thus? Why should we try to maintain distance, keep a hold on ourselves? It has been precisely the refusal to react with the horror that such scenes evoke that has kept women rotting in their tombs. Wittig invites us, as she has done all along, to leave our places as critics outside the text and go inside the nightmarish experience of finding one's body going to pieces:

> Suddenly at one side of the avenues *I* perceive trickles of your blood. It flows making a small noise, *I* recognize it, its colour leaps to m/y eyes, there is no other like it. Exactly parallel in a gentle wave flows the white of your eyes. *I* can no longer stand upright. . . . In the end *I* begin to run. The pain make m/y eyeballs start from their orbits. *I* bend down repeatedly to pick them up groping in the sand of the main avenue. *I* cry out with impatience, *I* search on my knees. [P. 53]

Body parts are strewn everywhere in *The Lesbian Body*. And as the body fragments, so does the prose: "They lead m/e to your scattered fragments, there is an arm, there is a foot, the neck and head are together, your eyelids are closed, your detached ears are somewhere, your eyeballs have rolled in the mud" (p. 79, TM). Just as the parts of the body lie disconnected, so do the components of the sentence. They separate from each other; the sentence becomes a list.

Wittig literalizes the body as a list in *The Lesbian Body*. Scattered among and interrupting the hundred-odd vignettes or prose poems that make up the text are pages of lists in bold type, lists of parts of the female body, its movement and secretions:

THE PLEXUSES THE GLANDS THE
GANGLIA THE LOBES THE
CALLOSITIES AND BONES THE
CARTILAGE THE OSTEOID THE
CARIES THE MATTER THE MARROW

[P. 40]

The female body is a list: words next to each other, parts next to each other, without any apparent connections. By their syncopated appearances in an already discontinuous text, these

200

lists represent the final reduction of the female to a selfless and random agglomeration of word-objects.

Fragmentation becomes extreme when the speaker-writer loses all sense of connection to her absent self-companion. Even her dismembered parts disappear, and she becomes discontinuity itself. The erasure of women's wholeness is complete; in fact, woman is, in this passage, that very erasure, the precise process of absence:

> There is no trace of you. Your face your body your silhouette are lost. In your place there is a void . . . *I* walk beside the sea, m/y entire body is sick, m/y throat does not allow m/e to speak, *I* see the sea, *I* gaze at it, *I* search, *I* question m/yself in the silence in the lack of traces, *I* question an absence so strange that it makes a hole within m/y body.   [P. 35]

When the separation from others and other selves becomes complete, when all traces of connections are lost, then there is no way even to inscribe the loss. The voice is silent; a hole opens up in the body-text, a void that is not the empty place left by a lost memory but lostness itself.

In the space between the various sections, in the spaces between the items in the lists, and especially in the incongruous juxtaposition of prose and list, *The Lesbian Body* outlines these voids, these intermittences, these disconnections. As the speaker-writer descends into gehenna with her companion-reader and the past is unrolled, as she sheds the gracious surface of her heterosexual body-discourse, like Eurydice, she passes through the tortuous chambers where women's minds, bodies, memories have been truncated, mutilated, and left to die in a language that is itself slashed up and dismembered. There is no history here, no continuity, no narration; only moments, lists. And finally silence, holes, severance.

Coming Apart/Together

By its continuous and insistent process of fragmentation and erasure, the text of *The Lesbian Body* undoes accepted assumptions about connections and relatedness. Our habitual ways of linking things to each other, words to each other, people to each other, are put into question by the very existence of this book as a text. The puzzles presented by connections and disconnections, parts and wholes, are the main questions posed at all levels of *The Lesbian Body*. Wittig reveals, though, that taking things apart—pronouns, bodies, stories— not only is a way of undoing false connections; it may also be the discovery of new ways of putting them together:

> *I* discover that your skin can be lifted layer by layer, *I* pull, it lifts off . . . *I* tear off the skin brutally beneath the hair, *I* reveal the beauty of the shining bone traversed by blood-vessels, m/y two hands crush the valut and the occiput behind, now m/y fingers bury themselves in the cerebral convolutions, the meninges are traversed by cerebrospinal fluid flowing from all quarters, m/y hands are plunged in the soft hemispheres, *I* seek the medulla and the cerebellum tucked in somewhere underneath, now *I* hold all of you silent immobilized every cry blocked in your throat your last thoughts behind your eyes caught in m/y hands, the daylight is no purer than the bottom of m/y heart m/y dearest one. [P. 17]

The desire to be under the skin of a loved one is here expressed in the literal gesture of pulling off the outer coverings of the lover's body. The brutality, the exquisite strength of that desire, the radical wish to touch in some essential way, is conveyed in the motions of the writer's hands flaying, crushing, plunging their way into the very center of the lover's being. Traditional—that is, heterosexual—erotic body codes are replaced here by a desire to experience some other kind of shared innerness with the loved one. The female body parts that have conventionally figured in love literature written by men are absent. Other parts of the body that most certainly have never before appeared in erotic discourse are touched, crushed, fondled. The female body as it has been presented/fragmented in male literature is dismantled by a different sort of taking apart that reveals another body with new openings, new vulnerabilities, other possibilities of desire.

The violence in this passage is combined with new, unexpected elements: a vivid aesthetic sensibility, a care for precise, scientific nomenclature, a kind of awed tenderness. Vocabulary, modes of sensibility, discourse from widely divergent spheres are brought together in this passage in a way that shocks our expectations. While the lover's body is being taken apart, so are our habitual modes of understanding.

This disruption of our reactions is achieved precisely by the juxtaposition of what is conventionally kept apart: science and love, eroticism and guts. Wittig shocks our sense of propriety by transgressing the property boundaries in language; she crosses linguistic territories divided off by specialists and dividing up our sensibilities. Her radical undoing of the female body and of the codes that have charted it into separate spheres of knowing and feeling undoes us as masters of a special kind of language. Our cry of protest blocked in our throat, we are obliged to put the text and ourselves together in a new way.

Just as in this passage, the very questioning of connections connects the various aspects of the functioning of the text. The interstices that separate and break up the m/e, the speaker/companion, the writer/reader, the body/discourse become the places of potential new articulations. By her very effort to inscribe the dismemberment of women, the writer has already opened up the possibility of remembering. By cutting up the language that had cut her up, the writer has already transformed the discourse that was her undoing. To express in language exactly what that language has been constructed to hide is to have changed already the very conditions of speaking and writing in that language. By means of her recognition and inscription of "the hole within [her] body" and her language, the speaker-writer discovers joyously that that hole and the new connections it creates have already created a new language:

Already you return with the news. The first to waken have announced the pure and simple disappearance of vowels. . . . Your lip your tongue modulate the new language in guttural sounds, the consonants pronounced jostled one against the other produce gruntings gratings scrapings of the vocal cords, your voice untried in this pronunciation speeds up or slows down and yet you cannot stop talking. The novel effect of the movement of your cheeks and mouth the difficulty the sounds have in making their way out of your mouth are so comical that *I* choke with laughter, *I* fall over backwards, m/y tears stream.   [Pp. 103–4, TM]

A (funny) new language has been created by the disappearance of vowels from the old language. Those letters and sounds that for some reason have traditionally been associated with the feminine—especially the so-called mute *e* that is the feminine marker in French—have disappeared, leaving behind the "male" consonants. Where the gracious women-vowels had been, shaped and defined by the surrounding men-consonants, there are now holes. Or more precisely, not holes at all, but new connections.

Paradoxically, rather than fragmenting language, these holes created by the disappearance of the women-vowels open up—in their jostling, scraping, grating way—new possibilities of meaning. By inscribing the erasure of women in a heterosexual economy, these women have already erased that economy itself. And surprisingly, what is left when traditional women-vowels disappear from discourse is not a male residue but an entirely new, undetermined, playful way of making connections that restores speech to females.

Reassuming their rotting bodies, touching each of their severed parts, gruesome as it is, in and of itself, heals these women's wounds and resurrects from the tomb of the underworld the subtext, a living body in the place of the old, dead one. By rehearsing their loss, they regain themselves and discover that, in a sense, they were never lost at all. It's so funny you could cry.

The Text as a Whole

The entire structure of *The Lesbian Body* demonstrates the new kind of writing that Wittig proposes. The text does not operate in the mode of discursive narrative but rather reproduces the episodic nature of women's history. The juxtaposition of the episodes seems random, just as the arrangement of the lists appears arbitrary. This arbitrariness of order or association is not emphasized, however, as it might be in absurdist literature or in the *nouveau roman.* Wittig does not shatter meaning or even multiply it in the conventional way.

The way these pieces and these passages fit together is, finally, not important. A virtual form does not preside over this process as its intention and final aim. The act of fragmentation is in itself the aim, for it is also a way of loving each and every part—of the body, of the text—in and for itself, without subordinating one to the other, without putting one in the service of the other. Wholeness, healing, may come as an afterflash of this loving dismemberment, but it can never be the project of the discourse.

Wittig refuses hierarchies of sensibility and meaning. The trip down to the underworld is the same as Eurydice's trip up to the surface of the earth. Levels coalesce; there is no mystery to be solved here, no code to be broken. No hidden truth lies beneath the surface of the text. No mastery is called for because nothing is concealed. A prior meaning is not fixed by the author and then offered to us as a puzzle to be solved. Her last thoughts are caught in our hands; meaning is an aftertaste that comes while we savor the scattered parts of *The Lesbian Body.*

Ecstasy and Beyond

Wittig's text describes the birth of a new kind of writing. The speaker-writer prays to Sappho, who causes a purple, lilac-scented rain to fall. As the companions bathe in the rain, they begin to sing for joy:

> You begin to stir singing, you whistle between your teeth, you sing, loudly *I* praise Sappho the all-attentive, you recapitulate m/y phrases in your song, you spin them out, you modulate them interminably . . . you take hold of my fingers so that they

may touch your body so *I* may familiarize m/self with your new appearance so *I* may interpret you m/y most mauve one, glory to Sappho over centuries of centuries. [P. 116]

The mauve-colored rain, the gift of Sappho, bathes this scene, creating a continuous background out of which the song of the lovers emerges. As depicted in this passage, language does not mark off a distinct symbolic domain separate from a preverbal matrix that it organizes. Nor is language detachable from the body whose perceptions and movements it expresses as a discourse. Words emanate rather from the same impulse that generates gesture. As Wittig describes it, language fuses the separate agencies we call "body" and "mind." The mutuality of gesture and speech is emphasized in the French by Wittig's use of the present participle: "Tu commences à bouger en chantant," you begin to move while, or even by means of, singing.

Wittig's depiction here of the creation of what we might call a text serves as a parable for a new process of writing-reading. In her model, the individual text can arise only in an already established context. To Wittig, this means specifically a mythic and historical female community where language is shared in a nonfamilial, voluntary association. The individual subject emerges simultaneously from and with other subjects, not as rivals but as partners in a structure of mutual interdependence. In the context of a community that validates the intelligibility of language without enforcing particular meanings, individuals can exchange words without incurring debts and obligations. As in the dance of Leduc's lovers, here the song of one becomes the song of the other—not identical but recapitulated and modulated, much as Wittig's text repeats and modifies the words of other writers.

That this model of female language emerges in a community of equals is paramount. In that context, language cannot be ᴜn instrument of oppression or a substitute for a loss. Wittig demonstrates the interdependence of historical political structures and philosophical conceptualizations of language: the one necessarily reflects the other. Because power is shared, language also is communal. Because material goods are available to all, writing is not a substitute for a thing but rather a kind of spill-over of its enjoyment. As a surplus of ecstasy, writing communicates its own desire: "you take hold of m/y fingers so that they may touch your body . . . so *I* may interpret you m/y most mauve one." Fulfillment precedes desire, or rather it has its own desire—to be read, to be interpreted.

Although women have been pulled to pieces, their own language is not based on an idea of themselves as an emptiness, a hole. Although they may be nothing to men or boxes or gashes or slits, women loving each other are full of themselves. Their being, then, is based on an economy of abundance that calls meaning to it as a surplus. In this passage of *The Lesbian Body*, Wittig elaborates precisely the scene that is unimaginable in the Lacano-Freudian sexual schema: female *jouissance* producing its own meaning.[6] Without envisioning this model specifically as an answer to their provocative rhetorical question—"What does woman want?"—Wittig nevertheless demystifies the denial of women's status as subjects insidiously implied by that question.

The Dance of the Goddesses

The notion of a validating community and tradition is, as we have seen, absolutely essential to Wittig's version of writing-reading. In another passage she describes more precisely how that female tradition might be constituted:

> On the hillside they do round dances in the evening. Often and often *I* watch them without daring to approach. *I* know them all by their names from having studied them in the library books. *I* list their attributes, *I* consider their bearing, *I* am not sorry that their severity should have remained attached to the characters of the books since they are here before m/e so totally devoid of it.

6. Jacques Lacan, *Encore* (Paris: Seuil, 1975), pp. 56, 69, 75.

> My heart beats at times when *I* see you among them m/y best
> beloved. . . . Amicably you share the sacred mushroom, each
> one bites the edge of the cap, no one asks to be bigger or smaller.
> At a sign from the blessed Aphrodite all around you exchange
> their colours. Leucothea becomes the black one, Demeter the
> white . . . the transformations spread from one to the other, the
> rainbow of the prism passes across their faces. [Pp. 69–70, TM]

The goddesses who both give and are the shape of women's
past have come out of the libraries, the palaces of official
knowledge. Differing radically from the solemnity of their representations in those closed institutions, they graciously receive mortals among them and share the source of their visions. The writer is linked to them by her reverence and
knowledge—she recognizes and names them—but also by her
love for her companion-reader, who participates in their ritual.

The shaping element in this scene is the daily ritual of the
dance. It is a ritual marked by rhythm and repeated forms
connecting past to present, reverence to desire, knowledge to
pleasure. But although this ritual is a fixed form, it is not a
closed structure. Its very essence is transformation in a circuitry of exchange. Again, this exchange is not the result of an
economy of need or lack: unlike Carroll's Alice, "no one asks
to be bigger or smaller." Rather they share and exchange what
they already possess: the signs of their identity. To write, even
to use another's words, does not, then, involve competition,
aggression, and dis- or replacement. The signs of meaning that
formally punctuate the shared continuum of space and time
already belong to everyone—goddesses and mortals, givers and
receivers alike.

The exchange of signs among the goddesses who conventionally represent the principle of identity itself opens up the
process of the production of meaning in a fundamental way.
Within the punctual field of the language of the dance, these
transformations betoken the possibility of a radical change.
Identity—of the person, of the word—no longer means coincidence with the self. It is not even suspended or ambiguous; it

208

does what is specifically contradictory to the very notion of identity—it becomes something else.

From Metaphor to Metamorphosis

This revolutionary revision of meaning as the perpetual circulation of infinitely malleable and extensible signs is not, in fact, altogether new. Like most of the discoveries and unconcealments of *The Lesbian Body*, this revision is also a return to the past; it reactivates a long-forgotten way of conceptualizing change and transformation, or, to use the Greek-rooted word appropriate to the setting, metamorphosis.

The companion-lovers of *The Lesbian Body* are not always themselves. They are liable to turn up as horses, wolves, fish, swans, mud, spiders. Often we witness the change:

> *I* have long been prepared for this phenomenon by various palpitations traversing m/y body at every instant. An urgent wave descends emitted by m/y brain under the touch of your fingers on m/y shoulders. M/y back opens between the shoulder-blades to release the fan-shaped membranes compressed by the ribs. Violet and translucent they at once unfold and begin to quiver. . . . The wings are born incessantly with ever-increasing speed. M/y arms are attached to m/y sides by two gigantic wings of a black colour. . . . The multiplication proceeds the wings now extend as far as m/y hips, at my feet two membranes arise and open at once diaphanous violent palpitant transmitting waves. A quiet hissing issues from your throat while *I* stay motionless body petrified before you wings all outspread traversed throughout by vertiginous movements which at this moment make you cry out while sombrely m/y desired one *I* enfold you. [Pp. 73–74]

The metaphoric possibilities of this passage are overwhelmed by the weight of precise anatomic detail. Yet this can't be real; people don't grow wings. As in the dismemberment passages, we are left in some disarray concerning the status of the language we are given to read.

Just as our confusion before was significant and marked off the specific path of our reading, here it highlights a significant characteristic of language, a confusion in language itself: that is, metaphor is syntactically indistinguishable from literal predication. Our ability as readers to tell metaphor from literal statement depends not on any inherent difference of form but rather on conventional definitions of reality and fiction existing outside any particular text. Transgressive playing with these invisible but well-defined boundaries has traditionally been tolerated in literature. But to go too far in the erasure of these limits is to enter into a realm of confusion usually reserved in our society for children and the mentally deranged.

While, since Aristotle, metaphor has been regarded primarily as a linking mechanism, a trope that brings together disparate elements, in fact metaphor can operate as trope only and precisely because the boundaries between two linked elements are strictly maintained. Metaphor creates a new meaning by bringing new elements into proximity, but the final separation of these components is absolutely necessary for the maintenance of this meaning.

What Wittig does in the above passage and generally throughout *The Lesbian Body* is to refuse the external system of conventional authority used to demarcate the boundary line between literal predication and metaphoric linking. By rejecting the forces of authority that hold the elements of metaphor apart, she collapses the metaphor in on itself, producing a new assertion of identity.

As we have seen, both Duras and Cixous moved in this same direction. But both accepted, if even provisionally, the traditional label of madness applied to such a project. Wittig rejects such reductive mappings of human experience. Rather than accept internment within the confines of madness, even though madness may eventually be redeemed, she steps totally out of the boundaries defined by traditional structures of social power. In the same kind of gesture of return to forgotten sources which marked her evocation of a lost female history predating traditional male narrative, Wittig returns to an archaic past, the retroactively created sources of another male text, Ovid's *Metamorphoses.*

In the ancient world whose remnants Ovid records, gods appear and interact with mortals, people are transformed into animals and objects, and nothing is thought mad. The speaker-writer in *The Lesbian Body* is a winged creature or a horse, a swan, a shark, just as in Ovid the nymph Cyane becomes a spring or Arethusa a river:

> Then freezing sweat poured down my thighs and knees.
> A darkening moisture fell from all my body
> And where I stopped a stream ran down; from hair
> To foot it flowed, faster than words can tell.
> I had been changed into a pool, a river.[7]

Wittig refuses the structures of hierarchical power maintained in the symbolic operation of language by reference to an authority outside itself. She insists, rather, on the radical possibilities of transformation in language by transforming the very reference to authority into a process of changing form. The shift from metaphor to metamorphosis, so slight, so uncanny, changes everything. Reality is no longer a rule to be observed; authority and identity are always liable to be transformed.

By abolishing the boundaries between body and imagination, subject and object, fact and fiction, reason and madness, Wittig also abolishes the dominant aggressive drive that maintains the partitioned structures underlying discourse and the definition of the subject. The erotic energies dammed up by this zoning of our lives are then free to surge together in a powerful new current:

> Your nostrils inhale m/y perfume spreading wide whenever you do so and your head is thrown back. The blue sunlight falls on m/y pale blue flowers . . . the silk of m/y flowers tautens

7. Ovid, *Metamorphoses,* trans. Horace Gregory (New York: Viking, 1958), bk. V, p. 158.

spreads everywhere. . . . Your fingers splay out, they alight thus on a heap of m/y flowers a cluster, you utter a cry, you lack the impulse to withdraw your hand, your fingertips the skin of your palm are touched by the skin of m/y sleek flowers, then your entire hand plunges into them up to the wrist then the other, now you progress with both hands up to the shoulders in the thick of m/y flowers, *I* take you by surprise, your breasts are touched your throat is touched, your belly is touched, your loins are touched, your buttocks are touched, suddenly the nape of your neck is heavily burdened with an armful of m/e a massive branch, as you advance the cascade of m/y flowers closes over you, your head too becomes submerged, *I* am terribly tall big strong, you do not complain while *I* stream over you all flowers all colours all odors . . . *ad vitam aeternam,* amen.   [P. 144]

In this remarkable passage Wittig steps over the threshold of propriety that has kept women out of the flowers to which they have so often been likened. No longer the object but the subject of desire, she speaks from inside the flower and from inside herself at the same time. When the two elements of the metaphor are no longer kept separate, when they merge as a new reality, the woman, the flower, and the metaphor are simultaneously transformed. Very different from the beautiful but fragile objects of men's desire, these flowers are soft and strong at the same time, flowing, powerful, ecstatic. Like the dancing goddesses who escaped from the libraries, these flowers are more supple, more powerful than any described in books.

Even though metaphor appears to propose new ways of thinking and imagining, its propositions are always provisional and can be retracted at any time as a manner of speaking. Under the pretext of bringing together, the traditional practice of metaphor effectually maintains sharp boundaries between different levels of experience and knowing. It operates, therefore, not only as a trope for all figurative language but also as the symbol par excellence of the power structures of patriarchal society. By enforcing particular definitions of what is fictional and what is real and thus between action and consciousness, metaphor subverts and, what is worse, potentially trivializes the very combinations it proposes.

Wittig reveals these positivistic power structures underlying the gracious fictions of metaphor precisely by taking metaphor seriously, by refusing to accept it as fantasy. When metaphor is thus literalized as metamorphosis, it liberates an awesome power within language. If the distinctions between fact and fiction, action and thought no longer hold, then neither language nor reality can be divided up into distinct territories to be possessed and controlled by any group or individual. Life and language become, radically, common ground.

Wittig challenges and transforms male literary tradition not by taking it apart but rather by putting its separated fragments back together. And as she puts those fragments together, she puts herself as a woman together in and with language. For the first time she can speak from within language as she speaks from within the flower. She demonstrates thus a model of attack unimaginable in male tradition: an erotic model of fusion and transformation. This is war by union.

Wittig does not undermine male tradition or subvert or ironize it; on the contrary, she takes it very seriously. But by insisting on taking language at its word, she ends up turning the high seriousness of "literature" into a joke. When fact and fiction flow together, writing becomes a liberating kind of play.

The Incomparable Sappho

Since the power and play of language ultimately resonate with the structure of the society it both expresses and shapes, the liberated language envisioned by Wittig can occur only, as we have seen, in a validating female community. Although the power to become a subject in language cannot be the gift of another, neither can it emerge in isolation, without a reader.

But even beyond the confirmation of particular meanings furnished by a female community whose history she retroactively creates (remembers), Wittig yearns for a more permanent grounding of her self in her writing: a myth that would inscribe the meaning of her words in the structure of the world; a force that would connect her particular truth with the timeless truth of the universe. Without this link to a confirming universal, Wittig's metamorphic writing could drift into deviancy or chaos.

Sappho is the name Wittig gives to this linking force that guarantees the authenticity of her writing. Literally and figuratively the point at which history and myth merge, Sappho is not only the founder of lesbian literary tradition, she is not only a muse, she is, as Elaine Marks points out, a "potent goddess, the central figure of a new mythology."[8]

In the case of Sappho as with all else in this women's book, Wittig is dealing with fragments. Sappho's destiny as a writer is typical, symbolic of all female "success" stories in a male-dominated tradition. Although Sappho's contemporaries considered her to be such a great poet that they called her "the divine Sappho," the "tenth Muse," her work has survived only as fragmentary references in male writing. Of her entire poetic production, which some critics guess probably amounted to some 8,000 lines, we now have only 500 lines, many of which are only fragments themselves.[9] Even though legend covered over the lesbian content of Sappho's poetry, endowing her retroactively with a male lover for whom she supposedly committed suicide, her works were still considered immoral and were reputedly burned by the church in the early Middle Ages.[10]

In one sense, *The Lesbian Body* represents an attempt to restore wholeness to Sappho's fragmented work, to reconnect

8. "Lesbian Intertextuality," in *Homosexualities and French Literature,* ed. George Stambolian and Elaine Marks (Ithaca: Cornell University Press, 1979), p. 376.

9. C. R. Haines, *Sappho: The Poems and Fragments* (London: Routledge, n.d.), p. 15, and Maurice Hall, *The Poems of Sappho* (London: Staples, 1953), p. ix.

10. D. M. Robinson, *Sappho and Her Influence* (Boston: Marshall Jones, 1924), p. 134.

recursively the scattered pieces of her poetry. But in a larger sense, Sappho is herself a principle of connectedness binding women and their writing to each other and to the world. Her name alone generates a universe over which she presides as first principle and protective deity. Not only does she come to the aid of the faltering writer as she struggles for words (p. 16), Sappho "writes" on the lovers, tracing their love in a cosmic benediction:

> *I* am kneeling at the seashore, you, you are standing before m/e arms folded, m/y mouth opens to *I* entreat the divine incomparable Sappho. . . . entreat Sappho she who gleams more than the moon among the constellations of our heavens. *I* implore Sappho in a very loud voice. *I* ask Sappho the all-powerful to mark on your forehead as on m/ine the signs of her star. *I* solicit all-smiling Sappho to exhale over you as over m/e the breezes which make us pale when we contemplate the sky and night comes. . . . *I* await the arrival of the comets with their smoky flashes, they are here thanks be to Sappho, the stones of her star are fallen, those which marked you above your cheek . . . with a violet seal exactly like m/y own, glory to Sappho for as long as we shall live in this dark continent. [P. 57, TM]

No wan moon maiden but the hurler of stars and smoky comets, Sappho becomes the original female writer, marking the companions with the seal of their connection. As universal force and sanction of female desire, Sappho replaces a male-dominated cosmology of love. The "dark continent" at the end of the passage is an unmistakable reference to Freud.[11] Since he declared female psychology and sexuality to be a mysterious domain that he could not or would not enter, Freud left female psychic life, female desire, disconnected from a theory of interpretation in modern psychology which claimed to be comprehensive and is still so regarded. And because women left a dark blotch on his map of the psychic

11. Sigmund Freud, "Lay Analysis," in *Standard Edition of the Complete Psychological Works of Sigmund Freud,* trans. James Strachey et al., 24 vols. (London: Hogarth, 1953–74), 20:212.

world, because they appeared as a fragmenting force in the psychoanalytic cosmos, Freud saw women as mutilated, incomplete beings.

The bright light of Sappho's constellations illumines this dark domain. But more important, she orders it with the inscription of intelligible signs. These seals of connection to larger forces of will and desire ensure that women-love will not lapse into anomaly, but that it is rather at one with the charted forces of the universe. The generous, all-powerful Sappho represents, then, beyond the ebb and flow of human history, the dream of a grounding force of female language. She at once creates and guarantees a space, a medium, in which speech and writing can emerge from and in new forms of female relationships.

Monique Wittig writes of and for women, just as men have written of and for men for literally thousands of years. Over those millennia a male subject, a male discourse, a male way of thinking have evolved. Necessarily a reflection of the patriarchal social structure it in turn helps to define, this male practice of language is grounded in the same value system that supports patriarchy. Although language is purportedly equally available to everyone in this culture, in fact men have consistently asserted control over language, especially written language, whether it takes the form of sales reports, sacred texts, legal decisions, or lyric poetry. The false pretension of male discourse to universality has been perhaps its most destructive aspect for those it has excluded from recognition. If they wish to speak for themselves, they must work their way out of and into language at the same time.

Like the broader practice of language, writing has been shaped by aggressive power models of family and social organization, and thus reveals the same charting of territories, prerogatives, and rules designed to regulate conflict and competition between males and to keep the disenfranchised out of the running. As a consequence of women's false inclusion in writing and their resultant objectification, their own experience of

216

themselves and of the world has been distorted, fragmented, mutilated. Denied as the origin of their own experience, women could not be the source of expression in writing; any woman who wrote and claimed public attention was by definition outside of herself and outside social norms at the same time. She was, by definition, crazy, eccentric, deviant.

In *The Lesbian Body*, from a position defined, then, as deviant, Wittig seizes this alienated language in a radical and logically impossible gesture. She makes an end run around male tradition and starts the game over at a point before the cheating started, before the long history of exclusion began. By retroactively recovering a lost female history, by assuming a present that that history might have produced, she recreates a language that can express desire as women experience it. Her remembering of female history, her re-creation of female discourse, and her reclaiming of her own and other women's bodies are all part of the same gesture of recovery and healing, since the exclusion of women from the status of subject entailed precisely the disconnecting of these realms of female experience from each other as well as from the main flow of "human" history.

The recuperation of past loss also includes the recognition that loss has occurred. As part of the process of healing, Wittig painfully repeats in *The Lesbian Body* the pain of fragmentation that has for so long been a part of women's lives. Transgressing one of the most powerful taboos in our society, Wittig—in an impolite, blatant, brutal way—brings the violence done to women out of its hiding place in gracious metaphors and up to the literal surface of the text. Spurning the numbness that women have cultivated as a response to mistreatment and that has turned them into hysterics, Wittig plunges into and embraces all feeling, all experience, whether painful or ecstatic, with the avidity of the chronically deprived.

Wittig's resurrection of the lesbian body from its burial in male tradition entails transformation of that tradition from within. Although silenced and fragmented, women have always existed in male language in the form of a fiction. In order to take her place in language, Wittig does not need, then, to compete with men or fight against them; all that is required is the uncannily slight but revolutionary shift from metaphor to metamorphosis. To literalize metaphor is to convert women from figments of male imagination into real, living beings.

Erasing the boundaries traced in the signifier by patriarchal authority, Wittig frees metaphors-women to become what they always were—statements of identity. As the two components of metaphor flow together and fuse to form a new unity, a new truth, so the writer puts herself and her words together. With the enormous energies of Eros thus liberated, as Wittig gathers together the scattered fragments of her body and feelings, she also reunites the community of women.

The Lesbian Body creates simultaneously a new mythology of the female subject and a new mythology of writing grounded not in the rivalry of the patriarchal family, with its hierarchical system of "natural" authority and debts, but rather in the sharing of a voluntary community of women linked by ritual, erotic ties, and a common history and language. Self-centered in a new way, these women can enunciate their desire in a female context of meaning which affirms rather than trivializes their words. That women have a truth, that they are a truth is signified by the continuity of the name Sappho—designating no longer an add-on tenth muse in the hierarchy of male inspiration but the first principle and moving spirit of this realm where women love themselves and each other.

A new body and a new discourse are shaped by this love that flows not out of but into desire, this ecstasy that founds a language. In a repetition and redemption of old sacrificial rituals, Wittig fingers entrails and finds herself singing a song.

In this punctual but open structure of meaning, nothing can be lost but everything can be exchanged. Everything, including identity, is provisional, a game. The old compartmentalization of function in and of writing therefore no longer makes sense. Old titles fall away, and Author, Text, and Reader, like the dancing goddesses, not only change places but trade identities as well. As the writer and the writing play, so can we the readers, shedding, with what relief, the responsibility to be right.

The Lesbian Body has fused the underworld of its project with the surface of its writing. No fictional behind or under or out there is projected by this text. There is no secret we must guess, no hidden intention it is our duty to unearth:

> You sing with strident voice your certainty of triumph over m/y death, you do not heed m/y sobs, you drag m/e to the surface of the earth where the sun is visible. Only there at the exit toward the trees and the forest do you turn to face m/e with a bound and it is true that looking into your eyes *I* revive with prodigious speed.   [P. 20]

What you see is what you get. The surface is all. At the end of our journey up through the underworld of women's writing, everything moves toward the sunlight. Like Eurydice looking into the eyes of these triumphant texts, we can shed the dead skin of scholarship and play perhaps a livelier game—taking apart its/our pieces, coming together, ripping, fusing, dancing. *Ad vitam aeternam.*

Conclusion

In her article "Gynesis" Alice Jardine points out that the "vague territory of *modernity*" has been almost entirely avoided by Anglo-American feminist theorists.[1] Although I covered some of that "vague territory" in the Introduction, I would like now to scan it again to see where and how, if at all, the books we have just read fit into or relate to it. Our exercise in topography will help us not only to situate the authors and their works in relation to the intellectual currents of their time—the "tradition" of the future—but also to determine more precisely the strategies these authors employ with respect to that tradition and to see what, if anything, their strategies have in common.

To begin with, the central motivation that generates the narratives of these French twentieth-century writers appears to run directly counter to what Jardine calls modernity and what in the United States is more commonly called postmodernism. Their effort to discover and define the self assumes precisely what postmodernism rejects: the notion of a coherent, definable self.[2] Indeed, talk about the "motivation" of

1. Alice Jardine, "Gynesis," *Diacritics* 12 (Summer 1982), 55.
2. Discussions of postmodernism may be found in ibid. and in Ihab Hassan, *The Dismemberment of Orpheus: Toward a Postmodern Literature,*

220

these texts would be seen in the postmodernist light as equally unacceptable, as it also suggests a belief in a psychological entity as origin of the text: in an "author," who might resemble a person. In the domain defined by postmodernist thought, the words "self," "author," and "motivation" and the beliefs they imply seem naive, behind the times.

In contrast to postmodernist thought, the French movement, centered on the urgent call to inscribe women's experience in a peculiarly female idiom (*écriture féminine*), often ignores the complications of split selves and the elusiveness of adequate expression in language. While insisting that women have been excluded from the practice of writing and that they are therefore alienated from its exclusively male code, many writers associated with this movement at the same time imply or even state that women are somehow essentially "closer" to language than men: "A woman is not separated from words," writes Michèle Montrelay. "They live through her and do not contain any secret that could have been hidden from her. . . . Words come out of her with total immediacy."[3] Later in the same paragraph Montrelay speaks of a *texte-jouissance*, a kind of "orgasm-text" in which women's language may emerge without any circuitry through social or intellectual symbolic systems.

Based on what one might call the mirage of the real obstacle, the presupposition of some natural proximity of women and language pervades much of the discourse of the *écriture féminine* movement. Hinting that if only male syntactic and semantic codings could be thrown off, women would be free to enter language—to embrace it, to bathe in it—without hindrance, Cixous, for instance, exhorts women to "write your

---

2d ed. (Madison: University of Wisconsin Press, 1982), who states that "as an artistic, philosophical, and social phenomenon, postmodernism veers toward . . . disjunctive, or indeterminate forms, a discourse of ironies and fragments, a 'white ideology' of absences and fractures, a desire of diffractions, an invocation of complex, articulate silences" (p. 271).

3. Michèle Montrelay, *L'Ombre et le nom* (Paris: Minuit, 1977), p. 153. See also Luce Irigaray, *This Sex Which Is Not One*, trans. Catherine Porter (Ithaca: Cornell University Press, 1985).

self. . . . To write. An act which will not only 'realize' the decensored relation of woman to her sexuality, to her womanly being, giving her access to her native strength; it will give her back her goods, her pleasures, her organs, her immense bodily territories which have been kept under seal."[4]

Although other women, such as Julia Kristeva, speak against "naive romanticism" and "a belief in identity," in general the basic assumption underlying the call to inscribe the woman or women or the feminine in writing is that some referent supports the word *féminine* and that it can be inscribed directly in language.[5] The same kind of longing for an uncomplicated relationship with language and the hint that it would be possible if only men were evacuated from the scene appears at several junctures in *The Vagabond*, *She Came to Stay*, and *La Bâtarde*.

From one point of view, then, the enterprise of women's writing as it exists both in fiction and as a theory runs counter to the current of postmodernism; the two appear to be, as Jardine suggests, "oxymoronic" (p. 55). From another point of view, though, women's writing and postmodernism appear to flow in similar directions. They share the project of deconstructing the certainties of the past, especially those having to do with the assumptions built into a traditional practice of language. Inasmuch as each is based on a radical questioning of the status of truth and fiction and on a rejection of dialectic, inasmuch as each places a positive value on nonmastery, twentieth-century women's writing and postmodernism share important characteristics. Colette's and Leduc's exploration of language as a disguise, Duras's valorization of silence and her confounding of dialectical oppositions, Cixous's problematizing of identity are but a few examples of what might be called postmodernist strategies in the texts we have read.

4. Hélène Cixous, "The Laugh of the Medusa," in *New French Feminisims*, ed. Isabelle de Courtivron and Elaine Marks (Amherst: University of Massachusetts Press, 1980), p. 250.
5. Julia Kristeva, "Woman Can Never Be Defined," in *New French Feminisims*, ed. Courtivron and Marks, p. 138.

Women's writing in fiction and as a theory also shares some characteristics with postmodernism as an avant-garde movement, including its defiance of the authoritarian past and its extension of language to aspects of human experience previously unexplored or unexpressed (female experience, in the case of women's writing). Many women, as we have observed, have even adopted the common avant-garde strategy of protest which includes choosing the enemy's insult as their emblem (the hysteric, the whore, etc.).

But the women who have attempted in their writing to dismantle the structures of the past are, even as members of an avant-garde movement, hopelessly out of date. They do not disdain their public; they do not write in secret, hermetic, or intellectualized codes. Finally, they appear to believe that what they write has some relation to social reality, that liberation in writing may lead to other forms of liberation.[6]

The paradoxical anachronism of twentieth-century French women's writing in relation to postmodernism highlights our original thesis, that is, that men and women have significantly different relationships with literary tradition. It may look as if the twentieth-century men who have dominated the postmodernist movement and the women writers represented here are reacting to and against the same tradition; but that similarity is an illusion.

Men may undermine mastery and valorize nonmastery, for instance, but they do so in the mode of those who have known from the inside what mastery may be. If a woman writer puts the authority of past tradition into question, she does so as one who never possessed authority herself. The writers represented here hardly need to explore the territory of nonmastery, for they already know it all too well. Their experience of nonmastery is therefore vastly different from that of men: they know it not as a self-willed divestiture but as a destiny. Nonmastery for them is not the reverse of mastery, which they

6. See Renato Poggioli, *The Theory of the Avant-Garde* (Cambridge: Harvard University Press, 1968), pp. 39, 62–98.

have never known, but rather something else: something in the nature of the doubly denied. And just as a double negative produces its own kind of affirmation, so the questioning of mastery by the nonmaster also paradoxically produces a positive. While this positive—that is, the movement into non-nonmastery, or into non-nonselfhood—looks like a return to the original positive pole—mastery, the self—the movement leads, in fact, in an altogether different direction, or rather, it opens up a new dimension. While the character of women's writing, with its projects of self-definition and achievement of authority, gives the appearance of being naive, simplistic, or behind the times, it is in fact already on the far side of the postmodernist project. The asymmetry of men's and women's representation in tradition means that their reaction to tradition not only will be qualitatively different, it also will determine a recursive structural redefinition of that tradition from the point of view of the misrepresented (women).

The writers here are indeed attempting to define themselves in language; but already suspicious of authority and intimately acquainted with the anxieties of a split and fractured self, they seek a mode of definition that is based neither on a lack nor on a credulous assertion of presence. In fact, in attempting to define themselves, they radically redefine the old notion of the self as an isolate, a unit—whole or split—and resituate "it" in a network of exchangeability (Duras, Cixous), the differences of the same (Beauvoir, Leduc), or the possibility of metamorphosis (Wittig). These women, who have all had the experience of turning themselves into a disguise, know that identity has nothing to do with self-coincidence and everything to do with the possibilities of transformation.

If all the authors here, like many of their postmodernist male counterparts, draw on biological and psychological analogies to deconstruct writing as a type of production, they do so because the ability to produce offspring and the ability to produce writing have long been regarded as mutually exclusive. If they undo writing as production, they do so not, then, to assert language as a radically heterogeneous and autonomous do-

224

main, but rather to assert its connection with life in another way. The whole question of the referentiality of language is at once eluded and assumed in these books. Coming from a place where their definitions of things had no "meaning" at all, these writers seek less to problematize old relationships of words and things than to redefine language itself.

"Double discourse" is a concept often used by feminist critics to describe the narrative and linguistic strategy by which women attempt to express their peculiar experience of being both "inside" and "outside" language at the same time.[7] But in these twentieth-century French texts, the doubleness of discourse has itself been doubled (undone) to produce a startling multiplicity of places. The authors have fused the story of their dispossession into a new language, a new narrative, which goes beyond the futility of old dualities.

The new narrative tells the story of being in possession of one's words at the same time that one recognizes that language is radically unpossessable by anyone. The flight/theft of the swallow in *The Vagabond*, the desperate and healing waltz in *La Bâtarde*, Lol's white lies in *The Ravishing of Lol V. Stein*, the not-quite-murdered body of Xavière in *She Came to Stay*, the double doors in *Portrait of Dora*, the split pronouns in *The Lesbian Body* are all symbolic condensations of a newly realized logic in which multiplicity and wholeness do not exclude each other. Paradoxically, the undoing of proprietary models of language and the exclusionary mapping it entails do not produce what one might logically expect in a postmodernist model: the double disinheritance of women. Rather, by the logic of the double negative, the unpossessability of language makes it an especially fitting vehicle for the vagabonds and the dispossessed, for those who do not "fit in," who do not have a place.

Because the relationship of women and language is a process

7. For a review of the notion of double or oscillating texts, see Elaine Showalter, "Feminist Criticism in the Wildnerness," in *Writing and Sexual Difference*, ed. Elizabeth Abel (Chicago: University of Chicago Press, 1982), p. 34.

of opening a mutually defining space, because it is, therefore, always in flux, it cannot be expressed in a static formula, a definition that would last. The contradictions between the multiplicity and mutability of position in women's writing and traditional notions of critical discourse have led such writers as Hélène Cixous to insist that no theory of women's writing can ever be constructed.[8] But Cixous's understandable mistrust of hypostatic formulations should not be used to justify the relegation of women once again to the outlands of rational thought. The lack of fit between women's writing and theoretical discourse does not mean that one or the other must be disqualified or supplanted. Rather, if women's writing and theory, as it is now practiced, generate incompatible models, what is required is a re-vision of theory from the inside of women's writing, from the point of view of the (misrepresented) objects of theory.

When we look at theory from the point of view of the misobserved, we can see how central spectacle is to speculation. But theory's function of distancing and making meaning visible is challenged by the double dealings of women's writing. The multiplicities, shifts, and transformations there produce an indescribable blur that used to be mistaken for foolishness.

The distance and stasis of theory as it is traditionally conceived will never make sense of this blur, for it is itself a kinetic process. What is required of the reader (theoretician), rather, is a movement toward, with, and into the text. The process of reading created by the writing of these texts is expressed better in the vocabulary of movement and position than in that of vision. The meaning of a text lies not in the perception of a summation, the discernment of a pattern hidden in it, but in a movement in relation to it. Just as the establishment of gender or the definition of the self in language is a never-ending movement oriented toward a goal that it never attains in any final way, reading is also a process that denies closure.

8. Cixous, "Laugh of the Medusa," p. 253.

The unmasking of the illusions of closure in these texts does not, however, betoken the eternal deferring of meaning, as it might in a postmodernist interpretation. The double undoing of meaning puts meaning, rather, on the near side of writing. It is the beginning of writing, not its end, or rather, there is no more beginning or end, since beginning and end are fused/undone by the movement of the text into a paradoxical multidimensional surface where hierarchies and antinomies coalesce.[9]

The construction of a theory of this writing would involve, then, not a distant view of the object-text but a moving closer to it. A distance so small that distinctions between text and reader blur does not necessarily involve, however, complicity or identification or fusion, those antimyths of the split self. The kind of proximity in which mutual transformation becomes possible might best be described as *a standing with*, expressed by the French word *constater* (from the Latin *constare*, "to stand together, to rest upon, to correspond to"). In later usage, the word came to mean "to stand firm, to stand still, to remain the same," and, by extension, "to be established, certain, sure." I would like, in a move akin to Wittig's, to return to the ancient meaning of the word before it hardened into certainty, to a time when to stand with each other was the same as to rest upon each other.

In this new constative mode, reading is a gesture, a standing together, a resting upon each other of reader and text in a relationship of mutual definition, mutual transformation, like that of the individual and language. The process of reading and the constitution of theory resemble, therefore, the practice/undoing of metaphor we discovered as a major strategy in

9. In *L'Hysterique entre Freud et Lacan* (Paris: Editions Universitaires, 1983), Monique David-Ménard proposes a new explanation for women's conflation of knowledge and desire, which she derives from a new reading of the female Oedipus complex. She points out an obvious but neglected aspect of this stage in female development: the girl is in a position very different from the boy's because she desires erotically the person who is also the representative of the Law and hence the origin of the symbolic systems underlying representations of knowledge. What is split for males—erotic desire and the domain of the symbolic—is fused for females (pp. 195–207).

these books. The deconstruction of the traditional practice of metaphor, with its implications of controlled distance and hierarchies of meaning, produced not an antimetaphor (except perhaps in the case of Beauvoir) but the metamorphosis of metaphor itself into its paradigmatic opposite, metonymy. Retracing, perhaps, an earlier voyage, metaphor changed its identity, slid into something else, became the trope not of resemblance but of the change proximity brings.

If standing next to something, as the reader does to the text, inevitably creates relationship and the possibility of community, it creates at the same time the unpredictable, uncontrollable chanciness of change. But while the modes of community may mutate from text to text and from reader to reader, the possibility of transformation remains the same, the possibility of trading places, of replacing oneself in some exchange which, in the old language, might recall a gift.

Index

Index

Empathy, 133–35. *See also* Replacement

Emptiness. *See* Nothingness

Eros, 25, 28, 62, 82, 197, 211–13, 218

Eroticism. *See* Eros

Eurydice, 108–99, 201, 205, 219

Evisceration, 20, 187, 189–91

Exchangeability, 142–46, 150–52, 163, 178, 218, 224

Exclusion of women, 9, 13–14n, 17–19, 29, 32, 66–67, 162–64, 178, 193–94, 216, 221

Exhibitionism, 40–41, 47–48, 72–73, 124. *See also* Tradition: and negative inclusion of women

Father, 58, 79, 105–8, 115–16, 132

Fiction, 39, 47, 77–80, 90–91, 129–30, 217–18

Flaying, 187, 202

Flowers, 211–12

Fragmentation, 29–30, 41, 49, 52, 57, 65, 101, 115, 167–70, 180–81, 185–86, 191–95, 198–205, 214–16. *See also* Subject: split

Freud, Sigmund, 18, 23, 158–66, 173, 175–77, 181–82, 184, 207, 215
Fragment of an Analysis of a Case of Hysteria (Dora), 158–65
Interpretation of Dreams, 158
Psychopathology of Everyday Life, 158n

Gap, 10, 29, 166

Gehenna, 188–89, 201

Gender, 7–8, 11–13, 21–22, 78–80, 104–5, 118, 154–56, 159, 192–98
and art, 6, 9–10
of authors, 10–11, 71–73, 97–100
and language, 8–9, 11, 17–19, 67–68, 99, 173–74
as masquerade, 106
See also Tradition

Genet, Jean, 10

Genitals, 42, 48, 106–7, 117, 118, 176–77, 179–80, 184

Genre, 13, 38–39, 77–80, 103, 191

Gift. *See* Language: as gift; Writing: as gift

Goddess, 27, 60, 207–9, 214, 218. *See also entries for individual goddesses*

Grandmother. *See* Mother

Heroine, 68, 71, 74, 93, 135

Heterosexuality, 41–43, 51–52, 63–64, 69–71, 82–83, 85–87, 90–91, 93, 100–101, 106, 201–2. *See also* Marriage

Hierarchy, 10, 12–13, 17, 78, 137, 161

History, 5–6, 11, 25–26, 71, 189, 198, 217

Hole. *See* Gap

Homosexuality, 33, 72, 93–94, 105, 117–21, 164–65, 184, 187, 214–16

Humor, 25, 191, 204, 213

Hysteria, 23, 72, 158–84, 185, 223

Hysterical discourse, 162–63, 166–75, 179–81, 183

"I," 30, 49, 83–88, 132, 147–51, 169–70, 191–94

Identity, 7–8, 11, 58, 71, 143–46, 208–10, 218

Illegitimacy, 105–6, 108–9, 113, 118, 121–22, 124

Images of women. *See* Representations of women

Indifference, 56, 149, 152, 154–56

Jardine, Alice, 18, 220

Joke. *See* Humor

Jouissance. *See* Ecstasy

Kristeva, Julia, 222

Lacan, Jacques, 13–14n, 17–18, 173, 192, 207

Lafayette, Mme de, 40n, 69–70

Language, 8–13, 15–19, 24–25, 35, 44–48, 60–62, 83–84, 92, 95–97, 121, 136–37, 174–76, 203–7, 213, 216–18, 222
as gift, 25, 60–62, 69, 71–72, 117, 119, 154–55
See also Gender: and language

Lautréamont (Isidor Ducasse), 191

Leduc, Violette, 5, 22, 23, 27, 29, 102–22, 124, 224
Affamée, 102
Asphyxie, 102, 103, 107–8, 122
Bâtarde, 5, 20, 23, 24, 25, 29, 31, 33, 102–22, 222
Ravages, 102, 120n

List, 200–201

Love, 51, 56, 67, 80, 138, 145

230

Index

Selflessness, 27, 50, 111, 136, 139, 154–55, 201
Sex, 7, 11, 14, 32
Silence, 10, 13–14n, 24, 35, 37, 43–44, 50, 57, 70–72, 136, 166, 181–83
Socrates, 194
Solitude, 20–21, 66, 69
Style indirect libre, 88–90
Subject, 8–10, 23, 28, 71, 144, 206–7, 217–18
split, 18–19, 49, 192–93
Symbol, 9, 10, 11, 28, 30, 56, 61

Text, 28, 38–40, 43, 55–56, 68, 87, 90–92, 110–11, 187–88, 191, 194, 199–202, 204–6, 218–19
Theft, 25, 63, 66, 107–8
Theory, 4, 6, 17–19, 158–59, 226–27
Theory of the Avant-Garde (Poggioli), 21, 33, 223
Tradition, 4, 12–13, 15–16, 19, 24, 27, 30, 32, 71, 125–26, 129, 140–41, 152–54, 185, 189, 195–98, 213, 223–25
and female autonomy, 22–24, 26, 43–44, 106–7, 212–13
male relation to, 21–22
and negative inclusion of women, 13–17, 19–22, 32, 44, 67–68, 125, 189–91, 193–94, 207, 217
revision of, 23, 26, 196–97, 217–18, 223–26
Transformation. *See* Change
Translation, 64–5, 128, 188–89, 196–97
Triangle, 82–83, 100, 142–43

Verlaine, Paul, 197–98
Violence, 28, 35, 80, 86, 182–84, 193
Vision, 147–51
Vowels, 204
Voyage, 25–6, 38, 54–55, 69, 135, 187–89, 190, 198–99

Weil, Simone, 93n
Wholeness, 66, 73, 194, 201, 205
Whore, 23, 25, 29, 44, 124, 146–47, 151–52, 155–56, 223
Wittig, Monique, 5,23, 29, 186–219, 224, 227
Guérillières, 186–87
Lesbian Body, 5, 20, 23–26, 29, 31, 33, 185–219, 225
Opoponox, 186
Wound, 41, 42, 48, 62, 115–17, 183–84, 194, 204
Writing, 28–29, 33–37, 42, 50, 68–74, 91–101, 103–4, 112–13, 118–22, 133–35, 139–40, 166, 182–84, 204–7, 216–18
and anxiety, 12–13, 94–97, 123–24
and binary marking, 12, 23, 78–80, 104–5, 160–61
French influence on, 4, 16–17
as gift, 111, 117
as graphics, 55–56, 193–94
as heroism, 36, 126, 129, 131, 137–38, 152–53, 164, 188
and speech, 12, 31, 34, 168
as transgression, 12–13, 20–21, 25, 44, 81, 124

Zeus, 109, 197
Zeyna, 196–97

Library of Congress Cataloging-in-Publication Data

Evans, Martha Noel, 1939–
    Masks of tradition.

    Includes index.
    1. French literature—Women authors—History and
criticism. 2. French literature—20th century—History
and criticism. 3. Women and literature. 4. Feminism
and literature—France—History—20th century. I. Title.
PQ149.E83 1987   840'.9'9287   87-6685
ISBN 0-8014-2028-8 (alk. paper)